1985

A GRISEZ READER FOR BEYOND THE NEW MORALITY

Germain Grisez
Russell Shaw

Edited by

Joseph H. Casey, S.J.
Boston College

UNIVERSITY
PRESS OF
AMERICA

LANHAM • NEW YORK • LONDON

Library of Congress Cataloging in Publication Data

Grisez, Germain Gabriel, 1929–
    A Grisez reader for Beyond the new morality.

    Bibliography: p.
    1. Ethics–Addresses, essays, lectures. I. Grisez,
Germain Gabriel, 1929–   . Beyond the new morality. II.
Shaw, Russell, B. III. Casey, Joseph H. VI. Title.
BJ1025.G725   170   81–43481
ISBN 0–8191–2243–2   AACR2
ISBN 0–8191–2244–0 (pbk.)

ACKNOWLEDGEMENTS

The Reader selections listed under "Publications" (pp. 211-212) are reproduced as copyrighted material printed with permission of the publishers and the author. The editor warmly thanks them all: Germain G. Grisez, University of Notre Dame Press, St. John's University Press, Glencoe Publishing Company (subsidiary of Macmillan Publishing Company, owners of copyright of Bruce Publishing Company's volume: Contraception and the Natural Law), Edizione Domenicane Italiane, New Catholic Encyclopedia, and the editors of the following journals: Ethics (University of Chicago Press), The American Journal of Jurisprudence (University of Notre Dame Press), Philosophy in Context (Cleveland State University, Department of Philosophy).

CONTENTS

BEYOND THE NEW MORALITY, the authors tell us, is the "joint
enterprise (of Germain Grisez and Russell Shaw), for which they
are willing to share not only blame but (they continue to hope)
also praise." However, "One of the authors..., Grisez, is a professional philosopher.... The ethical theory...is, properly
speaking, Grisez's." (p. XIX) "Grisez has set forth his ethical
theory at length and in the language of technical philosophy in
other publications...." (p. XVI)

The Reader provides selections from those publications which
can be read along with the text. The selections explain and
develop the pivotal insights of BEYOND THE NEW MORALITY. Each of
the eight sections indicates the chapters of the text to which the
readings relate.

As a guide to the readings selected I shall identify these
pivotal insights as "planks" in the building of Grisez's ethical
theory.

First Plank: We possess freedom of self-determination.
Section 2 - Chapter 1

Second Plank: The central, pervasive problem of life is to live
as a person able to make free choices. In this way we create
the selves each is to be.
Section 3 - Chapter 2

Third Plank: Everyone wants to be happy: the ultimate overarching goal of living.
Section 4 - Chapters 3 and 4

Fourth Plank: To be happy is to be fulfilled as being a complete
person.
Section 4 - Chapter 4

Fifth Plank: To be human involves belonging to many different
communities. We are constantly acting as members of these
communities.
Section 5 - Chapter 5

Sixth Plank: Ethical relativism is false. Therefore there must
be standards by which we can determine whether what we choose
is right and whether our reasons for choosing it are right.

Utilitarianism is a "dead-end" street, a non-viable ethical
theory.
Sections 6 and 7 - Chapters 6 and 10

Seventh Plank: A. To be a complete person one must provide for
eight ultimate aspects of oneself.

1

B. The eight ultimate goods involved in all possible choices provide for these eight ultimate aspects of oneself. They are: life, play, aesthetic experience, speculative knowledge, integrity, authenticity, friendship, religion.
C. These goods are irreducible oné to the other and so are incommensurable.

Section 8 - Chapter 7

Eighth Plank: A. Moral good is not a ninth good, an addition to the eight goods.
B. Moral good is choosing whatever good inclusivistically. Thus moral good fosters human being, leaving one open to further self-realization.
C. Moral evil is choosing whatever good exclusivistically. Thus moral evil puts limits on human being, amounting to a kind of existential suicide.

Section 8 - Chapters 8 and 9

Ninth Plank: Eight modes of responsibility specify the first, basic principle of morality: one ought always to choose inclusivistically.
1. Be committed to selected basic purposes and see that they lead to a harmonious lifestyle.
2. Be open to all the fundamental goods as they apply to oneself and to all others.
3. Be willing to help others even outside structured relationships.
4. Be detached in your commitments so that their loss will not drain life of meaning.
5. Be creatively faithful in your commitments.
6. Be efficient in selecting and pursuing specific objectives in fulfilling commitments.
7. Be responsible in fulfilling your genuine duties within a just society and honest in resolving conflicts between duties.
8. Never act directly against any of the fundamental human goods.

Section 8 - Chapters 11, 12 and 13

Tenth Plank: Resolving the ambiguous case:
A. If the action is an indivisible unity and if it directly realizes a human good, persons performing the act for the sake of the good need not be wrongly disposed toward the good which is simultaneously damaged.
B. If the two aspects of an action are related as means to end (the good result is attained in an act distinct from that in which the bad is caused), it is immoral to perform the action because it is never right to do evil to achieve good.

Section 9 - Chapter 14

1: INTRODUCING GERMAIN G. GRISEZ

Brief biographical data to identify Grisez. Selections and poems from an unpublished essay and a Christmas letter reveal the human, personal dimensions of the author as husband and father.

"American Catholic Education"

My experience of higher education is the following: From 1947-1950 I was an undergraduate, majoring in philosophy, at John Carroll University, Cleveland, Ohio. John Carroll is a Jesuit institution and at least during the time I was there it was less a university than a slightly expanded liberal arts college. During 1950-1951 I was admitted as a layman to study philosophy at the Dominican House of Studies, River Forest, Illinois. This institution was a seminary, but my courses were selected for my own purposes of philosophic formation from various parts of the curriculum. Thus, although I did not live in, I came to know many of the seminarians in various years of the program. From 1951-1957 I was in residence at the University of Chicago, working on my Ph.D. in philosophy. The philosophy department at Chicago during those years was pluralistic, representing various types of philosophy. It did not include Thomism: Mortimer Adler and Yves Simon were at the University of Chicago but were not members of the philosophy department, and I had little contact with either of them. From 1957-1972 I was a member of the faculty in the department of philosophy at Georgetown University in Washington, D.C., where I taught both at the undergraduate and at the graduate levels. In 1972 I moved to my present position, as professor of philosophy at Campion College, which is a Catholic college federated with the provincial University of Saskatchewan Regina Campus, in Regina, Canada. My teaching at Campion is strictly undergraduate.

(p. 41)

"Charity and Dissenting Theologians"

Dr. Germain Grisez, a layman, has been appointed to the newly created Rev. Harry J. Flynn Chair in Christian Ethics at Mount Saint Mary's College, Emmitsburg, Maryland. He is now beginning work on a volume of principles of Catholic moral theology.

(p. 13)

A Christmas Letter

Dear Friends,

We have been living here on campus since September 1979. Our apartment is a unit in a new dormitory, which normally would house five students. But it has all the amenities in itself. It is very adequate for the two of us.

Last year we were so busy getting settled that we did not get out cards. And we've had time to visit or talk with few friends in the last two years. The main reason—and our reason for being here—is that Germain is working on a volume on Christian Moral Principles. This will be a textbook in moral theology. He teaches the course to first-year theology students in the seminary and at the same time writes and improves the text.

Our third son, Joseph, who was born in 1956, went with us to Canada when we moved there in 1972. When we came back in 1978, he stayed. He was driving trucks, often on long trips north during the winter. On March 23 of this year, while on one of these trips, Joe encountered thawing weather, failed to make an up-grade, and was killed when his truck slid back. We had his body returned here and buried on the hill overlooking the college. Our grief still comes and goes in waves, and we often walk up to pray at his grave. But we look for the resurrection of the dead and life everlasting.

Our other boys are married and live nearby. We see them fairly often. There are now six grandchildren, two of them born this year. All three boys are doing well in their jobs—Tom as an electrician, Jim in the bindery of a printing plant, and Paul as an auto painter.

Our own life here is quite simple. We work together more of the time and more closely than ever. When the seminarians are here, we go to Mass and to prayers with them regularly. Otherwise we go to a nearby parish for morning Mass. Because nothing is more than fifteen minutes walk away, we usually go back and forth without starting our car. The office and the apartment are within five minutes walk, which makes it easy and pleasant to go back and forth, even several times a day, for meals, to pick up things, and so on. After years of going back and forth to work, it really is nice to live and work in the same place.

Sometimes the seminarians come over for a good meal, and we socialize with them. When we have time, we often go for a walk, sometimes right here, and occasionally down in the national park, where Camp David is located. We do not do much traveling or

4

meeting-going not connected with the work. Because a chair was set up for the project, Germain has a light teaching load and we have two offices, with quite adequate facilities.

We hope that you have a joyful Christmas and that this next year will be kind to you. We do like to hear from friends and family. If you are down this way, give us a call. We have one spare room!

Peace and joy!

(Germain and Jeannette Grisez)

"Fidelity"

All the talk about love has put fidelity in the shade, if not buried it. I would like to uncover fidelity, to bring it into the light again, and what is more, to praise it, and even to sing its praises.

. . .

Love, in many current discussions, is set in opposition to law. I seriously doubt that this opposition is sound. It arises, perhaps, because love has been brought onto the battle field to serve as a big gun in attacking the fixed defenses of certain moral positions, positions strongly defended by moral law. Putting aside the question of the value of these positions, one wonders at the propriety of making use of love as a weapon in an argument. Isn't this employment of love something of a degradation? I think that perhaps the right weapon for attacking bad law is good law, and that love—if it is genuine— will not become an implement of war, but will remain serene and true to itself, a sacred presence above all the conflict.

At any rate, shouldn't we consider that perhaps the real enemy of love may be escaping our attention? While we are getting ready to lynch the law because of its alleged violation of love, may we not be allowing the real violator of love to slip away unnoticed? I think it may be that infidelity, not law, is the real violator of love, and I want you to ask yourselves whether sound law is not really the eyes and hands of a heart full of genuine love.

. . .

Genuine love, confirmed by fidelity, does not of course reject the change that belongs to consistent growth. The healing up of wounds, the filling out of what is incomplete, the unfolding of potentialities always hidden in the true self of one's beloved--fidelity never rejects these changes, but always welcomes them. Yet they are welcome neither because they are changes, nor because they bring something new. If fidelity does not live in the past, it does not live in the present, nor at some mythical point in the future.

Fidelity aspires to stand outside time, to transcend change, to reach the immortal and the eternal. If anyone does not understand this aspiration, he does not know what real love is. Not anxiety about one's own security, not fear of losing some possession, but the fidelity of love itself demands that the true self of one's beloved and the bond of union be unalterable.

Spanning the distance between time and eternity, love confirmed by fidelity is subject to the incursions of change but it longs for the stability of perfection, as each lover commits himself irrevocably to the goodness of the other and seeks to rescue the communion of love from the torrent of time. That was why, many years ago, I wrote for my wife:

> "Jeannette--"
> How often have I uttered it, your name,
> And felt its softness gently run my tongue.
> But still the sound is never quite the same,
> For each new sounding gives it meaning new.
>> For me and you there is too little time.
>> The years of youth, our youth, fly quickly past.
>> Some day that passes will carry by the prime
>> Of life and love from us. Oh, never change!
> Though changing ever, never change in this:
> Our love once given must never be recalled.
> The joy of knowing you, your glance, your kiss,
> Your gentle soul and goodness must remain.

Not only one's beloved, but the bond of union must be unalterable. This bond of union cannot simply be something subjective, something that is felt, but that remains within. It must be objective, because the only bond that can unite two persons must be common to both of them.

More profoundly, words of love and acts of love cannot express or communicate unity unless the unity already exists. Love must be there first, then words and acts can have their meaning. And love must exist as a common and objective bond. This bond is fidelity. Fidelity is neither expression nor communication. It is a pledge, a bond, an objective unity and confirmation of love.

. . .

If the unity of fidelity is objective, however, still it is not something extrinsic to the two who love each other. It is the bond common to them and within them, which unites them into one--they leave father and mother and cleave to one another. But how can one so commit oneself to another person, knowing that the other is deficient and imperfect as oneself? Only because fidelity is to the true self of the other person, to the true perfection of the other.

But is not this perfection merely an unreal possibility, an abstraction? No, for the union of fidelity introduces the two within the unity of Goodness Itself, within the unity of divine perfection. There the perfection of the other is real, and one can thus be faithful to it without committing oneself to a mere ideal. By virtue of fidelity, lovers thus can say to each other:

We are two. Our love is a third.
So we are three.
But by the third we are one.
    We are old. Our love is young.
    We aged, it new.
    And in its birth, we are reborn.
We are weak. Our love is strong.
We fall, it rises.
And by its power we are heartened.
    We are small. Our love is great.
    We diminish, it grows.
    Through its growth, we are magnified.
We are human. Our love divine.
We fail, it wins.
For its victory, may we be crowned.

. . .

Certainly, in the life of each individual, no one of us has certitude what he will find if he lives his life in a constant effort to discover and perfect his true self. Simply because there are setbacks, simply because there are all kinds of shocks and surprises, that does not give us a right ever to say that the effort is hopeless and that we are therefore authorized to quit. The same thing is true of marriage. A married couple must continue to seek what they shall be, and try to discover the mystery to which their fidelity directs, no matter how many masks must be set aside.

Such a quest requires courage. While we may gain confidence from the past, if it has gone well, we cannot know that the future will resemble the past. Nevertheless, fidelity will allow us to turn toward the future with light hearts, for fidelity, like faith, is childlike:

> I glance back and see behind me twelve who smiled.
> I glance ahead and see only impenetrable mist!
>> Who can tell whether the face of the next will be
>> frowning or smiling?
>> Who can know what lies in the path to trip him
>> as he passes?
> I look aside and see there one who smiles,
> Unafraid to accompany me along the unknown path that
> lies ahead.
>> Stand close to me; hold my hand tightly.
>> Forgetting fear, we will walk on together.
>> Like children on a summer's day, we'll skip through
>> life's year.

. . .

...The two must become one by their dedicated cooperation in view of something really "greater than both of us," as they say. They must be possessed by a common cause they can love more than themselves; they must become the servants of a reality beyond themselves, and work together in this service. Not face to face, but side by side the two of us really become we two. And out of we two comes the genuine I and thou.

The unity of marriage has its meaning from such a reality beyond the couple themselves. They are enlisted in the service of life, they are invited to cooperate together with the Creator of life to pass on to men yet to be all the gifts they received from their own parents. In the child, the two become one flesh, and it is fully so only in the child, for the child is really one, and yet is really the flesh and blood of both. Thus the child is necessary, not as an accomplished fact but as a beloved hope, if communion in marital love is to be possible.

. . .

But perhaps all this is too complicated? Then listen to the way a young man said it a long time ago to his bride. He put the whole thing much more simply:

> To what shall we compare our love, Jeannette?
> It is a rose too young to blossom yet
> That needs long months of patient care until
> One quiet night when all is warm and still
> It will put forth a single, tender bloom.
> This little life will grow within your womb
> Until you bring him forth one day in pain

8

And hold in flesh our love for whom we've lain.
You are dear earth; our love shall grow in you.
And I the water and the air for it,
But God must bathe us in the sun of life.
Be fertile soil, and be we always true
To vows we've made for doing what is fit
To gain Perfection as a man and wife.

. . .

If an act is to be truly spontaneous, it must come from the
personality of the agent himself, it must originate in the freedom of self-determination—that is what spontaneity in human
action means. The adolescent who thinks of spontaneity as "doing
what comes naturally" is actually a slave of his conditioned
reflexes.

. . .

That is why we have reason for confidence that fidelity need
not crush spontaneity, and that true spontaneity of genuine love
need not threaten the unbreakable consecration of fidelity.

Flying bending, silent speeding,
Rising slowly, slowly falling,
Red-brown goldness shyly calling,
What beyond this veil impeding?
    Hot soft firmness, hope exceding;
    Primal peace perhaps recalling?
    Past and future both forestalling;
    Now, the now, this only needing.
Flying curving, now receding,
Lifting gently, calmly falling,
Past and future now recalling,
You and I, love once more heeding.

. . .

Meanwhile, if we wish to live faithfully, we must begin early
to cultivate fidelity. It is never too soon. Marriage will not
make a different person of you. It will not solve moral problems you have never faced before. Even in marriage, one must
seek the grace of fidelity, and fight to keep it. But this fight
is not always something dramatic. It can take the most simple
and commonplace form, and be the slightest step in an effort of
building that must be lifelong. Shall we end our meditation by
recalling one little step, taken very early in a marriage?

9

Darling,
Last night, as you and I, having kissed goodnight,
Parted, one of us oneither side of our door,
And I heard the lock click as you locked it tight,
My memory stirred with other nights and other partings.
 Just then, as I began to climb the steps,
 Heading toward the train to town and to work,
 A warm breeze lifted the corner of my coat and
   flapped it,
 It was like the first night of spring.
I imagined you getting ready for bed.
I felt an urge to return to you,
I wanted so much to kiss you once more, just once more,
And then to remain with you all night, not to leave.
 You could tell them: "He isn't feeling well tonight,
 He can't come in to work."
 And we could talk and stay up late
 And then, finally, go to bed together.
But there is work,
I must make a living for us now,
And if I'm not sick, I'm not sick,
And so I left you there alone and went on.
 Alone?
 I forget, you are not alone now,
 You are with child, our child; he is with you.
 He waits now, to burst forth when the trees bud,
 To find the world and his first spring.
Darling, God love you and him and keep us all.
 Wake me at 8:30 tonight; I have to leave at 10.
 There's fresh bread in the box.

(passim)

Background for Chapter 1, "Freedom Means Responsibility"

Sensitive to the contemporary demand for freedom,
Grisez begins his treatment of ethics by identifying the
kind of freedom involved in ethics. It is hard to conceive
serious ethical decision-making or reflection on ethical
theory which does not presuppose freedom. Students, I find,
seem to take for granted that they are free but the freedom
they treasure is "freedom to do as one pleases." They seem
unaware of the centuries-long dispute about free choice—the
freedom so essential for ethics that it should be carefully
distinguished from other kinds of freedom and its reality
firmly established. It is free choice which grounds responsibility: this action would not exist except that I chose
to do it.

Grisez in collaboration with two other philosophers
addresses those two concerns. They clearly distinguish
free choice from other kinds of freedom and, in my opinion,
provide an argument which definitively establishes the
reality of free choice.

First Plank: We possess freedom of self-determination.

Free Choice

The philosophical controversy about free will and determinism
is perennial. Like many perennial controversies, this one involves
a tangle of distinct but closely related issues. Thus, the controversy is formulated in different ways by different philosophers.
At different times in the history of thought the focus of attention has been on different issues.

The issue with which we are concerned in this work emerged
most clearly in early modern philosophy. Jewish and Christian
religious beliefs about man and moral obligation had shaped an
interpretation of the common human experience of making choices.
Within the theistic perspective, it seemed evident that whenever
a person makes a choice he could equally well choose an alternative other than the one he does. Many early modern philosophers,
such as Hobbes and Spinoza, replaced traditional theism with a
naturalistic conception of the world and of man. This naturalistic
conception became part of the worldview of science and gained in-
creasing plausibility from the progress and fruitfulness of modern

science. Within the naturalistic perspective, it seems evident that whenever anything happens, however contingent it might be, what does happen is the only possible outcome of conditions given prior to the event. The state of the world at a given time and the way the world works settles whatever is going to happen in the world at any later time.

As soon as the naturalistic view was applied to human choice the incompatibility between the modern view and the traditional one became evident. Either a person who chooses can equally well choose another alternative, or the alternative he is going to choose is settled prior to his very act of choosing. Philosophers like Hobbes faced this issue squarely and argued for the position-- one unpopular at the time--that human choices are no exception to determinacy of nature.

The heretical thesis of Hobbes is the orthodox position today. So much is this the case that most of the contemporary literature relevant to freedom and determinism is concerned with issues other than that on which Hobbes and his contemporaries concentrated their attention. However, we are as dissatisfied with the position prevalent today as Hobbes and others were with the position prevalent in their day. Thus, in this work we attempt to establish a thesis which few contemporary philosophers regard as defensible: that human persons can make free choices--choices such that only the act of choosing itself settles which alternative a person will choose.

"Freedom" has many other senses, but in this work we are not concerned except incidentally with questions about freedom in these other senses. The question whether someone can make a free choice has implications for morality and law, but in this work we are concerned only incidentally with such implications. Not only philosophers, but also scientists and theologians, have a stake in the controversy over free will and determinism. But in this work we not only concentrate on a single issue--whether someone can make a free choice--but we limit ourselves to philosophic methods of dealing with the issue. Even within the ambit of philo- sophical inquiry, we almost wholly avoid problems in the philosophy of science and the philosophy of religion. The present work be- longs, then, in the field of philosophy of mind or philosophy of action.

In our attempt to show that someone can make a free choice, we use self-referential argumentation. We argue that any affirma- tion of the thesis that no one can make a free choice is self- refuting. Either the proposition that no one can make a free choice is falsified by any rational affirmation of it, or any attempt to rationally affirm it is self-defeating. The method

12

of the argument we develop is called "self-referential" because
the argument works by showing the implications of the reference
which one who affirms that no one can make a free choice must
make to his own act of affirming his position.

Before summarizing the argument we lay out in chapter six,
we introduce the following abbreviations which we use throughout
the book. "Sfc" will name the proposition that someone can make
a free choice. "Nfc" will name the proposition that no one can
make a free choice. These two propositions articulate states of
affairs incompatible with each other. According to Sfc, there is
nothing about the world which precludes a human capacity to make
free choices, and at least some persons have this capacity.
According to Nfc, there is something about the world--about the
act of choosing, about human nature, about the natural world, or
about the nature of things--which precludes a human capacity to
make free choices. A proponent of Sfc is anyone who affirms Sfc,
anyone who thinks the world and human persons to be such that Sfc
is true or more reasonable to think true than its contradictory.
We use "PSfc" to name the proponent of Sfc; PNfc for the person who
affirms Nfc, anyone who thinks the world and human persons to be
such that Nfc is true or more reasonable to think true than its
contradictory. We need a name for the precise issue with which
we are concerned, both to make it easy to refer to this controversy and to make it clear that the issue we are considering is
distinct from all of the other issues involved in the controversy
over free will and determinism. We use "Sfc/Nfc" to name the
controversy between those who hold that someone can make a free
choice and those who hold that no one can make a free choice.

Thus, "Sfc" and "Nfc" name the contradictory propositions
which are the positions at issue; "PSfc" and "PNfc" name the persons, real or imaginary, who defend the respective positions; and
"Sfc/Nfc" names the controversy over the precise issue with which
we are concerned in this work.

We begin our argument in chapter six after having made clear
in previous parts of the book that Nfc is neither an evident
matter of fact nor a logical truth. The PNfc cannot rationally
affirm his position without offering some grounds for it. He has
opponents who are not merely ignorant of facts nor merely without
insight into logical necessities. The considerations which the
PNfc adduces in favor of his position must be relevant to the
issue and must have argumentative force. The PNfc, then, must
assume some norms by appeal to which he can, if challenged, show
the relevance and the argumentative force of the grounds he adduces for the position he defends. For example, the PNfc might
suggest his thesis as a hypothesis which should be accepted because Nfc is simpler than Sfc. The norm in this case is some

sort of simplicity rule. Again, the PNFc might suggest that Sfc ought to be rejected because the notion of free choice is somehow unintelligible. The norm in this case is some sort of principle that whatever is real must be intelligible.

Norms demanding simplicity in explanation and intelligibility in being are not easy to classify. They are neither factual descriptions nor formal truths. Their normativity or prescriptive force is odd. They do not have the normativity of a standard of psychological normality; one cannot simply write off one's philosophical opponents as mentally ill. They do not have the normativity of technical rules which make clear what will be required to achieve some optional goal; one cannot expect one's philosophical opponents to accept the same optional goals one accepts oneself. They do not have the normativity of certain rules of logic—those which cannot be violated without falling into incoherence; one who refuses to accept a conclusion drawn in accord with a rule of simplicity or some version of a principle of intelligibility does not fall into incoherence, even if he is unreasonable. They do not have the normativity of esthetic standards; one cannot refute one's philosophical opponents by showing that they have bad taste.

A PNfc maintains that his position is more reasonable unconditionally, and that everyone ought to be reasonable enough to accept Nfc. Yet he cannot maintain that Sfc is impossible, for it is a coherent possibility. Thus the PNfc's affirming of his position depends upon some prescription which directs persons interested in the issue to accept one of two coherent possibilities and which directs with unconditional normative force. Such a prescription presupposes that persons to whom it is given can choose the option which is prescribed although some one might not choose it. In other words, the norms to which the PNfc must at least implicitly appeal when he tries to show that one ought to accept his position have no force unless one can accept it although one need not accept it. Thus, the normativity the PNfc needs to justify his own position and to exclude Sfc as less reasonable presupposes that some human persons have a capacity to choose freely, for no one can accept the PNfc's demand that he be reasonable—a demand which is unconditional and yet can be rejected without logical absurdity—unless he can make a free choice.

Since a PNfc's very affirmation of his own position implies the demand that one be able to make a free choice, a PNfc cannot affirm his position without either falsifying it or asking that an impossible demand be met. If Sfc is true and one can meet the PNfc's demand, then Nfc is false, and the PNfc's position is falsified by the demand implicit in the very act of affirming it. If Sfc is false and one cannot meet the PNfc's demand, then the

PNfc's act of affirming his position is pointless, for it is
pointless to attempt what cannot succeed unless an impossible
demand be met.

Since any affirmation of Nfc must be either false or pointless, there is in principle no way to exclude Sfc. If Nfc is
false, then its contradictory is true. If any attempt to affirm
Nfc is pointless, then no one can rationally affirm anything
against Sfc. Yet there remains the common experience of choice,
which grounds a judgment many people make: that they do choose
freely. Furthermore, the normativity required to make rational
affirmations is a fact, and this fact--unless it is illusory--
implies Sfc. In this situation, Sfc must be affirmed to be true.
To refuse to affirm it would be to dismiss the data which support
it, although it is in principle impossible to have any rational
ground for affirming Nfc and dismissing these data.

Our interest in Sfc/Nfc partly arises out of the importance
of the issue to ethics. Since ethics seeks to answer questions
about the moral quality of human actions, and since free choice--
if it obtains--is a property of certain human acts which conditions all their other properties, one's ethical theory will be
distorted if one's position on Sfc/Nfc is mistaken. We realize
that many hold otherwise: that the truth about free choice makes
little or no difference to ethics. We disagree, although we do
not argue this point here.

Another motive for our interest in Sfc/Nfc is theological and
cultural. Judaism and Christianity view the human person as a
responsible agent, made in the image of God, capable of making
a free choice to accept or to reject God's self-revelation. If
Nfc is true, this theistic view of the human person makes no
sense. Likewise, we believe, the contemporary concern for the
autonomy and dignity of the person makes no sense unless Sfc is
true.

Meanings of the Word "Freedom"

In one sense, "freedom" means physical freedom. In this
sense, anything which behaves spontaneously--that is, without
external constraint or restraint--can be said to be free.

In this sense of "freedom" even nonorganic entities can be
called "free"; one speaks, for example, of "freely falling
bodies." Animals also are called "free" in this sense: an animal in the wild is free while one in captivity is not. Similarly,
a person who is drugged so that he is in a coma lacks physical
freedom. A person can be called "free" in this sense if he

acts spontaneously, not being constrained by someone else or restrained by prison bars and chains.

Physical freedom is subject to degree and depends on conditions. The more restrained something is by circumstances, the less room there is for its spontaneous behavior, and the less free it is. Also, the more constrained something is in its behavior, the less its behavior is its own, the less it seems active and the more it seems passive; hence the less free one takes it to be.

In a second sense, "freedom" means freedom to do as one pleases. In this sense, a person is called "free" if there is no one ordering him to do what he does not wish to do or forbidding him to do what he desires to do.

The adolescent demand for freedom from authority is often a demand for freedom in this sense. In this sense of "freedom," a slave, to the extent that he is a slave, is not free. A slave's lack of freedom need not reduce his physical freedom, although this too may be restricted. But a slave lacks freedom precisely in the sense that his action fulfills the demand of another, and only indirectly if at all any desire of his own. Historically, the quest for personal liberty from enslaving institutions also involves a quest for freedom in this sense.

Freedom to do as one pleases is subject to degree; how much of it one enjoys depends on circumstances. The more burdened one is by requirements laid upon him by others, the less scope he has to do as he pleases. The more influential one is in his relations with others, the more scope he has to do as he pleases.

"Freedom" is also used, but less commonly, to signify what we call "ideal freedom." In this sense of "freedom," individuals and societies are said to be "free" if they are not prevented from acting in accord with an ideal, whatever that ideal might be. If one is free in this sense, he has overcome or successfully avoided the obstacles to fulfilling an ideal.

With ideal freedom in mind, St. Paul considered the sinner not to be free, since the sinner is bound by his sin to fall short of the ideal of uprightness. Paul considered Christians free, because their redemption by Christ freed them for uprightness. Similarly Freud considered the neurotic not to be free. But the cured patient, freed of his neurosis, is able to behave in accord with a psychological ideal.

One has ideal freedom if he is not blocked in efforts to do as he ought to do. Often, what one ought to do and what one would like to do are opposed to each other. However, most ideals for human behavior are proposed with the expectation that, at some point, doing as one pleases and doing as one ought will coincide.

Ideal freedom has as many varieties as there are diverse conceptions of the ideal condition of the person and diverse views of the obstacles to be faced in fulfilling the ideal. One way of conceiving the ideal human condition is as a perfect society, such as Marx's ideal community. Ideal freedom in this case cannot be attained by isolated individuals but only by society as a whole. Yet the general concept of ideal freedom remains the same: persons have it when they <u>can</u> act as they ideally <u>would</u> act.

Another unfamiliar concept can be expressed by "freedom"—the emergence of novelty. This freedom obtains when factors which tend toward repetition are overcome.

The creative artist may be called "free" in this sense because he introduces something new and is not merely repeating previous accomplishments. Some philosophers have regarded the whole of reality as an ongoing process—rather like the creative process of art—in which novelties regularly emerge. Such philosophies admit an element of indeterminism in nature and do not reduce emerging novelties to antecedent conditions and their laws.

Freedom as emergence of novelty is distinct from physical freedom, because physical freedom is defined by the given spontaneity of the entity in question, whereas freedom as emergence of novelty can involve the emergence of a new spontaneity. Freedom to do as one pleases can be as repetitive and noncreative as one's desires happen to be, whereas freedom as emergence of novelty can involve an emergence of new desires. Ideal freedom presupposes a given principle in accord with which action should proceed; freedom as emergence of novelty can involve the creation of novel principles and the emergence of new ideals.

In one sense, "political freedom" means a version of freedom to do as one pleases which applies to nations. In this sense, a country is said to be "free" when it is not subject to the rule of some other country. Nations, like individuals, can be bound in slavery or can enjoy liberty.

But there are other senses of "political freedom." In one of these, "freedom" means the participation of individuals in governing their own polity. There is political freedom of this sort in a nation to the extent that factors which would inhibit such participation are excluded. In this sense, children are not politically free. In Western liberal democracies, practically all adults are, at least to some extent. "Political freedom" can be used to refer to the social analogues of the referents of other senses of "freedom" previously distinguished.

"Free Choice" Defined

The word "freedom" also can be used to refer to freedom of choice. Since this work is concerned with Sfc/Nfc, we have distinguished other meanings of "freedom" mainly in order to forestall confusion. In this section, we define what we mean by "free choice" as it occurs in "Someone can make a free choice." We do not consider our definition of "free choice" arbitrary for we think that our use of the expression is the same as some uses of it in ordinary language. Moreover, the definition we propose captures the essentials of the experience on the basis of which people often think their choices are free. This experience will be articulated in sections C through F.

Someone makes a free choice if and only if he makes a choice $\underline{C}$ in the actual world, and there is a possible world such that he does not make $\underline{C}$ in this possible world and everything in this possible world except his making $\underline{C}$ and the consequences of his making $\underline{C}$ is the same as in the actual world.

The following remarks will clarify the meaning and implications of this definition.

If a choice is free the causal conditions for that choice are such that they would also be the conditions for not making that choice except insofar as these conditions include the person's very choosing itself and the consequences of his choice. Thus, a choice's being free is consistent with its having necessary causal conditions other than the choice itself; such necessary causal conditions would be called "causes of the choice" provided that "cause" not be taken to mean "sufficient condition."

Normally, one chooses not merely to do an act or not to do it, but to do one act or another. Obviously, the two positive possibilities do not share all the same necessary conditions. However, one can choose either only insofar as the necessary conditions of both are given--or, at least, expected to be given. The two alternatives have a common set of conditions necessary for either of them being chosen--the person about to choose must be interested in both, must be aware of both, must regard the joint realization of the two as impossible. The person's very choosing-- if choice is free--makes the difference in that all other conditions necessary for carrying out both alternatives being given--

18

or expected--and all other necessary conditions for choosing either
being given, one's very choosing is the only factor which brings
it about that one alternative rather than the other is pursued.

Moreover, on our definition, a free choice would not be a
chance event. Its causally sufficient condition could be specified: the necessary conditions other than the choice together
with a person's very choosing. Choosing is not a wholly isolated
event; it is something a person does.

Choice--What it is Not

We must next describe a distinctive way in which someone is
said to "make a choice." The expression is used in the relevant
sense in the sentence: "John made a choice to join the Peace
Corps." In this experience, we think, are to be found the phenomena which give rise to the conviction that people make free
choices. Of course, the mere fact that someone has an experience
which leads him to judge that he makes free choices does not of
itself guarantee the reality of such freedom.

The experience we are concerned with often is called "making
up one's mind" or "decision." "Choice" and "decision" and "making
up one's mind" have other uses. "Choice" sometimes refers to
overt behavior--for example, taking a certain french pastry from
a tray. Such picking of one object from an available set of objects may or may not involve the experience of choice in which
we are interested. "Decision" sometimes refers to an act which is
essentially cognitive--for example, a literary critic decides that
Shakespeare indeed wrote "Hamlet." The experience of making such
a judgment is not an experience of choosing what to do. The expression "to make up one's mind" also is sometimes used in an
essentially cognitive sense. This expression, however, brings
out the reflexive character of the activity we are going to describe. The same aspect of the experienced activity is emphasized
by certain expressions in other languages, for example, by the
French, "Je me décide."

For brevity's sake, we refer to the experience with which we
are concerned simply as "choice."

Choice is not a theoretical construct, but is a phenomenon
which can be described. There are, however, certain related
phenomena which must be distinguished from choice. These include
being interested, wishing, and behaving.

One is interested in anything of which he is aware and which
makes a practical difference to him. Interest can be prior to

choice. One must be interested in at least two different possibilities before any question of choice arises.

"Wishing" does not indicate an indeterminacy to be settled. It is often used in contexts in which there is some obstacle in the way of effective action. Wishing can precede deliberation and choice, and then the obstacle to action can be the need to choose how to act for that for which one wishes. Wishing also can follow choice, as when one finds a chosen course of action blocked but still wishes for the attainment of that for which he had chosen to act. Then too, one can wish for what he thinks is simply unattainable; such wishing neither precedes nor follows choice but is irrelevant to it.

Behavior which comes about by choice is obviously distinct from choice. It is possible to choose to do something and then to discover that one cannot do what one had chosen to do. For example, one can make up his mind to take an automobile trip but be prevented from doing so by lack of gasoline. The distinction between choice and behavior is clear from their separation in such cases.

Besides the experiences of interest, wishing, and behavior, there are also certain experiences of being drawn into action without deliberation. These are not experiences of choice; they must be distinguished from it. There are various such experiences.

One may feel an overwhelming need which cannot be resisted--for example, a starving man may feel an overwhelming need to eat, so that when food becomes available he eats it without hesitation. A person under torture may resist for a time, but, finally, overcome by his agony, blurt out information which is sought. In such cases, one does not choose to act; one is driven to act. No making of a choice is experienced; in fact, the experience can be one of being compelled to act contrary to what one had chosen to do.

There are also many cases in which one's behavior follows an impulse without reflection or hesitation. For example, as one is reading he becomes aware that he is thirsty, and as he comes to the end of a section goes for a drink. If someone were to ask why he behaved thus, he might reply: "I just felt like it; I felt thirsty." This reason was not a ground for choosing to drink rather than not to drink. Rather, he was aware of no alternative. Given the motive, without awareness of anything opposing, one acts without hesitation.

Experiences of acting in accord with a habitual pattern of behavior are very common. For example, one gets up in the morning, dresses, has breakfast, and sets off for work--all without hesitation, deliberation, and choice. The habitual pattern perhaps was established by choices at some more or less remote time in the past, and the habitual pattern could perhaps be altered if one reflected upon it and saw any reason to alter it. ·However, as the habitual behavior pattern is usually carried out, it simply does not involve any choices at all.

Acting in accord with overwhelming need, acting spontaneously, and acting habitually must be distinguished from acting upon choice. Choice follows hesitation and indecision. One must make up one's mind because it is unmade; it is in some disarray.

An Example of Choice

A young man receives a notice to report for induction into the army. He considers various possibilities. He might leave the country; he might stay in the country but not report for induction; or he might report as the notice requires. Each course of action has potential advantages and disadvantages. If he leaves the country he could live in safety and avoid reporting for induction to serve in a war which he might consider immoral. But this alternative carries the disadvantage of extended, perhaps permanent, exile. If. he stays in the country and evades the draft, he avoids both exile and service, but risks imprisonment. If he reports as required, he accepts all the disadvantages of military service, including participation in a military action which he perhaps considers immoral. But if he reports, he pre- serves his citizenship and avoids the risk of prison. The young man considers the possibilities and makes up his mind, let us suppose, to report for induction.

There are many other examples of choice. A student considers whether to spend an evening at a beer party, or to stay in his room to study for an important test; he makes up his mind one way or the other. Someone considers whether to go out of town for a holiday weekend, or to stay and visit with a friend who will be in town that weekend; he chooses one alternative. A young per- son considers whether to go into law school, with the idea of entering practice in that profession, or to go on to graduate school and a career in scholarship; he decides for one or the other.

The experience of making choices occurs repeatedly throughout life; it is not unusual.

The Beginnings of Choice

The initial context for choosing is an experienced conflict of desires or interests. If the young man of our example had not felt an aversion both to reporting for induction and to the consequences of refusing to do so, he would not have had to make a choice. The situation opens incompatible possibilities, at least the two possibilities of either acting or refraining from action. Some felt emotion, interest, impulse, or inclination draws him toward each of the alternatives. The conflict leads to hesitation; immediate behavior is blocked. He stops and thinks.

The experience of choice is framed by definite alternatives, each of which presents itself as attractive in one or more ways. Yet each alternative also has its limitations; none promises complete satisfaction. The first stage of the experience of choice is being moved to consider alternatives, rather than simply being drawn by an unopposed motive to act without reflection.

It is important to notice that many factors--of which a person might or might not be aware--limit the alternatives which present themselves. If one's disposition and temperament have been formed in such a way that certain possibilities do not arouse interest, then he will not consider them as alternatives for choice. If one is ignorant of certain possibilities or mistakenly thinks courses of action impossible which in fact are possible, then such alternatives will be excluded from the very beginning. For example, a young person being brought up in unfavorable conditions of poverty and discrimination might be aware of very few possibilities, and his early formation might allow even fewer of these to become live options.

Another important point is that moral conflicts are not the only cases in which choices are called for. Situations requiring "will power" to overcome a temptation against one's moral standard can give rise to deliberation and lead to choice. But moral concerns are only one sort of motive which can give rise to choice situations, and moral conflicts are absent from many such situations. A student choosing between law school and graduate school need not see his option as one between moral good and evil.

The beginnings of choice are present in any situation in which one is unsettled about his own future action. Choice does not concern the actions of others, except insofar as one is acting with them, or they are acting under one's direction. Alternatives must be open, or at least must seem to be open. Choice is concerned with the future, not with the past. The past appears settled, and choice is directly concerned with prospective action. The outcome of the situation is felt to be open only to the extent that one supposes it can be affected by what one can actually do.

The possibilities which appear to be open--the alternatives confronting the young man who has received his draft notice-- seem to be live options. They are genuine possibilities for him; he is really interested to some extent in each of them. Of course, an apparent alternative might not be real--perhaps the border has been closed so that the alternative of going to a foreign country is no longer available. It can still appear to be an alternative and can even be chosen, so long as the young man is not aware of its impossibility. In other words, the possibility must be open so far as he knows; it need not really be open.

To one who is faced with the necessity of making a choice, it seems that the alternatives are really open and unsettled, all things considered. Normally the first thing one does is to examine the situation to see whether there are not factors already taken for granted which can settle the apparently unsettled situation, thus obviating the need for real deliberation and choice.

For example, a couple wishes to make a month-long tour of Europe. A number of factors are already settled, and they take these factors for granted when they go to the travel agency. For example, the tour must leave after the first of July and return before the end of August. The total cost cannot exceed $4,000. The tour must allow them time to visit a small town in Eastern Germany, from which the husband's family emigrated. The travel agent produces information about a number of tours, which he thinks might be of interest to the couple. Studying this information, they discover that some of the tours leave too early or return too late; some cost too much, or will not allow them time to visit the village in Eastern Germany. In fact, only one tour which they can find satisfies all of the conditions they had set in advance. They decide to take that one. They might say that they "choose" that tour.

In one sense of "choose," of course, they do choose it. However, the same choice could be made by a computer, if it were properly programmed and fed the information concerning the conditions a tour would have to meet to satisfy the couple's requirements. Given the assumptions and the actual conditions of the alternatives, there really is no open possibility except one. However, it might have seemed to the couple, when they first received the information from the travel agent, that they faced several live options, and that they would have to choose among them by criteria supplementary to those already settled.

Many choice-situations are similar to this example, and someone might argue that all choice-situations are of this sort. However, sometimes an individual feels that he has considered all available information but thinks that alternatives still remain open and does not think that anything already given will lead to a unique resolution of the question as to what is to be done.

Of course, when a person does something following a calculation which has led to the exclusion of every possibility but one, just as when he does something without needing to stop and reflect, he can proceed with a sense of "freedom"--meaning physical freedom or the freedom to do as one pleases. He need not feel constrained, compelled, restrained, or in any way forced. But he is not deliberating and choosing, and thus there is no question of free choice.

In cases of this sort, deliberation and choice perhaps occurred previously. If the couple of our example chose the conditions which settled their decision in favor of the tour which they took, then this prior choice might have seemed to them free and the later decision also might seem free. The sense of freedom might be especially strong in a person who is prepared at any time to reconsider his choice of the conditions of a decision. Thus, if the couple were not altogether committed to making the tour until they chose the particular one they accepted, then their choice of that particular tour included the final decision to make the trip. Until then, the choice was only tentative and conditional.

Deliberation and Choice

Given alternative possible courses of action, one must settle among them if one is going to act at all. This settling among alternatives begins with active, practical reflection upon the alternatives--such reflection is called "deliberation." Deliberation forms a bridge between the opening situation, in which hesitation occurs in virtue of a conflict of desires or interests, and the closing act of making a choice.

Deliberation is active thinking; it is not merely vacillation. The opening situation does include vacillation, as motives for each alternative present themselves, and no alternative seems satisfactory in every respect. Deliberation begins when one starts to reflect on the possibilities, to consider the various motives, to seek actively for a resolution of the impasse.

The possible reasons for each choice need not all be present and clearly articulated at the beginning of deliberation. The marshalling of considerations and clarification of possible reasons are part of deliberation. As one proceeds in deliberating, one sees that certain possibilities which seemed viable at the beginning are not, while one comes to see other alternatives of which one was not initially aware. Deliberation prepares a clear reason for acting in accord with each alternative which remains under consideration. Whatever choice is eventually made, one will be in a position to say why that choice was made by recalling the considerations already adduced in deliberation in favor of the alternative finally chosen.

Deliberation begins with uncertainty. One does not know what he is going to do. But uncertainty about one's future action often carries with it a certain unsettledness about one's present self. In important choices one has the feeling that whatever one chooses, the outcome will more or less significantly alter or confirm one's identity. As a person deliberates, he considers what difference it would make to himself to carry out each of the alternatives.

One can deliberate about possible actions without knowing when the opportunity for action will arrive. For example, a person can deliberate about where he will spend his next vacation without knowing when he will next have a vacation. Such deliberation can lead to a choice based on a condition not within one's power, provided that the condition is not known to be impossible. For example, a person can make up his mind to go on a certain vacation if he is given enough time off from work or a large enough bonus to finance the trip. Such advance deliberation also can lead to a tentative decision; one can decide to take a certain trip unless some other, more interesting possibility arises.

There is no incompatibility between carrying on deliberation and having a basis on which one can guess the outcome. Perhaps a person has a strong inclination to one alternative at the outset and on the basis of past experience with similar inclinations judges that he will most likely decide to follow it, for he has usually followed similar inclinations in similar situations before. A person in this frame of mind is still able to deliberate. However, if he knew for certain what he was going to do, there would seem to be no alternative and the possibility of deliberation would be removed.

A person engaged in deliberation feels he can go on deliberating or can stop. After a time reflection no longer yields any additional considerations. One finds himself reviewing the same ground. Still, further reflection might turn up something new. So one can continue to reflect. If choice is not urgent, one can set aside the deliberation with a view to considering the matter later when some further factors might come into view.

25

It is worth noting that deliberation itself can become the subject of a second-level deliberation and choice. Thus, one can shift from deliberating about the original problem to deliberating about whether to terminate deliberation or to go on with it.

While a person is still deliberating, he sees alternative courses of action as possibilities. He sees the various choices to initiate those courses of action as all genuinely possible. He expresses this possibility: "I can make this choice, and then again I can make that one." This possibility is not mere contingency. It is not as if a person were expecting one or another set of events, all of which were beyond his control. Rather, the possible choices appear to be within his power. "It is really up to me what I am going to do," expresses this experience.

When one sees an animal vacillate between two courses of action—for example, pursuit of food and obedience to a command to stay—one might say that it "can do either one." By this one would mean that one knows of nothing constraining or restraining the animal—that it has physical freedom. One need not suppose the animal to be considering possibilities, as if it were about to choose. Rather, one supposes that the animal's impulses settle the issue, that the stronger impulse prevails. A human person, however, when he is about to choose thinks that he himself is going to settle the issue.

Thus, when the youth of our example considered that he could submit to induction, leave the country, or stay and risk going to prison, "could" did not mean mere logical possibility or causal contingency. A person supposes that he himself makes his choice and that nothing makes him make the choice he makes. In other words, he thinks that the causal conditions apart from his own choosing are not sufficient to bring his choosing about.

The act of choice involves focusing of attention on one alternative, the one chosen. But there is more to choice than focus of attention. Even in the very act of choosing, one can remain aware of what he is not choosing, as evidenced by the feeling one sometimes has of surrendering what was attractive in the rejected alternative. After choice, the choice does not come unmade when one turns his attention to other matters.

As we have seen, a person deliberates with an awareness of possibilities and with a belief that he can and must settle among them. He does not experience something happening which he can identify as the choice itself. A person does not encounter his choices; he makes his choices. The experience of choice is an experience of doing something; it is not an experience of undergoing anything.

26

The connotation of passivity in the word "experience" is
misleading if it makes one suppose that consciousness of choos-
ing--at the moment of choice--is passive in the way in which
having a dream, feeling dizzy, or hearing a noise is passive. A
person's own choosing is not given to himself; in this sense,
choice is not a datum.

Even if choosing is not a datum at the moment of choice, one
is directly aware of it. One can tell that he has made a choice
immediately upon making it. In retrospect, of course, choice can
be noted to be a datum. One is clearly aware of having moved
from deliberation about possibilities to the state of having made
up his mind; choice divides the two. Thus one's knowledge of his
own choices is not inferential.

From Experience to Judgment

Reflecting upon the phenomena described, we distinguish
three aspects of the experience. First, one experiences a state
of affairs in which his desire or interest is aroused by alternative possibilities, without experiencing anything limiting the
possibilities to one. Second, one feels that it is within his
power to take one alternative or another, and that nothing but
the exercise of this power will realize one of the alternatives.
Third, one is aware of making his choice, without being aware of
anything else making him make that choice. We call these three
aspects taken together "a sense of freedom."

But having a sense of freedom must be distinguished from the
judgments one makes on the basis of this experience. Corresponding to each aspect of the experience, there is a judgment.
These judgments might be expressed as follows. Corresponding to
the first aspect: "I could do this and then again I could do
that; the alternatives are really open possibilities." Corresponding to the second aspect: "It is in my own power to do this
or that; it is up to me alone to settle which I shall do."
Corresponding to the third aspect: "I made up my own mind, and
nothing made me choose as I did." If someone asserts any of
these three judgments, he implies that the choice to which he
refers is free.

Each of the three judgments has a positive and a negative
aspect. The positive aspects of the judgments--"I could do this
and then again I could do that," "it is in my own power to do
this or that," and "I made up my own mind"--reflect what is present in the experience. A person is aware of possibilities as
desirable but incompatible; he is aware that no possibility is
attractive in every respect; and he is aware that he can make
his own evaluation of the diverse respects in which various

27

possibilities are desirable. The negative aspects of the judgments—"the possibilities are really open," "it is up to me alone," and "nothing made me choose as I did" —cannot in the same way express what is present in experience.

In a certain sense, any judgment involves more than experience. If one experiences rain falling on his head, in judging that rain is falling on his head, he makes a truth-claim which he does not make simply by having the experience. An experience can be illusory, but an experience cannot be false. Many judgments based upon experience also presuppose the truth of assumptions which are so much taken for granted that they are not noted. For example, one who experiences himself flipping a switch and seeing a light go on thinks that his flipping the switch makes the light go on, since he takes for granted assumptions about the way in which the electrical apparatus works.

Some negative judgments—for example, a judgment distinguishing two objects of perception—do not go beyond experience in ways other than affirmative judgments do. However, some negative judgments require a further step beyond experience. For example, if one looks in the refrigerator for cheese and finds none there, the judgment that there is no cheese in the refrigerator is not based upon data alone. The negative judgment can be false without the experience being illusory—for example, if the cheese is there but hidden from sight. A negative judgment based on the absence of data presupposes a framework of expectations in which the absence of those data normally grounds the negative judgment; although this framework is an epistemic condition for making the negative judgment, it is not part of the state of affairs articulated in the proposition asserted in the negative judgment.

Other examples might help to clarify the point. If someone asks me whether I have eaten breakfast and if I do not recall having done so, I judge that I have not yet eaten breakfast. One assumes that the absence of memory of an event which would have been so recent warrants the judgment that it did not occur. But this assumption is a framework of the judgment, not a premise from which the proposition affirmed is deduced. I do not infer that I have not eaten breakfast, although the judgment could be mistaken if the usual conditions set by the appropriate framework happen not to be fulfilled. Similarly, if I perceive nothing which would prevent me from doing something which I know how to do, then I judge that I can do it.

If this analysis is correct, it follows that when someone judges that he has made a free choice, his judgment is likely to seem to him self-evident, since it is not an inference but is grounded directly in his experience. At the same time, since this judgment presupposes a framework of expectations, the judgment will be false if the expectations are mistaken. Therefore, the judgment can be challenged without challenging the data as they appear to the person who makes the judgment.

For example, the judgment, "I have not yet eaten breakfast," made by someone who has just suffered a severe blow to the head, could be challenged without challenging the accuracy of the individual's description of his current experience, since in such a situation there is a plausible ground for questioning the assumption that absence of memory of an event which would have been so recent warrants the judgment that the event did not occur. Similarly, the judgment, "I freely chose x," can be challenged without challenging the accuracy of a person's description of his experience of choice. There are plausible grounds--for example, grounds suggested by modern psychology--for questioning the assumption that absence of awareness of awareness of a causal condition other than one's own choosing warrants the judgment that there is no such condition.

The phenomena summed up in the "sense of freedom" are not identical with the judgment that one is free. The sense of freedom and the judgment that one is making a free choice are to be distinguished.

The preceding point makes clear that in describing the experience of choice we have not asserted that people make free choices. One can admit the entire description of choice presented here, yet still hold that no one makes any free choice. One who holds this will challenge the framework of expectations in virtue of which many people make the judgment that they have made a free choice. For this framework, he will substitute some such assumption as the following: "Even if I am not conscious of anything which makes me choose as I do, there must be something which brings my choice about."

The significance of the experience of choice, as we have described it, is that if someone accepts it at face value, including the negative aspects, he will judge that he chooses freely; in retrospect, he will think that under the very same conditions he could have chosen otherwise than he in fact chose.

The foregoing description of the experience of choice and the analysis of the corresponding judgments show that the expression "free choice" has a reference in experience. While there are other semantic problems which must be treated prior to an attempt to resolve Sfc/Nfc, one serious obstacle to considering the controversy genuine is removed by establishing a reference for "free choice" without prejudging whether there are free choices.

Should anyone challenge the foregoing formulation of the experience of choice and the corresponding judgments, our reply is that at least some people would accept this formulation as an expression of their experience and the way they talk about it.

Whether Sfc or Nfc is true remains to be settled. Some have argued that the experience of choice is sufficient to establish Sfc. In chapter two, section A, we show that arguments articulated along these lines are question-begging.

The Affirmation of "No Free Choice"

If Nfc is true, then no one's affirmations and utterances can be freely chosen acts. Affirming and uttering certainly are among a person's acts, but if Nfc is true, no one can freely choose to do these acts any more than he can freely choose to do any other acts. If no one's affirmations and utterances can be freely chosen acts, then no PNfc's affirming or uttering can be a freely chosen act. The PNfc is a man among men; if no one can make a free choice, neither can he. If no PNfc's affirming or uttering can be a freely chosen act, then no PNfc's stating of Nfc can involve a freely chosen act. Whenever a PNfc states his thesis, he performs an instance of the kinds of acts which are affirmations and utterances. Thus, if Nfc is true, any statement of it, in excluding the possibility of free choice generally, excludes free choice from the very act which affirms it.

A proposition's truth or falsity depends upon whether the state of affairs it picks out obtains. Whether or not the state of affairs a proposition picks out obtains, the reference of the proposition remains the same. Thus, the reference of Nfc remains the same whether it is true or false. Nfc has an instance referring to any possible human act; thus, it has an instance referring to any possible act of affirming or uttering, and so to any possible act of affirming Nfc and uttering sentences which express Nfc. Hence, it is clear that Nfc is a performatively self-referential proposition.

We argue in chapter six that Nfc is self-refuting--that any affirmation of Nfc relevant to Sfc/Nfc either falsifies Nfc or renders the affirming of it self-defeating. To prepare for this argument, we now clarify what is involved in the affirming of Nfc. To do so, we must clarify what is involved in making any grounded affirmation.

At the beginning of this chapter, we defined an "act of affirming" as any propositional act by which someone holds a proposition to be true or reasonable to accept. Assenting to a proposition by faith, accepting it as a hypothesis which has some likelihood, and asserting it are among the ways of affirming it. Thus, one affirms a proposition whenever he holds it to be true or more likely to be so than not.

"To affirm" sometimes is taken to mean to publicly assert a proposition as absolutely certain. In this sense of "to affirm," its contrary is "to disavow"; one only denies a proposition in this sense if one publicly rejects the proposition as certainly false. Between affirming and denying in these strong senses, there obviously are many propositional acts which involve holding a proposition true or likely. By contrast, according to the definition of "affirming" which we have adopted, any propositional act by which one holds a proposition to be true or reasonable to accept is an affirmation of the proposition.

In Sfc/Nfc, it is clear that the PNfc must affirm Nfc. If one merely proposes the proposition as an interesting possibility, neither affirming it nor denying it, he is not a PNfc, for his propositional act in respect to the proposition is no more that of a PNfc than that of a PSfc. In a dispute about which of two contradictory propositions is true, one cannot be located on either side unless one expresses at least very tentatively a propositional act leaning toward one side.

To put the same point in other words, Nfc describes a world from which the ability to make free choices is absent. If any such world exists, then in that world no one can make a free choice. But the mere proposition, Nfc, does not claim that the actual world excludes Sfc. This claim is made only when someone holds Nfc true or likely true of the actual world—in other words, only when someone affirms Nfc. The mere proposition, Nfc, can be doubted or denied as well as affirmed. One who doubts it or denies it does not exclude free choice from the actual world, but leaves room for it.

Affirmations can be made in different ways; they can be groundless or they can be grounded.

A groundless affirmation is a gratuitous preference for one of a pair of contradictories. One of the pair is held without any epistemic warrant to be true or more likely. For example, a person knowing nothing about space exploration might affirm that travel to distant stars will be achieved within the next century, and another equally ignorant person might dispute this by saying that such travel is impossible. Of such groundless affirmations and denials, barroom arguments are made. One also can make an affirmation despite the availability to him of grounds for making the contradictory affirmation. For example,

31

a person who is told that he is dying of incurable cancer might affirm for many months that he is not seriously ill and that he surely does not have cancer.

In such cases, the groundless affirmation and the irrational affirmation remain affirmations. One proposition is held to be true or likely; its contradictory is held to be false or unlikely. A person who publicly affirms a proposition without grounds asks others to accept it and to reject its contradictory, but if anyone asks why the proposition should be accepted, no reason can be given for accepting it. The reasonableness of accepting it, or even of considering it, is not shown.

If the PNfc affirmed his position in this way, he would exclude Sfc only by an ipse dixit. However, Sfc/Nfc is a controversy to which the parties are scientists, philosophers, theologians, and others who are, or who at least claim to be, engaged in the serious pursuit of truth. In such company, anyone who makes arbitrary affirmations is ignored as soon as the arbitrariness of his affirmations becomes clear. Thus, the PNfc not only affirms Nfc but also proposes it as a grounded affirmation.

Affirmations can be grounded in different ways: by direct evidence, by logical insight or analysis, and by other procedures—for example, inductive argument.

If one has direct evidence for a proposition, one's affirming of it will be epistemically legitimate. For example, if one sees rain falling, one's affirmation that rain is falling has epistemic legitimacy. In such a case, the grounds for the affirmation are immediately given. If one has evidence of this sort, it is reasonable to affirm the proposition for which one has it, but it is not merely more reasonable to affirm the proposition than its contradictory. It is unreasonable and perhaps impossible to deny a proposition for which one has such evidence.

If one understands the formula of a logically true proposition, one's affirmation of it also will be epistemically legitimate. For example, if one understands $6 + 7 = 17 - 4$, then one's affirming of the equation has epistemic legitimacy. The same can be said for one's affirming of the conclusion of a more complex logical or mathematical proof. Here again the claim is not that it is more likely that the proposition is true or more reasonable to accept, but rather that it is perhaps impossible not to assent to it.

Statements of fact based on immediate evidence and statements of logically true propositions are not the only sorts of grounded affirmations. There are many statements--for example, interpretations of data, generalizations, and hypotheses--which one reasonably affirms, although they are based only somewhat indirectly on evidence. There are also propositions which are shown to be true by the analysis of language or by conceptual clarification which are reasonably affirmed, although they are neither self-evident nor logically necessary. There also are propositions supported by authority which one reasonably affirms. A great many--if not most--of the truths people think they know are propositions which they affirm on the authority of parents, teachers, friends, neighbors, journalists, technical experts, scientists, religious leaders, and so forth.

We define as "rational affirmations" all affirmations which are grounded otherwise than by direct evidence or by insight into logical truth. One affirms rationally if and only if the proposition he affirms is one more reasonable for him to hold true or likely than its contradictory. The contradictory of a rational affirmation remains consistent both with the direct evidence one has and with the logically necessary propositions one knows.

In the present work, we are concerned with a controversy regarding a set of facts--the phenomena of choice. In chapters two and three we pointed out that some on each side of the controversy have suggested that the affirmation of their position is based upon direct evidence. But neither of these claims succeeds; both depend upon a failure to recognize the limits of what can be derived from the data alone. Nor does an appeal to logically necessary truths settle the controversy. A clear example of this is the failure of the fatalist attempt to derive Nfc from logical truths alone. It remains that the affirmation either of Sfc or of Nfc can be at best a rational affirmation.

Thus, as we have seen Nfc is affirmed as a hypothesis by physical and psychological determinists. Some psychological determinists and some who attack the intelligibility of free choice seem to regard clarification of the phenomena of choice or conceptual analysis as an important ground for their affirmation of Nfc. Operationalists consider their affirmation of Nfc to be justified rationally by its fruitfulness. Religious believers who affirm Nfc think their assent to it is justified by the authority of their faith.

In chapter six, we argue that any attempted rational affirmation of Nfc either falsifies Nfc or renders the attempt to affirm it self-defeating. Our argument will rest on the claim that there are necessary conditions for rationally affirming Nfc-- that is, conditions which must be fulfilled if the attempt to rationally affirm it is to succeed. To clarify the notion of conditions for rational affirmation, we note that many human acts have conditions which must be met if these acts are to be what they are intended to be.

As we mentioned previously, C.K. Grant points out that making a statement has what he calls "pragmatic implications," and that if these implications are false, the making of the statement is irrational. Somewhat similarly, John R. Searle explains that an illocutionary act such as promising has a set of conditions which must be satisfied for a successful and nondefective act.

In law, conditions are laid down for the success of acts such as making a contract or a will, indicting a person, passing sentence on a convict, and so on. If the conditions are not met, the attempted legal act can be held null and void. In religion, likewise, there are conditions for the validity as well as for the licitness of ritual acts, such as sacraments; the ritual is believed to be pointless if conditions for its validity, at least, are not satisfied.

It seems reasonable to suppose that there are analogous conditions for the propositional acts of affirming and denying. If there are such conditions and they are not fulfilled, then acts of affirming and denying will be defective in some way. Such conditions for rationally affirming a proposition would be neither a function of the meaning or truth of the proposition nor of the meaningfulness of the language used in stating it.

Assuming there are conditions for making rationally grounded affirmations, then if these conditions are not fulfilled an attempt to make such an affirmation fails to be what it was meant to be—a rational affirmation. Of course, one's affirming can succeed in this respect—when conditions obtain—and one's statement can still go wrong in some other way. For example, one can succeed in affirming a false proposition or a proposition inconsistent with other propositions of which one is more certain. One might have rational grounds for affirming a proposition—for example, one might have evidence which confirms a plausible hypothesis—yet the evidence itself might consist in faulty observations. For these reasons, an attempt to make a rational affirmation can succeed, although the proposition one affirms is false, inconsistent with other propositions which one should prefer to it, or actually without the ground one supposes one has.

Thus, it seems that certain conditions must obtain if one is to be successful in rationally affirming a proposition such as Nfc. Inasmuch as we regard Sfc as true, we obviously consider Nfc false and think there are many propositions inconsistent with Nfc which one should prefer to it. Moreover, in chapter three,

34

we have disputed the soundness of all the grounds we know of on which Nfc has been affirmed. However, we have not disputed--in fact, we have made clear--that Nfc is rationally affirmed. Thus, we assume that the conditions for rationally affirming Nfc can obtain. We next consider certain of these conditions.

The normativity involved in the affirmation of Nfc has properties partly common to the normativity of logical norms and technical norms.

Like a logical norm, the norm required to rationally affirm Nfc has an unconditional force. Logical norms are conditioned neither upon one's purposes nor upon contingent states of affairs. Whatever one might wish to do or to think, one must be consistent. The exclusion of Sfc in the rational affirmation of Nfc is also unconditional.

However, the normativity needed to exclude Sfc is like that of a technical norm in that it prescribes one from a set of coherent alternatives. Sfc is coherent, yet it is rationally excluded by the rational affirmation of Nfc.

Thus, the normativity required to rationally exclude Sfc unconditionally prescribes one of two coherent and incompatible alternatives. However, the unconditionality of this prescribing is distinct from that of logical norms. Also, the openness of the alternatives presupposed by this prescribing is distinct from the openness of the alternatives presupposed by technical norms.

The unconditionality of a logical norm consists in the fact that its violation is irrational in the sense of being incoherent. The unconditionality of the normativity required to rationally exclude Sfc consists in the fact that the PSfc's violation of it-- as the PNfc sees it--is irrational in the sense that it violates a rationality norm which both the PSfc and the PNfc must respect.

The alternatives, one of which is prescribed in rationally affirming Nfc, are not only logically coherent, but also physically and psychologically possible, and they are not such that either of them is indispensable for achieving a purpose necessarily shared by everyone. There are open alternatives; both Sfc and Nfc can be affirmed. However, if the affirmation of one alternative is rational, the other alternative is not open to a person who is committed to the rational pursuit of truth.

A PNfc might object to the foregoing analysis by saying that the normativity of the rationality norm which he assumes in affirming Nfc either precludes open alternatives to his affirmation or prescribes only conditionally. However, as we showed in chapter five, section E, in the context of Sfc/Nfc, Nfc must be

35

rationally affirmed. Unlike other grounded affirmations—those based on immediate evidence and/or derived from logical truths—a rational affirmation does leave an alternative open as a possibility, but as one less reasonable to accept. Moreover, the PNfc who attempts to ground his affirmation by an appeal to a technical rule for achieving a particular purpose rather than to a rationality norm finds that he cannot exclude rational opponents. We made the latter point clear in our analysis and critique of operational grounds for affirming Nfc in chapter three, section F.

In this section we have shown that in rationally excluding Sfc the PNfc requires a normativity which prescribes unconditionally and between open alternatives. This clarification of the kind of normativity required to rationally exclude Sfc permits us to dispense with the empirical assumption we made in our first formulation of our argument in section B. The second formulation of our argument will show that if the conditions obtain which are necessary to rationally affirm Nfc, then Nfc is inevitably falsified by any rational affirmation of it. After stating this argument in E, we will show in F that the prescriptivity of the PNfc's rational exclusion of Sfc cannot be in force unless Sfc is true.

Second Formulation of the Argument

1) The PNfc rationally affirms Nfc. (By assumption.)
2) If Nfc is rationally affirmed, then the conditions obtain whereby Sfc is rationally excluded. (By the clarifications in chapter five, section E.)
3) The conditions obtain whereby Sfc can be rationally excluded. (From (1) and (2).)
4) If the conditions obtain whereby Sfc is rationally excluded, then some rationality norm must be in force. (By the clarifications in chapter five, section F.)
5) A rationality norm adequate to warrant an affirmation which excludes Sfc is in force. (From (3) and (4).)
(The preceding steps are identical with the corresponding steps in the first formulation in B; the following steps are different.)
6*) Any norm by which a PNfc can rationally exclude Sfc has a normativity which prescribes unconditionally and prescribes one of two open alternatives. (Established in D.)
7*) Any norm which prescribes unconditionally and prescribes one of two open alternatives is in force only if the person to whom it is addressed can make a free choice. (To be established in F.)

8*) Any norm by which the PNfc can rationally exclude Sfc is in force only if the person to whom it is addressed can make a free choice. (From (6*) and (7*) together with the clarifications in chapter five, section F.)

9*) Someone can make a free choice. (From (5) and (8*).)

10*) Nfc is inconsistent with (9*).

11*) Nfc is falsified by (9*). ((9*) states what the PNfc does in rationally affirming Nfc, assuming that the conditions obtain whereby one can rationally affirm Nfc.)

The present formulation differs from the formulation in B; the present argument is based upon a statement of the property of any rational affirmation of Nfc in virtue of which the PNfc's act of rationally affirming Nfc performatively falsifies Nfc. This property entails Sfc as we shall show in F; yet no rational affirmation of Nfc can lack this property. Thus, if the conditions obtain whereby the PNfc can rationally affirm Nfc, Nfc is inevitably falsified. We consider in G what follows if these conditions do not obtain.

Our present argument includes (7*) as a key premise. The proposition in (7*) is one of the most important theses in this work. If it is true, then no PNfc can avoid appealing in his very attempt to deny Sfc to a norm which entails Sfc. We next prove (7*).

Normativity and Free Choice

In this section we show that a norm which prescribes unconditionally between open alternatives has, as a necessary condition for its being in force, the ability to make a free choice on the part of the person directed by such a norm. We do not argue in the present section that Sfc is true. We are concerned here only with a conceptual relationship--that between a certain kind of norm and free choice. We express the necessity in this relationship by saying that this kind of normativity "entails" free choice.

There clearly is some sort of close connection between the relevant normativity--the normativity required by the PNfc in his rational exclusion of Sfc--and free choice. A choice is free if and only if there is a choice between open alternatives such that there is no factor but the choosing itself which settles which alternative is chosen. The normativity in question directs a person with respect to an act which he might choose as one of two open alternatives, and this norm directs him by prescribing unconditionally.

37

Nevertheless, the relationship between such normativity and free choice is not one of mutual entailment. If choices which are experienced and naturally judged to be free actually are free, then among such choices are many to which no normative demand seems relevant. For example, one might have the experience of choosing between staying in town over a weekend to entertain a visiting friend and going on a weekend vacation with another friend. One experiences such a choice as his own and experiences nothing requiring either alternative, not only in the sense that he is aware of no condition determining him but also in the sense that he experiences no normative demand to choose one alternative rather than the other. In fact, his experience is simply that both possibilities are attractive, but the two are incompatible, and there is no way to settle which to do except by choosing.

Although the relationship between free choice and a norm which prescribes unconditionally between two open alternatives is not one of mutual entailment, still it is clear that if one is free, he could be bound by the kind of demand which the PNfc makes in rationally affirming Nfc. If one is free, then the two alternatives must be regarded as open; one can choose either of them. Yet one of them is prescribed--that is, one is rationally preferable.

For our argument, the important aspect of the relationship between free choice and a norm which prescribes unconditionally between two open alternatives is that free choice is a necessary condition for the fulfillment of such a norm. We argue for this thesis as follows. If one is determined by any factor whatsoever either to fulfill the norm or not to fulfill the norm, then there are not two open alternatives. The alternative to which one is determined will be the only one which can be realized, whether or not he is aware of this fact. But the sort of normativity relevant here is just the sort which implies that there are open alternatives; this was shown in D. Thus, nothing determines the fulfillment or the nonfulfillment of the norm. Although nothing can determine the fulfillment of the norm, still the norm does prescribe; it prescribes unconditionally. Thus, the norm must be able to be fulfilled, but it cannot be fulfilled by a necessitated or determined response. In other words, if the norm actually prescribes, then the person to whom it is addressed both must be able to bring it about that the norm be fulfilled and must be able to bring it about that the norm not be fulfilled-- that is, he must be able to choose freely.

The preceding argument can be stated in another way. If a norm which prescribes unconditionally and between open alterna- tives is such that the one to whom it is addressed can fulfill it, but is not determined to fulfill it, then he can choose to fulfill it. Clearly, if one can but need not choose one of the alternatives, then he is free in that choice. The norm in question is such that a person directed by it can fulfill it but need not fulfill it; if he were determined, then the alternatives would not be open. We showed in D that the alternatives of affirming either Nfc or Sfc are open. If one were determined either to fulfill or not to fulfill the norm, thenthe norm would not prescribe unconditionally. We showed in D that the norm does prescribe unconditionally.

A performatively self-referential proposition is self-defeating if the self-referential instance renders the affirmation of the proposition pointless. For example, unrestricted skepticism is self-defeating in this way. The performatively self-referential instance of "All affirmations are groundless" is "The affirmation that all affirmations are groundless also is groundless." Thus, skepticism is removed by the assumption, implicit in that affirmation, that skepticism is true.

Any rational affirmation of Nfc--assuming Nfc true--is self-defeating in this way. Nfc implies that at least one condition required to rationally affirm Nfc never obtains. The reason why one condition for rationally affirming Nfc never obtains if Nfc is true is that the truth of Nfc entails the falsity of Sfc. The falsity of Sfc in turn entails the impossibility that the norm to which any PNfc must appeal in attempting to rationally affirm Nfc can be in force. The impossibility of this norm being in force entails that the rationality norm required for a rational affirmation of Nfc cannot be in force; thus the truth of Nfc entails the impossibility of rationally affirming Nfc.

As we have just shown, the performatively self-referential instance of Nfc requires that any rational affirmation of Nfc be impossible. If Nfc is assumed to be true, then it cannot be rationally affirmed. One might seem to rationally affirm it, but one's act would be putative, not genuine, for it would be conditioned upon a norm which was itself void inasmuch as what it required for its validity could not be given. The performatively self-referential instance of Nfc renders ineffectual any attempt to rationally affirm it. This instance requires that any affirmation of Nfc not be a rational affirmation, since any rational affirmation is conditioned upon a norm which cannot be in force unless Sfc is true. Thus, if Nfc is true any attempt to rationally affirm it is self-defeating.

The argument from immediate experience was sound, at least to the extent that there is an experience of choice; any attempt by a PNfc to deny the elements of this experience is mistaken. Moreover, the experience of choice does lead to judgments--"I have made a free choice"--which on the whole surely are sound. These judgments, as we have explained in I, are not undercut and cannot be undercut by theories which attack as in principle mistaken the framework of expectation within which one considers his own experience. We have concluded that the individual who thinks he knows he has made a free choice does know it.

The defect in the argument from immediate experience is that it fails to provide any serious response to the challenge of arguments for Nfc. Many who defend Sfc on the basis of experience proceed as if Nfc simply does not exist in the field of philosophical controversy. However, if anyone--PNfc or PSfc--proceeds as if he simply has no opposition, he is dogmatic. Moreover, those who argue from immediate experience contribute little to the clarification of the nature of free choice or to the issues at stake in Sfc/Nfc. Only through developing arguments, we believe, can these issues and concepts be clarified. For our part, we think that in developing the argument for Sfc in B through I we have also clarified the concept of free choice.

Thus, if we are correct, our development of the argument for Sfc has remedied the defects of the argument from immediate experience.

The argument based upon moral responsibility certainly is correct in claiming that there is a normativity which entails Sfc. The normativity to which the PNfc appeals when he attempts to rationally affirm Nfc is a normativity to which the PNfc must appeal if he is to remain in Sfc/Nfc. In fact, the same normativity belongs to all rationality norms. All affirming in rational discourse appeals to the same normativity. Thus, it is clear that there are undeniable examples of the sort of normativity which those who pressed the argument from moral responsibility use as their point of departure.

The PNfc, often in the role of compatibilist, tries to explain away the normativity to which the PSfc points in the argument from moral responsibility. However, the normativity to which the PNfc appeals in seeking to rationally affirm Nfc cannot be explained by reduction to any other sort of normativity. Thus, the concern of the PSfc, who argues for Sfc on the basis of moral responsibility, that Nfc would undercut morality is not an irrational fear.

The normativity which is discernible in any rational attempt to affirm anything whatsoever embodies a morality immanent in the intellectual life itself. As such, this morality is an epitome of man's moral responsibility in every field of action. This normativity is irreducible to any mere set of natural conditions;

one cannot reduce this "ought" to any "is" which does not already embody it. However, the exclusion of naturalistic descriptivism does not require that one abandon the intellectual life—or human life in general—to arbitrary options. The demand of this normativity is both rational and unconditional, although one can choose to disregard it.

The difficulty with the argument from moral responsibility is not that those who develop it appeal to anything unreal as their point of departure. The difficulty is that they simply assume the reality of a sort of normativity which they merely affirm to be incompatible with Nfc; they do not exhibit this sort of normativity and show its incompatibility with Nfc.

Precisely by showing in D that this sort of normativity is necessary for the PNfc's rational affirmation of Nfc, and that no other sort of normativity will do, we show the irreducibility of the moral normativity which those who argue from moral responsibility wish to defend.

Moreover, those who argue from moral responsibility generally assume a point which seems intuitively obvious—namely, that "ought" implies "can." We have clarified the soundness of this intuition in F, and we think the point to be in need of the sort of defense we provided for it there.

In clarifying this peculiar sort of normativity, we also have shown in what way it is unconditional. Kant and many others distinguish categorical from hypothetical imperatives. But they fail to distinguish the unconditional demands of logical norms from the unconditional normativity which prescribes one of two open alternatives.

Thomas Aquinas's argument for free choice is based upon a distinction between man's ultimate good and the goodness inherent in any alternatives between which a person can choose. Any particular purpose embodies only a limited goodness, which can never appeal to every aspect of the human personality. Thus, for Aquinas, the goods between which human persons choose are incommensurable in themselves. By establishing a personal order of priorities, choice makes limited goods commensurable with each other. In developing his argument, Aquinas provides one of the most accurate descriptions of the experience of choice. He also has a clear understanding of the normativity which corresponds to free choice and distinguishes this normativity from that of logical and of technical norms.

Aquinas's accurate understanding of free choice was most useful to us in clarifying the controversy. By stressing the special character of moral normativity and the incommensurability of goods, Aquinas provides insights which find their place in our argument's use of the special character of the normativity of rationality norms and in our account of the very possibility of action which is rationally directed but which, nevertheless, is not determined by the reasons which guide it. Aquinas's argument falls short insofar as he lacks the method of self-referential argumentation. Lacking this method, he is unable to show that Nfc is self-refuting. His exposition of free choice fails--if it is taken as a demonstration--to avoid question-begging.

(pp. 1, 2, 4-23; 139-144; 162-167; 178-180)

Background for Chapter 2, "Being a Person Is a Lifelong Job"

A. The Person

Grisez shuns legalism. We are free, so we are the
responsible agents of our lives. Being free involves our
entire lives. In our hands lies the creation of the self
we are to be. We create this self by third level actions. And our fulfillment depends on being complete
persons. Grisez's ethics is eudaimonistic and teleological, not deontological or legalistic.

These ideas seem simple enough until reflection
uncovers the mystery of person and self. Grisez has a
brilliant treatment of these mysteries. After criticizing traditional explanations of the human person, he
lays out an original interpretation of what it is to be
a person and a self, staying as close as possible to
experience.

Second Plank: The central...problem...is to live as a person
able to make free choices...create the selves each is to be.

Beyond the New Theism

The Human Person

This chapter clarifies concepts which will be used in the
following chapters dealing with divine persons and human persons.
These chapters also will deal with communities of such persons,
including communities made up of persons of both sorts. Throughout the present chapter I am speaking exclusively of human persons and human community. First, I clarify the concept of person,
then the concept of community.

The human person is complex. Both predicables ascribing
outward corporeal characteristics and predicables ascribing
states of consciousness can be applied to any normal person. For
example, "John is touching something hot; John's hand is moving
rapidly; John's hand is blistered" ascribes corporeal characteristics to John. The same sort of predicables can be applied to
any primate; somewhat similar characteristics can be ascribed to

certain plants and even to inanimate bodies. "John senses heat; John is frightened; John's hand hurts" ascribes certain states of consciousness to John. Similar states of consciousness might be ascribed to any primate, but they cannot be ascribed to a plant or a nonliving body. "John thinks that the problem is badly defined; he is committed to arriving at a solution; he is working out a model for developing a better answer" also ascribes certain states of consciousness to John. The behavior and activities of subhuman primates do not lead us to ascribe similar states of consciousness to them. Moreover, these peculiarly human predicables are both noncorporeal and different from other states of consciousness. One's thoughts, commitments, and projects do not cease to exist when one goes to sleep; unconsciousness of these entities during some time is compatible with them continuing to exist as dispositions for later specifically human experiences and acts.

In chapter fourteen I proposed a descriptive metaphysics of four orders of reality within experience—taking "experience" in a broad enough sense to include everything of which man has direct knowledge. These four orders are the physical, the intentional, the existential, and the cultural. The four orders are distinguished from one another; they are not reducible to one another; however, they are not separated from each other; each includes the content of the others in its own distinctive way. My view of the person presupposes this ontology.

Many philosophies treat the person as if he were primarily or even exclusively limited to one of the four orders. The fact that the four orders are distinguished within experience—"hearing another" has four meanings—indicates that human persons are related to one another in all four orders. Hence, human persons must be understood as belonging to all four orders and somehow embracing them all. The consequence is not that the person is four realities—quadralism instead of dualism—but that the person is a complex reality whose unity is other than the unity of entities which are limited to any one of the four orders.

The person considered as pertaining to the physical order is a plurality of vital and psychic functions, integrated into the personality which psychology studies. Psychic life gradually emerges in the course of evolution. The human organism is the product of a long process of differentiation and complexification by which organic nature achieved this level of fulfilling the potentialities of matter. Psychic functions realize potentialities of a biological substructure—the nervous system. The biological structure and vital functions of the human organism depend upon and integrate physiochemical processes.

44

I think that Aristotle's account of the unity of the sentient organism is plausible for animals other than persons and for persons as natural bodies. Aristotle takes care of the body/mind problem to the extent that this problem is a question of the unity of the body and sense consciousness. The fact that states and functions of sense awareness are not reducible to vegetative functions of organisms, and a fortiori not reducible to the characteristics of inorganic bodies, does not mean that sentient mind is not an aspect of the organism. The transcendence of sense-consciousness to bodies lacking it—for example, that sense consciousness is of all sorts of bodies and that consciousness itself is not outwardly observable—does not argue against the natural and material character of sense consciousness; all life is remarkably different from merely inorganic matter.

P.F. Strawson provides arguments which I consider sound for holding that the concept of "person" is primitive, and that the ascription of both objective bodily characteristics and conscious states to one and the same individual depends upon recognizing the indivisibility and irreducibility of the "person." The only difficulty with Strawson's theory is that it is not a theory of persons but of sentient organisms in general, including both persons and brute animals. Strawson deals effectively with the mind/body problem but he does not touch the self/body problem.

The person considered as pertaining to the intentional order is a self-conscious subject for whom things known are objects. The person can know anything, including himself; what is other than the person is known as belonging to—but does not know—a world of objects. As Hegel pointed out, the subject is reflexive; the subject can think of himself as other and then recapture himself in this very thinking. The person as thinking of himself and as thought of by himself is one as person but two as subject and object of thinking. Negation originates in such knowledge; negation belongs to the world of thought and not to the world of nature.

As I explained in chapter nine (pages 178-179), it is only because human persons are self-conscious subjects that human knowledge of the world is an objective knowledge of things themselves, not merely an indirect relationship with things as known. A person in knowing understands his own knowing; he grasps what his knowing itself contributes to knowledge. In understanding his own knowing he adjudges the content to be other than the knowing; the content is not reflexive. The content known thus can be posited in a proposition (pro-positio) or projected (ob-iectus).

The person considered as pertaining to the existential order is a self-determining agent, a principle of his own action by free choice. The person acts; the world is a scene in which one creates and plays the role of his own life. Choice depends upon and involves understanding. The reflexivity and negation characteristic of propositional knowledge also condition choice. In choosing, one proceeds upon prior deliberation regarding objective possibilities, one excludes at least one real possibility which therefore never will obtain as an empirical state of affairs, and one proceeds toward the realization of another possibility with which one partially identifies one's self. In the chosen possibility one finds some degree of self-fulfillment.

The person considered as pertaining to the cultural order is man symboling, man the maker and communicator. By thought and freedom man engages in a creative interplay with his environment. But this environment is not merely a natural world; it is a human situation. Man builds his home in nature and continues to build his cultural home as he lives in it. In using symbols and tools man becomes aware of himself as master of the things he uses; he also should become aware of his dependence upon these things, of his finitude, and hence of his obligation to respect and to wonder at the subhuman world even as this world comes under subjection to human persons.

Each of these four considerations focuses upon an important aspect of the complex unity of the human person. However, if one takes any one of these considerations and sets it up as the model of the person, something important will be downgraded or omitted. The discussion of various formulations of the body/self problem indicates the consequences of taking any of these considerations in isolation as an adequate model. A naturalistic consideration grounds Aristotle's model; the consideration of man as knowing subject grounds a dualistic model which tends toward idealism; an existentialist consideration grounds a moments-in-a-process model; the consideration of man as culture-maker grounds an operational-istic dualism which tends toward materialism.

A better model can be developed by beginning from the fact that the person is not limited to one of the four orders. A person is in all four of the orders, and he embraces all of them in himself. In the person the four orders are distinct, irreducible, yet normally inseparable. The unity of the person is unlike the unity of any entity which is enclosed within one of the four orders. The unity of the person is mysterious and must remain so. This unity is immediately given in human experience, and it cannot be explained discursively, since reason cannot synthesize the distinct orders in a higher positive intelligibility. One can reason from any order to the others only insofar as all the orders are included in any one of them.

A preliminary suggestion of the model of the person I propose can be given by means of an example in which certain important aspects of the person are reflected. The example is a statement (S̲): "This set of marks can be used to express a proposition the assertion of which can serve as a point of departure for articulating and communicating a new model of the person."

Like any other statement, S̲ unites the four orders in itself. First, S̲ is a set of ink marks—or a succession of noises—entities in the physical order. Second, S̲ expresses a meaning and it has a logical structure. Third, to assert the proposition S̲ expresses is a human act, and this act is oriented to the social purpose of communicating something. Fourth, S̲ is a use of natural objects to express meaning, and this use has a creative intent inasmuch as I am attempting to work out a new model for understanding the complex unity of the human person.

Unlike many other statements, S̲ is peculiar in that the proposition S̲ expresses is self-referential. Thus, S̲ refers to S̲, and S̲ says of itself that it has the four predicables mentioned in the preceding paragraph. This fact makes clear that the four orders which are present in S̲ are not so distinct that they are not also united. Still, the physical marks on the paper, the assertion, the act of asserting it, and the creative effort are distinct; confusion of any one of these with any of the others would make it impossible for one to understand S̲, since each of them is referred to by different propositions—namely, by the four propositions set out in the preceding paragraph.

Unlike many other statements including many self-referential statements, the act of asserting S̲, insofar as it is a human act, also has a reflexive aspect. The act of asserting S̲ promises to articulate and communicate a model of the person, and that very act itself is the first step in carrying out what is promises. The human act itself involves the use of physical objects which are ink marks or sounds; the act gets its meaning from what one is doing; part of what one is doing precisely is asserting this proposition; and the act aims beyond what one does in it to the ulterior purpose of creating and communicating the model set out below.

Again, unlike many other statements, including many self-referential statements, the creativity projected in S̲ also involves reflexivity. If the effort made here to set out a new model of human personhood is creative, then S̲ is a step in that creative effort. The creative effort uses the material objects, the proposition, the act of asserting—but the creative effort to develop a model of the person also uses the creative effort of formulating S̲ and setting it out. And, in aiming to go on from

S, as I am now going on from it, the creative effort of S also aimed toward producing a certain experience, developing a model (which is an entity in the intentional order), affecting human action, and completing the work of this chapter.

The statement S, considered precisely as a set of marks or sounds--natural entities in the physical order--makes possible but also limits the other aspects of the reality of S. The meaning, the human act, the creative attempt--all depend upon the physical reality of S and none could exist without it. These aspects of S are limited by the characteristics of its natural reality, characteristics which must be accepted as they are and respected for the possibilities they offer. The physical aspect of the reality of S is not isolated from the other aspects, although it is distinct from them as they are from one another. What is peculiar about the physical reality of S is that this aspect is not reflexive; it provides a fixity and a self-containedness which the other aspects lack. What is physically, is other than the reflexive self; physical objects cannot be transformed dialectically; a bodily entity is what it is in its self, regardless of what one thinks or chooses or makes of it.

The model for understanding the complex unity of the human person now can be proposed. In contrast with any model which would confine the person to one of the orders, the model I propose is that there are four distinct and irreducible aspects of the person. A person is a physical body; a person is a propositional knower in whose world of meaning logical entities exist in being thought; a person acts by free choice; a person is a maker and user who puts things to work for new purposes and brings into actuality values which are otherwise only ideal possibilities.

These four aspects of the person are united, as the four aspects of the statement S are united. This unity is unlike the unity of any entity which is limited to one or another of the four orders. The unity of the person is not an intelligible principle of a fifth order, distinct from the four, nor is it something like an entity belonging to one or another of the four orders hidden behind all of them. The four aspects of the person all involve and in a way include one another, as the four orders always do. Moreover, the four aspects of the person are mutually irreducible to each other, as the four orders always are. If it were not for both the unity and the irreducible diversity of these four aspects of the person, the distinct sorts of reflexivity belonging to one person as thinker, doer, and maker, and the irreflexivity of the same person as body, would be impossible. The person is the self who unifies these four distinct and irreducible but normally inseparable aspects. The self is a unifying principle; various aspects of the person are unified by the self but not identified with it.

48

The unity of the person, by which the person is one self, is evidenced, first of all, by the compenetration of the four orders. Each of the four unifies itself, in its own way, with the others. The person includes these four modes of unity. The body thus includes the other aspects of a person; the other three aspects of the person each includes the body; the bodily aspect of a person is not one thing divided against the rest of the person as another thing. Indeed, on this model the soul or self is not part of the body or something hidden within it; it would be better to say that the body is one aspect of the person, united with the others by the soul or the self. But this statement must not be taken in an idealistic sense, as if the body were not a material object—a sentient organism in the physical order.

The body of a person differs from the material reality of a statement in an important respect. A human body as such has a mind; a person's body is capable of sense consciousness. Sense consciousness, like materiality in general, is not open to dialectical transformation. But sense consciousness provides an imperfect reflexivity, as is evidenced in the guidance of perception by perception (noticing, paying attention), learning by experience, and the like. Reflexivity in such cases is imperfect, for the two terms of the relationship are distinct moments in a process. In other words, though both ends of the relationship are within the unity of a human organism, the feedback of sense consciousness cannot of itself establish a relationship which distinguishes its own terms.

The reflexivity of propositional knowing, in contrast with that of sense consciousness, is complete. Knowing, insofar as it is reflexive, distinguishes itself into subject and object; when knowing itself is known, the two terms are other only as opposite terms of the relation. If such reflexivity did not occur, one never could know his very knowing, something one does in any true self-referential proposition, for example: that any proposition is either true or false. It is worth noticing that this reflexivity, while complete in its single instance, is not total. The proposition has other instances which are not self-referential.

One could carry out an analysis of the reflexivity of choice and of symboling parallel to the preceding analysis of the reflexivity of propositional knowing. In making commitments a person determines himself; in using anything a person uses his own abilities. But the reflexivity in each case while complete is not total; one commits oneself to a value which is not wholly identical with oneself and one uses something other than the abilities immanent in oneself. Thus self as knowing subject, self as existential agent, and self as culture-maker are open to and dependent upon what is not self. For this reason the self which unifies the bodily aspect of the person and these three reflexive aspects of the person is easily distinguished from the creator.

However, the self which is the principle of the unity of a human person is not identical with the knowing subject, the existential agent, or the culture-maker. All of these are included in the self; they are aspects of it. But the constitutive self of a human person is revealed in the unity as well as in the distinction and interrelationship of the four orders.

As I argued in chapter twenty-one (pages 319-320), the created universe does have unity--that of being created--which transcends the diversity of the four orders. This unity cannot be reduced to a rational system, as can the order proper to each of the four orders. The unity of the human person somehow embraces the community of everything man experiences. The unity of the human person is the image within creation of the unity of the creator. The unity of the creator is the unity of the term of all arguments toward an uncaused cause; these arguments begin in the diverse orders. These arguments have nothing in common at their starting points except the contingency of everything which is experienced and the unity of the person who experiences.

Thus I conclude that the complex unity of the human person is a fact for which one ought not to expect an explanation. Nothing else within experience is precisely the same sort of complex unity, although a statement can serve as a model for the person as the human person can serve as a model for the creator.

When death happens to the bodily person, is the self totally destroyed? I do not think any conclusive rational answer can be given to this question. It is difficult, if possible at all, to know to what extent the other aspects of the person need bodily life and to what extent the self depends upon the distinct aspects of the person which it unifies. The statement, S, could have none of its other aspects without the physical reality of sounds or ink marks. But S is not a person; S is only a model of the person. The person has an additional unifying factor, namely, the self-hood which is the common principle of reflexivity in thinking, choosing, and using. The statement, S, participates in this unity only insofar as this statement is embraced within a person. Thus, one can think it possible that when death happens to the bodily person, the self is not utterly destroyed but perhaps survives, although, as it were, in a mutilated condition.

The very possibility of disembodied survival has been under attack in recent years. Believers, of course, were far more heavily committed to the resurrection of the body than to the immortality of the soul. However, I am not convinced by the

arguments that disembodied survival of a self is impossible.
Many of these arguments rest upon the impossibility of satisfying
a demand for a criterion of personal identity after death. The
demand for a criterion often involves covert verificationism, as
I explained in chapter seven (pages 119-120); in this particular
case those who argue against disembodied survival frequently seem
to assume that only a criterion exactly like continuity--which
more or less serves as a criterion for the identity of an organic
individual--would be acceptable. Moreover, many arguments against
disembodied survival reject various proposed criteria of personal
identity on the ground that these criteria might--mere logical
possibility--be met by two or more distinct individuals. Such
arguments presuppose a rationalistic theory of individuation--that
is, identity of indiscernibles and intelligible difference between
any two individuals.

On the theory of the person which I have proposed, it is in
principle impossible that one should provide a criterion--that is,
a logically sufficient one--for the self-identity of a _person_, but
this impossibility does not show that persons are not self-identical.
It merely shows that one cannot have a criterion for everything.
Of course, each self which survives--if any do--in a disembodied
condition is distinct by being the mutilated self of a person who
began to be when a certain organism was conceived at a certain
place and time. But this unalterable fact--which might be known
only to God--is not what is demanded by those who ask for a criterion by which a "disembodied spirit" could be identified as the
"soul" of a particular dead man. They are asking for a statement
of the criteria by which one could recognize mutilated selves
existing under conditions of which we have no experience.
Obviously, there is no way to satisfy this demand.

(pp. 343-353)

B. The Person Is a Body

Question: Do I _have_ my body? Or am I my body?
Many contemporary thinkers assume that a person has
his/her body. Grisez quotes Fletcher saying, "Physical
nature--the body and its members, our organs and their
functions--all of these _things_ are a part of 'what is
over against us,' and if we live by the rules and conditions set in physiology or any other _it_, we are not
men, we are not _thou_." Marcel, on the other hand,
uncovers the lived experience of both having and being
our bodies. I have my shirt, but I not only have my
arm, I am my arm. Imagine walking on the beach, a
dear friend on your right arm, an acquaintance on your
left. You can be touching him/her on your right, but

not him/her on your left. But it is he/she you
touch in touching the arm.

Grisez penetrates this issue and helps one
recognize that we are our bodies. Far from being an
interesting theoretical problem, this issue underlies
the diverse positions taken on contraception, abortion,
and euthanasia.

"Dualism and the New Morality"

The doctrine of the resurrection of the body is clarified by
the fact that the human person is a body considered together with
the principle that grace perfects nature. St. Thomas, commenting
on St. Paul, explains: "...homo naturaliter desiderat salutem
sui ipsius, anima autem cum sit pars corporis hominis, non est
totus homo, et anima mea non est ego; unde licet anima consequatur
salutem in alia vita, non tamen ego vel quilibet homo" (Super
primam epistolam ad Corinthios lectura, XV, lec. ii).

The human person is a body. The soul is not the self. The
soul is only part of the body. Man wishes to be saved. If the
body does not live in glory, then the self is not saved, for only
one part of the person is saved. But this will not do, since, as
St. Thomas continues, "homo naturaliter desideret salutem"; if only
the soul is saved, "frustraretur naturale desiderium" (ibid.)

. . .

This dualism, which pervades modern philosophy, is the basis
of contemporary evaluations—the "new morality"—of human actions
and attitudes regarding organic human life and sexuality. If the
person really is not his body, then the destruction of the life
of the body is not directly and in itself an attack on a value
intrinsic to the human person. The lives of the unborn, the lives
of those not fully in possession of themselves—the hopelessly
insane and the "vegetating" senile—and the lives of those who no
longer can engage in praxis or problem solving become lives no
longer meaningful, no longer valuable, no longer inviolable. If
the person really is not his or her own body, then the use of the
sexual organs in a manner which does not respect their proper
biological teleology is not directly and in itself the perversion
of a good of the human person. Masturbatory sex—which includes
many acts involving two or more individuals—is justified because
it relieves tension and gives pleasure, and thus contributes to
the good of the person, which is located solely in consciousness.
Sexuality can be liberated from regulation by mere biological
laws—as advocates of the new morality regard them—so that it

can be employed for "interpersonal communication" or for the "fostering of conjugal love."

A very clear statement of the dualism which is the foundation of the new morality is the following passage in a work of Joseph Fletcher: "Physical nature--the body and its members, our organs and their functions--all of these things are a part of 'what is over against us,' and if we live by the rules and conditions set in physiology or any other it we are not men, we are not thou. When we discussed the problem of giving life to new creatures, and the authority of natural processes as over against the human values of responsibility and self-preservation (when nature and they are at cross-purposes), we remarked that spiritual reality and moral integrity belong to man alone, in whatever degree we may possess them as made imago Dei. Freedom, knowledge, choice, responsibility--all these things of personal or moral stature are in us, not out there. Physical nature is what is over against us, out there. It represents the world of its. Only man and God are thou; they only are persons" (Morals and Medicine (Boston: 1960), p. 211; emphasis in original).

For Fletcher, the body and its members, our organs and their functions, belong to physical nature; physical nature is not the person; everything of moral significance is located exclusively within the person. Thus, Fletcher argues in another work: "The right of spiritual beings to use intelligent control over physical nature, rather than submit beastlike to its blind workings, is the heart of many crucial questions. Birth control, artificial insemination, sterilization, and abortion are medically discovered ways of fulfilling and protecting human values and hopes in spite of nature's failures or foolishnesses. Death control, like birth control, is a matter of human dignity" (Moral Responsibility: Situation Ethics at Work (Philadelphia: 1967), p. 151).

For Fletcher, the human body is a pure means. The body in no way is and an in itself. No personal value inheres in the body, its processes, and their immanent biological teleology.

Discussion is now going on of the possibility--not very distant--of manufacturing new human individuals to order by biological engineering. Such discussion generally takes for granted the acceptability of killing individuals at embryonic stages and the production of individuals apart from normal sexual intercourse. Those who accept Fletcher's conception of the person, or any similar dualistic conception, find it difficult to explain why anyone should have reservations about the production of "better model" human organisms.

Anyone who sees the human person to be a special kind of body, who sees that bodily life and the biological processes for transmitting it are in and of themselves personal values, can see what is wrong with the proposal that human individuals be manufactured. A manufactured individual will be a person; he or she will deserve our respect as one sharing in personal dignity, as one called--together with the rest of us--to share in divine life. But such an individual also will be a product.

...

The impact of dualistic concepts on moral thinking regarding human life and sexuality is not limited to extremists such as Joseph Fletcher and to those who are preparing to manufacture human individuals in laboratories. One finds this same thinking in the documents which were given unauthorized publicity expressing the "majority view" in the Pontifical Commission on Population, Family and Births--that is, the famous "birth-control commission."

In other words, in this view, just as in the view of Joseph Fletcher, sexuality in and of itself is a physiological process belonging to the physical world; the body in and of itself is not the person; the goods of the body are altogether subordinate to "personal" values. Moreover, the concept of "use" in this context is highly significant; it is not merely a matter of the technical expression, "use of marriage," which is a legal synonym for "act of sexual intercourse within marriage." Rather, in the context of this document, the concept of use means that the sexual organs of the human person are transformed into tools which can be used now for one purpose, now for another; persons using their sexual tools can prevent the merely biological consequence of a new life coming into being, because the coming into being of a new human life also in and of itself has been transformed into a merely biological fact. The rationale for contraception offered in this document implicitly but totally rejects the view that at conception a new bodily person proceeds from the two-in-one-flesh union of the parental bodily person; this rationale for contraception implicitly but firmly substitutes production for procreation. For these theologians, the human power to have children is not of itself specifically human; it must be "assumed into the human sphere."

...

In truth, the really dualistic view is that sexual organs are tools and that sexual performances are mere biological functions which persons can use for diverse purposes. The masturbator, not the chaste person, thinks of his or her genital organs as instruments at the disposal of his or her self; such a person identifies the self with conscious awareness in which alone value--in the form of pleasure and other desired experiences--is located. Dualists, not chaste Christian married couples who know

54

themselves to be united interpersonally in the very bodily act of
sexual intercourse, regard sexual acts as physiological processes
which can be used "to make babies" or "to make love"--where babies
and love are equally reduced from personal dignity to the status
of products. (Reference here is not to real persons and couples,
but to the abstracted types of persons and couples which figure
in pro-contraceptive argumentation). Only the chaste person and
couple has a completely liberated sexuality, for only chastity
perfects sexual acts by eliminating compulsiveness and automatism.
Only those who are always able to say "No" are ever able to say
"Yes" with its full meaning and value.

. . .

The bodies which become one flesh in sexual intercourse are
persons; their unity in a certain sense forms a single person,
the potential procreator from whom the personal, bodily reality
of a new human individual flows in material, bodily, personal
continuity. An attack on this biological process is an attack on
the personal value of life, not always, indeed, on an existing
individual's life, but on human life in its moment of tradition.
(pp. 324-330)

"The Value of a Life: A Sketch"

In this section I offer some reflections on the concept--
and the reality--of human life. There are four points. First,
life is intrinsic to the human person. Second, life permeates
the person. Third, life transcends the individual; it unites men
with one another and mankind with the natural world. Fourth, life
often has been regarded as sharing in sanctity.

Modern philosophy and modern thought generally have been
marked by various forms of dualism. The epistemological turn,
beginning with Descartes, involved highlighting the opposition
between thinking subject and object of thought. The thinker's
own body tended to be placed among the objects of thought, while
the self-conscious mind was reserved to the subjective side.

Cartesian dualism, of course, is by no means the only form
of it. Kant's distinction between the phenomenal world of objects
and the noumenal world of the acting self set up a sort of dualism
different from Descartes'. What Kantian dualism has in common
with the Cartesian form is that the human body is still alienated
from the center of the self.

Pragmatism and other forms of operationalism that attack the
subject-object dichotomy nevertheless do not overcome the
dualistic assumption.

55

For subject and object, the operationalist substitutes user and used. The true self is the user; the body, of course, is among things used. The body belongs to the world in which problems arise. Problem-solving intelligence stands back from the world in order to deal with it. If knowledge is power, the knower who has the power is altogether distinct from the subject matter over which this power is exercised. Medicine is not the least successful form of applied science.

Anyone who has had the misfortune to undergo extensive medical treatment knows what it means to be a patient. And the patient-role of the body is only intensified if "it" doesn't respond to treatment. To be ill is for it not to work right; the person is not sick, but his organs are not functioning. Physician and patient conspire in establishing and in maintaining the dualistic attitude, since it is an implication of the physician's technical point of view and it is a consolation to the patient's threatened sense of self-identity. "I'm not sick. It's just that the old lungs are rotting away."

Classical psychoanalysis did not improve matters even though it tried to get rid of the soul. The patient is still patient, and the conscious self in contact with reality is still confronted with an objective breakdown. The id and the superego are not getting along with each other.

Modern ethical theories are likewise thoroughly dualistic. Kant has been mentioned already. Classical utilitarianism locates value in conscious experience. For practical purposes, the person is the subject of the experiences of pain and pleasure, and the worth of the person tends to become a function of the proportion of pleasure to pain.

The real person is the consciousness that calculates, manipulates the world, including the body itself, and receives a pay-off in pleasurable experience. The body is like a slot-machine; one pulls the lever and waits for the jack-pot. Utilitarianism is an ethics of the masturbator as hero.

In recent decades, developments in theoretical philosophy have turned against the prevalent dualism. A great deal of work in phenomenology has pointed to the conclusion that the body is not simply a possession nor an instrument of the person. There is more to personality than bodiliness, but the body is intrinsic to the person. Similar conclusions have been reached by linguistic analysis. Language is communication; communication occurs in bodily behavior; any consistent dualism makes the self incommunicable.

56

But practice lags well behind theory. Human life is widely thought of as a set of organic processes—what goes on in the body that stops at death. But since the body is regarded as distinct from the person, human life is considered extra-personal. If life is a value, then, it is not regarded as a <u>personal</u> value. Rather, life is a necessary condition of personal value; it is somehow extrinsic and it belongs to the order of means, not to the order of ends.

On the principle that a sound understanding of values cannot go on assumptions that are theoretically untenable, I submit that the practical dualism of most current consideration of the value of life must be set aside. If the human body is not extrinsic to the human person, then human life also is intrinsic to the person. Whatever value human life has, this value is not infrapersonal.

This brings me to my second point. Life permeates the person. Existence is not one property alongside other properties of existing things. Neither is life a property of the organism. Life, rather, is the existence of the organism. A dead body is not an organism lacking one of its integral parts or usual properties. A dead body is the remains of an organism that no longer exists.

At the outset of this paper, I pointed out that the word "life" is ambiguous. I am concerned with the reality that medicine and safety precautions try to protect, that killers destroy, and that death terminates. But what, exactly, is this reality?

The temptation is to view life as a property or set of properties that living things have in common. Growth, nutrition, and reproduction are vital functions. These functions are the subject matter of biology. Biology is the science of life. Thus life is nothing but this set of functions. Biology does not study the human person as person. Thus life is extrinsic to the person.

The conclusion, of course, is another version of the dualism I have been pointing out. Where does the argument go awry?

In the first place, we must notice that even from a biological point of view, growth, nutrition, and reproduction are not really common functions of living things. At the level of abstract statement we can say, correctly, that living things are characterized by these functions. But in concrete reality, what is involved in the growth or nutrition or reproduction of one kind of organism is not what is involved in the growth or nutrition or reproduction of another kind of organism. That is why biology does not engage in lengthy dissertation upon these vital functions as such, but gets down to cases. The "common" biological functions of human beings are specifically human, even from a purely biological point of view.

In the second place, if organic functions characterize living things, if does not follow that the life of living things is nothing more than a collection of these functions. The organism is a unity; the functions in question are multiple. In some sense, the organism exercises its own functions _for the sake of the_ whole.

What I am arguing for is not vitalism, which is itself a version of dualism in the biological field. Rather, I am suggesting that there is real teleology, and this is nothing more than to say that an organism is really a unity, not merely a region of natural events and processes. In other words, I am assuming a metaphysics in which the physical universe includes a multiplicity of really distinct individuals, and I am rejecting the sort of metaphysics that regards the entire physical universe as the sole substantial reality.

From this it follows that life is more basic than organic functioning. Life is the mode of existence of organic entities. This mode of existence embraces the capacity for organic functions. The exercise of these functions is the actuality of life. Consequently, if all organic function ceases, there is no life and hence no organism. Yet life embraces all the vital functions, and thus no single vital function can be identified with life itself.

A third consideration is that even in the sense in which growth, nutrition, and reproduction are common vital functions, these functions do not exhaust the set of vital functions for all living things. Sensation and anticipation, thinking and choosing, and other functions belong to various kinds of living beings, with concrete diversifications, just as growth, nutrition, and reproduction belong to all kinds of living beings. Only a covert form of dualism drives a wedge between vital functions on the one hand and psychic actions on the other. (I of course do not mean to deny the distinctions that are to be made.)

The apparently obvious inference from "biology is a science of life" to "life is nothing but what biology studies" actually assumes a whole metaphysics. If we are concerned with the life that death terminates, such life is still intensely personal. That is why death is intensely significant from an existential point of view. The life that is terminated by death is not an extrinsic condition but rather is an intrinsic principle of the life that a biographer writes an account of.

This conclusion brings me to my third point. Life transcends the individual, uniting persons with one another and human beings with their natural environment.

Reproduction is a vital function involving at least two organisms; sexual reproduction involves at least three. Nutrition

involves both the organism and something not already united with
it; there is vital interchange with a natural environment,
directly or indirectly with the inorganic world.

In other words, if individuals that live are really substantial entities, they also have real relations to other living individuals and to the inorganic aspects of the natural world.

Dualism removes the organic foundation of community and the
natural foundation of appreciation of non-organic conditions of
life. If we reject dualism, we must reassert these grounds. The
person is not a monad.

These considerations are of the utmost significance in the
background of ethical reflections upon problems involving the
family, sexuality, and the human use of natural resources. All
too often such problems are treated on assumptions that clearly
isolate "mere biological processes" from "personal values," as if
human parenthood, human sexual love, and human engagement in the
natural world were reducible to one aspect or to the other, or
resolvable into an inadequately integrated juxtaposition of both
aspects.

My final point in this section is that human life often has
been regarded as sharing in sanctity. "Sanctity" means more than
ethical or legal inviolability. "Sanctity" means holiness, the
proper attribute of divinity. "Sanctity" is the inviolability
of what belongs to God or the gods.

I do not intend here even to sketch a philosophy of religion,
or to outline a metaphysics of divine reality. All I wish to do
is to point out some unquestionable historical phenomena, some
facts of human religious experience.

The concept of life is a basic theme of many religions, and
it is certainly central in the entire Judeo-Christian tradition.
God is the Lord of life. The idea of life undergoes a considerable
expansion in the course of this religious development, but at no
point does the Christian theme of salvation depart from the basic
conception of life as a reality opposed to death.

Thus, the central elements of Christian faith include the
death and restoration to bodily life of God incarnate. The hope
of Christians is for the resurrection of the body and everlasting
life. Death, which resulted from sin--that is, alienation from
God--is overcome by Christ who reconciles mankind to God.

Such ideas will seem odd to those who do not share Christian
faith. But these ideas also find other expressions. Children are

awed at the wonder and mysteriousness of life; the concept of
"reverence for life" does not seem nonsensical.

Of course, it is possible to purge oneself of all such
feelings. The question is, whether it is possible to expel all
feelings of reverence for life in its basic sense and still maintain an appreciation of the meaningfulness of life in its most expanded sense. Is it possible to reject the sanctity of life while
maintaining the dignity of the person?

If dualism were correct, clearly there would be no problem.
But if dualism is rejected, the difficulty begins to emerge. If
life does not come from God, it presumably comes about by accident.
Clearly, the meaning of life cannot be a matter of mere chance.
Meaning therefore must be taken as supervening upon the data. But
in this case, why should one set of data be more susceptible to
meaning than another? It seems to follow that the meaning of one's
life has absolutely nothing to do with what actually goes on in
the course of it.

The concept of the dignity of the person involves the idea
that human persons are ends in themselves, not mere means to ulterior ends. Either this arises simply from the fact that one
acting always is the end of his own activity, and then the dignity
of the person means nothing more than the inviolability of the
powerful, or there must be some metaphysical foundation beyond
human meaning-giving for the assertion that human persons are
equal. If there is such a metaphysical foundation and if dualism
is firmly rejected, then the same ground on which we establish the
claims of justice also will be a ground for regarding human life
as sacred. And it makes no difference whether the metaphysical
foundation of human dignity is expressed in traditional religious
categories or not.

Having considered the problem of theory of value in general
and having clarified the concept of life, I here draw the elements
together into a position on the value of a human life.

My conclusion can be stated briefly. Human life is an
unqualified value in the sphere of human action. Persons are
ends in themselves. Life is intrinsic to the person, not merely
an extrinsic condition or means. Objectively, then, each person's
life shares in his dignity. To the extent that action can be
undertaken on the presupposition of the formally normative principle, life is to be sustained and respected, the care of each
individual's life becomes itself a reasonable effort, part of a
meaningful existence.

(pp. 11-13)

C. Third Level Action Which Affects the Self

Third level action and its creative relation to the self is difficult to grasp. The self, as we saw earlier, is that by which the four aspects of the person are unified: body, knower, chooser, culture-maker. The self is primarily knower and chooser. I develop the self by choices: interior acts of the will, which, however, are related also to other actions, including bodily actions, to the extent they are expressions of, and guided by, the interior, elicited acts of the will. By such acts I realize myself, "I make my self real." For by the acts of the will I choose goods which are aspects of my self. These are the third level actions.

Arthur Miller in Playing for Time dramatizes in a powerful way a third level choice affecting the very self. Vanya, a Jewish musician in a concentration camp, looks at the piece of food Maryann has left her. Vanya has gently charged Maryann with giving herself away to her captors for bits of food. Although she had refused the food, now alone she picks it up, smells it, licks it. Puts it away. Picks it up again. Eats a bit--then all of it. She almost gags. The scene ends with Vanya pressing her head against the wall--in remorse, it seems. A scrap of food: yes, but she put all she was into that choice: a step toward re-forming the self years had created.

"Moral Objectivity and the Cold War"

Two conditions of moral values are indicated by calling them "objective." First, moral values are independent of mere inclination; they are obligatory. Second, moral values are good for a man in so far as he is a man. That obligation is a condition of moral values implies that they are attainable by choice. That moral values are a man's proper good implies that they are not defined by any restricted aspect of a man's life.

If moral values are attainable by choice, then they do not exist except through choice, for choice is causal. What I choose never is merely given. I did not choose a wife; I chose to marry a woman. What is chosen, in other words, always is a course of action. Moreover, the course of action chosen never is a merely physical action. What is chosen, concretely, is a completely interpreted course of action--that is, it is a course of action to be performed for a purpose. Choice, in short, is of a means in one's power. It follows that what is attained by choice exists through choice; nothing can be chosen unless its existence absolutely or in some respect can be caused by action subject to choice. In the case of a wife, for example, it is the existence of a marriage—or a maiden's disillusion—which the choice causes. Beyond that, if one chooses a wife, then the fulfilment of his capacity for fatherhood and marital companionship, his prestige, security, pleasure—one or several such purposes are achieved by his choice.

An organism integrates chemical processes; a psyche, like man's, integrates organic functions. The organism and the psyche make intelligible order of what otherwise would be merely random. Statistical laws of physical and organic nature admit abnormal variations from statistical norms; this indeterminacy is resolved by a higher integration. In a similar way a human personality integrates psychic factors. Only deliberation and choice organize all the factors in a human psyche; consequently, the personality is determined precisely by the process of making up the mind which is the unity of these two acts. This integration does not occur except through conclusions of deliberation. It is a curious fact, however, that deliberation cannot be terminated except by choice, and that choice cannot be make unless deliberation terminates. This fact is what we call "freedom." Motives are operative only through deliberation; deliberation is limited only by choice. Therefore, choice is free. If the notion is paradoxical, consider this analogy. If I walk for my health, then I walk because of my health and I am healthy because of my walking.

In freely determining his own personality a man acts as a psycho-physical unit. In neither aspect, however, is a man complete by himself; in both he is involved with his physical and social environments. A man's free acts, therefore, are both influenced by his environment and influence it. As for the conditioning environment, the degree of integration of the personality as well as the materials to be integrated may be limited by it. This limitation grounds the phenomena which have been called "cultural relativity." It is the other aspect, however, which interests me here. Free actions establish virtuous or vicious patterns of character. They also establish all types of conventions, the relations which constitute institutions, and alterations in things which, thereupon, are called "works of art" or "products."

Primarily, the personality himself is of moral value. Habits of virtuous and vicious action, because they release or restrict freedom, are of secondary moral value. Conventions, institutions, and products are of tertiary moral value. Still, none of these is inconsiderable, for all of them flow from a man's effort to make himself fully human and all of them react on that effort. One point, however, must be noticed. In relation to any one choice, only what is included in that choice--explicitly or implicitly, as material transformed or as the transformation itself--is of moral value. My whole value rides on each of my acts; I am as good or as bad as the choice I now make, for that choice is my personality. The past is gone; the future is not; now alone is.

Moral value, then, exists only through choice; moral value relevant to any single choice exists only through that choice. It follows that moral value is not to be called "objective" in any of the epistemological senses. The moral object is not prepared and waiting, a fruit to be plucked. The morally valuable never presents itself and demands, "Choose me!" Therefore, I reject moral transcendentalism which supposes that moral value is goodness itself, pure freedom, the absolute ego, or some other metaphysical object. I reject moral intuitionism which supposes that moral value is a schematic order, harmony, or some other mathematical object. Moral empiricism which supposes that moral value is a feeling of approval, a customary way of acting, a given quality of action, or some other empirical object--these views seem to me to lack cognitive meaning. All such theories claim an objectivity for moral value which would exclude it; none of them considers freedom morally constitutive.

If it is agreed that moral values do not exist except through choice, still it will be argued that choice is not irrational. The structure of moral values must be objective; if values are not realized without choice, still they are articulated by a purely rational process. The implication is that moral values are an objective--that is, that they are a defined goal attainable by limited means. One having such a theory of moral objectivity considers ethics an art of solving human problems, an art of living, an art of making human value. Just as a builder's action is conditionally necessary--that is, it is determined by the plan of the house--so man's action is rationally necessitated by his objective. And just as the builder accepts his plan from an architect, the false analogy concludes that man must accept his plan from the experts, from nature, or from God. If this argument were correct, only the execution of moral value would be in man's power; the design would be another's, and the function of deliberation would be merely to discover what is necessary if man is to be a good thing.

However, this analogy of ethics to art is false. Products do have important relationships to moral values and can be called "morally valuable" in a secondary sense; however, moral value primarily is in a personality himself. And a personality cannot be a product, for he is indefinable and he is not attainable by limited means. To prove this proposition, I distinguish between a man's needs and his capacities and draw a conclusion from this distinction.

In common with other living beings a man has needs which he must satisfy and capacities which he may fulfil. However, a man differs from other organisms, not only in having different needs and capacities on the whole, but also in the ways he satisfies his needs and fulfils his capacities. Let us try to clarify this distinction.

Ordinary language shows a certain wisdom in taking "I could use some money," to mean "I need some money." The satisfaction of a need is the actual use of its object. Now use involves working on something extrinsic, a process which may be as simple as running a glass of water or as complex as building a guided missile. At a certain point of complication we talk about "technique." If the use of the object consists solely in appreciating it, we talk about "fine art." Fulfilling capacities, on the other hand, is the effect of a man's acts on himself.   The point of the distinction is not that a human operation cannot both work on extrinsic materials to satisfy a need and act to fulfil a capacity. The distinction is, rather, like that between a wife and a homemaker. The same woman may be fully both, but we hope that both her husband and the iceman will understand the distinction and take proper account of it.

Every operation freely performed fulfils some capacity, but there also may be another side to the operation. On one side it is a work; on the other it is an act. It is a good or bad work according to whether we accomplish our objective in the matter on which we are working. It is a good or bad act according to whether we are more complete persons for doing it. In both aspects our actions differ from those of all other living beings. Any other organism satisfies its needs with objects which require, at most, simple processing; to the extent that processing is needed, the work is done in an instinctive manner. Man satisfies few of his needs with things at hand. The needs themselves are fairly constant, but the processing is done in a variety of ways which always seem capable of improvement.

But compare a man as he realizes his capacities with a man in his need-fulfilling role. Any other living being realizes itself to its limit in the satisfaction of its needs and in reproduction. But not so a man! Capacities differ from one person to another, and they surpass any assignable limit. A man is not complete when his needs have been satisfied and he has reproduced. No; he seeks to the ends of the universe and he builds his own universe of imagination. Play he hides under serious titles, ashamed to admit that much of what he does is useless. And a man dares hope he will live forever and perhaps see God.

In satisfying his needs man is presented with a definite problem. In realizing himself it is up to each person to state for himself what the question is to be. In satisfying needs intelligence is used to discern the objective, to plan action which can attain it, and to direct execution. In realizing his capacities each person adjusts, judges, and chooses possible activities in view of his own personality. Technical problems can be tackled one by one. In each, man tries to find a minimum means. To solve such problems action must be taken; but what is to be done can be calculated, given sufficient information. But in self-realization each person must consider at once himself as a whole. There is no adequate means, much less a minimum one, for each person in his situation is unique, and man is open to an infinite fulfillment. Efficiency has no place here. To be a person, a choice must be made, an action must be taken; yet what is to be done never can be calculated.

That every man ought to realize his capacities as fully as possible, that he ought to integrate himself, that he ought to keep himself open to an infinite fulfillment--this is the axiom of moral reasoning. Yet this axiom does not define an objective; it merely states a condition which any man's personality should meet. Deliberation cannot be an applied science; research and development in human engineering, confused with deliberation, only do away with morality. On the other hand, I by no means accept irrationalism in ethics as do those who advocate situationalism. The general conditions necessary for the integration of any man's personality, for the fulfillment of his various capacities, and for the maintenance of his open personality can be stated as absolute moral principles--that is, as natural law. Yet natural law only spells out the axiom of moral reasoning; its dictates are universal. Although necessary for rational morality, the principles of natural law are not sufficient. Practical wisdom, the wit to invent an integration of personality, which is not given, for the concrete materials of personality, which are not yet fully human--practical wisdom alone knows what ought to be done. The decree of practical wisdom is eminently reasonable, but it is not a deduction from prior knowledge for it depends on a unique insight.

Moral value, therefore, has structure only by deliberation; what is to be each man's moral value is as unique as his personality and as indefinable as his openness to God. It follows that moral value is not to be called "objective" in any of the technical or esthetic meanings. Not only does the existence of moral value depend on a man's choice, but also the structure of moral value depends on his practical wisdom; each man not only makes his own personality, he determines what that personality is to be inasmuch as he shares the providence of God as well as his power. Therefore, I reject all rationalism. I reject the rationalism of naturalistic ethics which supposes that personality is hopelessly finite. I reject the rationalism of that pragmatistic ethics which supposes that personality is an indefinite series of solutions to an indefinite series of technical problems. I reject the rationalism of that scholastic ethics which supposes that the structure of personality can be deduced from universal principles with metaphysical necessity and that the judgment of practical wisdom can be replaced by casuistry. I reject individualistic ethics which supposes that moral value can be produced automatically by the interplay of individual calculations. I reject socialistic ethics which supposes that moral value is determined adequately by social technology. In resolving the problem of his own personality each man must consider society, for a man cannot be a person outside his society; the manner in which society will be considered by each man will depend upon his precise social relations. In any case a man cannot keep his personality open unless he cares more for a common good than for himself. The common goods sought by men in societies, on the other hand, can be chosen only by single men and can be realized only in unique personalities.

(pp. 292-296)

Background for Chapters 3 and 4, "What Fulfillment Isn't,"
"Fulfillment Is Being a Complete Person"

"Everyone wants to be happy"--the opening sentence of
Chapter 3, has been changed to, "Everyone wants fulfillment,"
in the second edition. This very interesting change suggests
that it is easier to work with the idea of "fulfillment" as
the ultimate purpose of living than with the idea of "happiness." However, both "fulfillment" and "happiness" function
in the same way in Grisez's eudaimonistic ethics. In the
spirit of Aristotle, Grisez seeks to establish that end,
that goal, that target which the intelligent person will aim
at in order to succeed in being a human person. He identifies it as fulfillment: being a complete person.

Third Plank: Everyone wants to be happy: the ultimate overarching
   goal of living.

Fourth Plank: To be happy is to be fulfilled as being a complete
   person.

"Man, Natural End Of"

Historical Introduction

Because the history of this problem is so extensive, only a
few of the most important positions can be outlined in detail.
Major consideration is therefore given to the thought of Aristotle,
St. Augustine, and St. Thomas Aquinas, after which follows a sum-
mary treatment of the thought of modern philosophers on this
subject.

Aristotle. *Aristotle begins his study of the end of man by
observing that every activity implies a definite objective, since
every effort presupposes a good at which it aims. Different
spheres of activity have different ends, but each is unified and
guided by its final objective. The basic question of *ethics,
then, concerns the single, final objective of the inclusive sphere
of action called "human life as a whole."

Everyone agrees that the end of man is *happiness--living or
doing well--but people differ on what constitutes happiness. Some
people think it is bodily *pleasure, or external goods such as
wealth and status, or good *character. Aristotle maintains that

happiness must be examined precisely as the end of action. So considered, whatever true happiness is, it must be the ultimate objective, sought always for itself and never for anything else. Moreover, in order to organize all of life, happiness must be complete in itself, requiring no addition to be an adequate principle of organization. Hence Aristotle rejects the popular ideas of happiness, for they indicate only what belongs to the lower part of man (bodily pleasure), or what is only a means (external goods), or what is not desirable apart from action (character).

Platonic Solution. Although Aristotle follows *Plato up to this point, he rejects Plato's answer to the main question. To eliminate *relativism, Plato posited as ultimate end a pure form of goodness—the Good itself—independent of everything else. But an ideal goodness that is not a good something seemed to Aristotle unintelligible. Moreover, if there were a Good itself, either it would remain irrelevant to the peculiar good for man, or it would conflict with the differences among goods appropriate to man and to other things.

Still Aristotle agreed with Plato that happiness must not be defined subjectively by the desires one happens to have; that approach would lead to relativism. Aristotle's solution is to define happiness objectively by what fulfills the capacities from which human action arises. He concludes that man's true happiness lies in his distinctive action, the use of reason, which best realizes specifically human capacities.

Reason, Virtue, and Contemplation. Yet many use reason without becoming happy because they do not use it fully. For maximum use reason must be cultivated until it reaches habitual excellence. The Greek word for habitual excellence is translated *virtue, and so we find Aristotle concluding that the happiness that is man's end consists in continuous activity of the soul according to its highest virtue.

For Aristotle, the highest excellence of reason is philosophical *wisdom, and so he considers the philosophical life best. The truest human happiness is in the *contemplation of the truths the philosopher can know about the highest realities. Such a life is godlike, since it belongs to man only because he has intelligence like that of immaterial beings. But it is not supernatural in the theological sense, for it belongs to the higher part of man himself and is attained by his own efforts.

Prudence and Active Life. All human feelings, actions, and social life should be organized as a preparation and foundation for the philosophical life. But in organizing the rest of life, reason also functions in a properly human way.   ...This practical

life of affairs, then, also is a fulfillment of man's proper
capacities, and it constitutes happiness secondarily.

The goods people mistakenly think are the end of man are not
altogether excluded by Aristotle. Good fortune and external goods
take a subordinate place. Friendship is important to happiness,
but true friendship is a shared virtuous life. Moreover, the
truly happy life is the pleasantest, for pleasure is merely the
conscious aspect of the perfect functioning of any capacity.
Since happiness is the perfect use of man's highest capacity, it
includes the deepest and most human pleasure.

For Aristotle, then, man's end is not a quality or a state,
and it is not found in any good above man himself. Rather, happiness is in life itself, in the fulfillment of human capacities,
chiefly in philosophical contemplation, for there man's best
capacity is used to its fullest extent, not for any practical result beyond itself but simply for its own sake.

St. Augustine. *Augustine did not ask whether man has a
natural end or whether God could have created man without offering
him grace. Augustine did not deny a natural end; he simply did
not consider the possibility. Nevertheless, he is of interest
because he presented the Christian doctrine on heaven in contrast
with the philosophers' teachings on happiness and the end of man.

In his youth Augustine read in Cicero's Hortensius the
earliest, most Platonist version of Aristotle's ethics. The ideal
of happiness in philosophical contemplation inflamed Augustine's
heart, and he set out in quest of wisdom. But through many years
he lived in error and immorality. Nothing ended his inner conflict and frustration until he received the grace of conversion
to Christ.

From the vantage-point of faith, Augustine reflects that all
along he has sought Christianity, and he sees heavenly beatitude,
the hope of Christians, as the only fully satisfying end of his
previously fruitless quest. Thus from personal experience
Augustine knows that only God can satisfy man's yearning for
happiness, and this psychological discovery dominates his thinking
about the end of man. Man's heart is made for God and shall not
rest except in Him.

Pagan Neoplatonism. Augustine ridicules the pagan philosophers who placed happiness in natural goods or in virtue, and
who valued the social life of man in this world. The present
life is full of miseries; true happiness will be found only in
the peace of eternal life with God. Thus Augustine contrasts this
life to the next as false happiness is contrasted to heavenly
beatitude.

One sees better why Augustine took this step in noting that he greatly respected one pagan philosophy—*Neoplatonism. Itself indebted to Christianity as well as to *Greek philosophy, *Gnosticism, and perhaps also to Indian thought, to which it is similar, Neoplatonism teaches a natural mysticism. The basic notions are that man's mind comes from the divine by emanation, a kind of necessary creation, and that in this life the mind is unnaturally restrained (see Emanationism). The practical conclusion follows: man should free himself from the world by an ascent to philosophical wisdom, and eventually he can redissolve into his divine source.

Augustine corrected Neoplatonism by insisting that God creates freely, that in heaven man is united to God by knowing Him rather than by dissolving into Him, and that man's return to God depends upon divine grace through Christ rather than upon a human effort of philosophical ascent. Augustine found Neoplatonism, so corrected, a useful framework for exploring Christian faith in a way that would satisfy his own experience and ideas.

End as Final State. Aristotle defined happiness in terms of the end of action and identified this end with the highest perfection of man himself. Augustine, on the other hand, defined happiness as the fulfillment of man's fundamental desire and identified this fulfillment with heavenly beatitude, in which man's mind attains the perfect goodness of God by knowing Him just as He is. Although the two approaches are quite different, they are not directly opposed. Indeed, Augustine was not concerned primarily with the end in relation to action, but with perfect happiness in the attainment of the supreme good. He does not use "end" precisely in Aristotle's sense—an objective of action sought as a fulfillment of the agent. Rather, Augustine thinks of the end as the absolute limit and the final state. Thus he contrasts the "end of good," heavenly beatitude, with the "end of evil," eternal separation from God; in both cases "end" means supreme instance, and the two absolute limits are final states. Aristotle would not speak of an "end of evil," because no one acts for the sake of evil.

Effect on Boethius. *Boethius, a Christian philosopher who followed Augustine, also determined the end of man by examining man's desire for happiness. Man wants happiness and he does not find it in any particular good. Only complete happiness (beatitude), a state perfected by the conjunction of all goods, leaves nothing to be desired. Nowhere but in God, whose perfect goodness is the source of every created and partial good, are all goods presented together. Hence man's desire for happiness cannot be satisfied unless he shares in the beatitude of God.

St. Thomas Aquinas. *Thomas Aquinas used Aristotle's doctrine to bring the theological theory of the end of man to a new stage of development. The resulting teaching is complex; several points in it are disputed among scholars.

Three points must be noticed: (1) Aquinas teaches that there is a twofold end or beatitude of man. One is proportioned to his natural abilities; the other is supernatural, and becomes proportionate to man only if he is given divine grace (De ver. 14.2, 10; 27.2; In 2 sent. 41.1.1; ST 1a, 62.1; 1a2ae, 62.1-2). (2) He presents only one end, heavenly beatitude, as the absolutely ultimate goal of human life (C. gent. 3.1-63). (3) Beatitude means the perfect and stable attainment of a perfect good; it is a happiness that leaves nothing to be desired. Only the supernatural end is perfect beatitude. The natural end is an imperfect beatitude, a happiness that is somewhat like perfect beatitude but lacks the perfection required for it (ST 1a2ae, 3).

To understand these points and the disputes that have arisen, it is necessary to notice how Thomas transformed Aristotle's notion of end and his theory of man.

Notion of End. The transcendent aspect of end that Aristotle excluded by rejecting Plato's ideal goodness is restored by Thomas. He identifies perfect goodness with the reality of God and explains that God directs creatures to Himself by creating them as an expression of His own goodness, i.e., of Himself. Thus the ultimate end of all creatures is God. Creatures lacking intelligence attain divine goodness merely by reflecting it in their own perfection; intelligent creatures may attain it more directly by knowing God and loving Him (C. gent. 3.17-25; In 2 sent. 1.2.1-2). The end of every creature's action thus has two aspects. On the one hand, it is a perfection within the creature itself. On the other hand, it is the transcendent perfection of God.

Man and the Good. Aristotle held that man is complete in his own reality and that human desire is limited to human good. Thomas teaches that man's will is not oriented primarily toward himself but toward the good in general. Even by nature man should not seek his perfection because it is his, but because it is good and a reflection of divine goodness (De ver. 22.1-5). Because God is the end of all creation, He should be loved above all things, and but for original sin man would so love Him naturally (ST 1a, 60.5; In 3 sent. 29.3). Man necessarily desires happiness, which he understands generally as the good that would satisfy his will. In fact, man's will is indefinitely open toward good and is naturally oriented toward God. But men do not necessarily recognize and accept this fact (ST 1a, 82.1-2). Moreover, the greatest perfection man can receive, heavenly beatitude, would fulfill and surpass his capacities in a way he can neither suspect nor wish for without faith and grace. Man's desire for happiness thus also has two aspects. On the one hand, it implicitly refers to the perfect goodness of God. On the other hand, it refers to man's capacity for perfection, which may be considered either according to the limits of attainment established by man's natural powers or according to what man can receive from God and achieve with supernatural aid (In 3 sent. 27.2.2).

Issues of Interpretation. The following five issues arise in the interpretation of Thomas's teaching:

1. Does Thomas consider Aristotle's doctrine an adequate account of the natural end of man? Thomas never describes the natural end of man in detail; rather, he constantly refers his readers for details to Aristotle or, more vaguely, to "the philosophers." In commenting on Aristotle's Nicomachean Ethics, Thomas seems to accept the teaching as correct within its limitations (In 1 eth. 9). At the same time, in his own works Thomas so transformed Aristotle's notions of end and of will that most Thomists have not considered Aristotle's teaching to be an adequate account of the natural end of man.

2. Does Thomas restrict the natural end to the present life? His references to Aristotle, whose treatment deals with this world exclusively, and his use of the contrast between earthly and heavenly beatitude suggest that he does. On the other hand, Thomas knows that some philosophers have put the end of man after death (In 4 sent. 49.1.1.4). He teaches that the separated soul naturally can attain a certain perfection (De anim. 17-20). And he holds that the souls of unbaptized infants enjoy goods proportionate to natural abilities, although they do not attain heavenly beatitude (In 2 sent. 33.2.2; De malo 5.3).

3. What is the meaning of Thomas's teaching that man "naturally" desires perfect happiness in a knowledge of God that in fact can be achieved only in supernatural beatitude? Thomas argues from natural desire that the beatific vision is not impossible and that the hope of Christians is not mistaken and perverse (C. gent. 3.50-57; Comp. theol. 1.104; ST 1a, 12.1; 1a2ae, 3.8). But he also teaches constantly that without grace man can neither know nor desire heavenly beatitude (ST 1a2ae, 114.2; De ver. 14.2). How could a natural end be a true objective of human action if the desire of nature itself goes beyond all that man can achieve by his own abilities? In what sense does man "naturally" desire that which is

72

in fact his supernatural end? These questions have been debated from the time of Thomas's first commentators to the present day.

4. If man were created without grace, could he ever be truly happy? The explanation of the meaning of beatitude—the attainment of perfect goodness (God) by a perfect and permanent act—and the presentation of the supernatural end alone as absolutely ultimate suggest a negative answer (ST la2ae, 1-3). But Thomas explicitly considers the possibility that God could have created man without grace (De malo 4.1 ad 14; Quodl. 1.4.3). His teaching that man necessarily seeks happiness in something he knows and accepts as an ultimate end (In 4 sent. 49.1.3.3) suggests that a man created without grace could achieve a true happiness that would be an imperfect likeness of beatitude. The account of the state of unbaptized infants—they exist without pain and frustration despite original sin—indicates the minimum of which human nature is capable.

5. Given grace, does man have a natural last end as well as a supernatural one? The negative answer is indicated because man cannot have two ultimate ends. But Thomas's derivation of a complete doctrine on natural virtues and natural law from a consideration of goods proportionate to human nature (ST la2ae, 61, 94) suggests that man's natural end is not removed by grace; therefore, the natural end must take a subordinate place within Christian life. This conclusion agrees also with Thomas's general teaching that grace presupposes and complements nature but does not abridge it.

Toward A Solution

The present disagreement among Catholic thinkers concerning the natural end of man indicates that there is not yet a completely satisfactory resolution of this problem. However, Catholic theologians and philosophers who have studied the problem do generally agree that there is a natural end of man. All agree that the supernatural end, concerning which faith teaches, either replaces or subordinates the natural end. The present trend of thought is away from the position that had become common since the 16th century toward a view that accentuates the lack of parallelism between the natural and the supernatural ends.

Natural Desire and Happiness. No one approaching the problem of the natural end within the Christian tradition can avoid being influenced by St. Augustine. Thus Catholic thinkers have tended to focus upon happiness and man's desires rather than upon human

73

action and the principles of its moral quality. Generally they have tried to determine what in fact would give man the greatest happiness of which his nature would be capable if he were not called to the supernatural life of grace. This emphasis has significant consequences. If attention is focused upon the restless heart and the real possibility of absolutely perfect happiness, the comparative imperfection of any natural end is clarified, but its positive character remains obscure.

Of course, even Aristotle considered happiness the ultimate end of man, and Aristotle did not identify this end with supernatural beatitude. This fact should be a reminder that an examination of the meaning of happiness is necessary if the problem of the end of man is to be formulated as an inquiry into what constitutes true happiness.

The universality of the human desire for happiness shows that man naturally and necessarily seeks something as an ultimate end in the enjoyment of which his will might rest. But the variety of goods that different men in fact accept as their ultimate ends proves that the human will is not determined to any definite good, even the highest. From this point of view Buckley's analysis of the natural end appears to be correct.

Perhaps, however, a different formulation of the problem of the natural end of man would lead to a more positive result.

Nature and Moral Obligation. From a psychological point of view, what each man seeks as a concrete last end is determined by himself; but from an ethical point of view, what last end every man should seek is predetermined by the nature of man and by his inescapable place in reality. This consideration suggests the following formulation that avoids the difficult notions of happiness and natural desire: Consider man strictly according to the requirements and possibilities of his nature. To what end ought he to direct his entire life? What good should man seek for its own sake, while rightly treating all other goods either as its constituent elements or as mere means to it?

Because Catholic philosophers generally accept Aristotle's thesis that choice is only of means, never of ends as such, some object to this formulation of the problem. But Aristotle lacked a clear notion of will and had only a limited understanding of freedom of choice. Moreover, one need not suppose that the last end is directly an object of choice, but only that man either chooses to consider and act for the good he should accept as his last end, or that he chooses to ignore the end to which he is obliged in favor of some other good that he prefers. A basic commitment to the morally required end is the first and most

<u>fundamental</u> <u>means</u> <u>for</u> <u>attaining</u> <u>it</u>. Obligation with respect to
the end need not be explained by any ulterior principle, for the
last end is itself a first principle, the source of all obligations and primarily of the obligation to accept its own primacy.

<u>Infinite</u> <u>and</u> <u>Finite</u> <u>Good</u>. In attempting to describe the
morally required natural last end, the first task is to determine
whether the perfect goodness of God belongs to the objective aspect
of man's natural end. As previously mentioned, there is disagreement among Catholic thinkers on this point. Some confusion seems
to arise from a tacit assumption, most obvious in De Lubac, that
if God is the end of man even according to nature, man's natural
relationship to God would be the personal association that only
grace can open to man.

But the orientation to God that belongs to man according to
mere nature is other than the Christian's relationship to his
Lord, Redeemer, and Sanctifier. Even by nature, man should not
love any finite good as if it were the perfect goodness of God, or
commit himself to any particular good as if his will could rest
content in the enjoyment of it alone. Human reason can discern
the limitations of finite goods, and man is obligated by nature
to act according to reason. It seems to follow that finite goods
belonging to man's natural end may rightly be sought only so far
as they are participations in the perfect goodness of God, although
no act within man's natural ability can attain God as He is in
Himself, since intimate sharing in divine life depends upon divine
grace.

<u>Specific</u> <u>Perfective</u> <u>Goods</u>. However, even if it is agreed
that finite goods directly attainable by man belong to his morally
required natural last end only so far as they are participations
in the perfect goodness of God, it still must be determined exactly
what goods accessible to human abilities coalesce to form the
organizing principle of a good human life. Aristotle thought that
the highest perfection of man is some action desirable only for
itself and perfect by itself alone. However, human actions receive value from the goods attained in and by them, and no single
natural mode of human action has the perfection that Aristotle
required of the end. The fact that human nature can be elevated
by grace indicates that man is less closed upon himself than
Aristotle believed.

Hence, it seems that Farrell, Adler, and Maritain are correct
in holding that all goods truly perfective of man have a place in
his natural end. Most noble among these is the truth man can know
about God and about his own place in reality, but most fundamental
is man's physical and psychological health. Health truly perfects
man; it deserves cultivation and demands respect even when no

further perfection happens to be accessible. Truth, health, and other perfective goods underlie the fundamental precepts of *natural law, for as constituents in the natural end, such goods first require that man act and first guide human action.

As already noted, especially in Maritain and Buckley, the present trend among Catholic thinkers is to admit a certain indeterminacy in the natural end. The ensemble of perfective goods has this characteristic, both because none of them is perfectly attained in any single act and because among them there is a two-fold priority: that of nobility centering upon truth, and that of necessity centering upon health. Moreover, since each of these accessible goods must sometimes be subordinated to others and since none of them is self-sufficient, the dispositions of upright character, by which man avoids subservience to any particular good and maintains his openness toward God, are themselves desirable for their own sake. Thus the natural end of man includes complete moral virtue, a good in principle accessible to man's natural abilities although fallen man cannot attain it without healing grace. To determine the precise relationship within the ensemble of perfective goods between substantive goods such as truth and health and the peculiar good of moral virtue remains one of the most difficult tasks in the investigation of man's natural end.

(pp. 132-137)

Background for Chapter 5, "Persons Complete One Another"

Persons living on Kohlberg's fourth stage identify the moral with the customs and laws of their communities. When Grisez deals with community he is far from espousing such a conception of morality. For he operates entirely on Kohlberg's sixth stage, establishing the grounds for each plank of his ethical theory.

His concern is to avoid treating morality only from the perspective of individuals as individuals, omitting the social dimension of ethical living. For Grisez to be a human person is to be both individual and social. Ethics must attend to both aspects. Hence a proper understanding of interpersonal and community living is required. These selections form the basis for Grisez's seventh mode of responsibility (Chapter 12) and provide insights pivotal for understanding Chapter 18 ("Revolution and Reform"). His treatment of issues related to euthanasia and abortion likewise depend on this understanding of society.

Fifth Plank: To be human involves belonging to many different communities....

Beyond the New Theism

The Human Community

"Community" is a narrower concept than "interpersonal relationship." Some relationships among persons are not very different from the relations of animals to one another or of persons to nonpersonal entities. A community is a unity of many persons, achieved in all four orders of reality, which transcends the unity of any multiplicity of entities within any one of the four orders, just as the unity of a person transcends the unity of any entity within any one of the orders.

The natural unity of distinct persons is chiefly their biological relationship. In sexual reproduction a man and a woman become a single principle of a new human person. Human life is not caused in a child by any nonpersonal principle; rather, life is transmitted in a continuous stream. The sperm and the ovum live by the life of the parents until they unite to form a new human individual. All human persons are blood brothers, or at least blood cousins.

Mankind is an interbreeding population. Apart from this complex biological society no individual human person could exist. In this bodily community individuals do exist in distinction from one another. One does not die whenever any human person dies. Still, "humanity" not only signifies abstractly what is common to all human persons, in virtue of which one can say of each, "This individual is human"; it also signifies the concrete, living process of human bodily life, which is a natural species, a whole to which all individual human persons belong as parts.

Human persons also know together. Two persons think of the very same proposition; they agree or disagree about its truth. (If anyone disagrees with this position, he must be thinking of it, and this fact confirms the position stated and falsifies the disagreeing position.) In this way inquiry proceeds as a dialogue--as an argument which is free for all.

The unity of diverse persons as knowing subjects in the world of thought also becomes clear when we ask the question "Who, today, knows physics or any other field of study?" The answer cannot be the name of one person. No person, not even the most able, knows the whole of any science. The physicists know their subject matter, but only the whole group have all the knowledge which pertains to the discipline. Individual scientists must be specialists; even the scholar who is interested in general questions must specialize in them. His special field of interest is questions which bear upon principles of the whole subject matter, but these questions are specific in that they are only a few of the questions which must be asked about the subject matter.

The unity of distinct persons in common action is a very important aspect of community. Of course, two or more persons may be common agents in the sense that their behavior happens to conduce to a single outcome--for example, their carelessness in driving causes an accident--without uniting as persons. Again, persons can cooperate in a purely contractual relationship without sharing a common commitment. But common action also can originate in a unified principle of specifically personal action. Only such unity constitutes community.

For example, two persons who both have their hearts set upon some one value which they both regard as superior to their individual wishes, desires, or satisfactions can come to appreciate each other's judgments of value. They not only make similar judgments, but each knows that the other shares his view. They not only make similar commitments, but each knows that the other endorses the same value to which he commits himself. Moreover, the two individuals approve and encourage one another's judgments and commitments; in this way each includes the other within his own concern. In such a case the two persons will unite their efforts if they can.

The common good which binds them together cannot be some defined goal attainable by obvious and readily specifiable means. Such a goal would not take a person outside himself to a purpose he could recognize as superior; only an open-ended value can provide the content for a common commitment. The commitment of two or more persons to a single value sometimes is expressed in a community constituting act, such as the adoption of a national constitution.

Derivative from the basic commitment which constitutes a community of action is a set of institutions. These distinguish roles and shape behavior in accord with the basic commitment. The action of each individual person becomes in this way a contribution to a common good to which all alike are dedicated. Each person does his own work, not for himself alone, but as a share in serving the good cause to which all are committed. Each person's dedicated action thus becomes less exclusively yet more truly his own; it becomes his share in what all do together. Each person's contributions are accepted by all as "ours." In a true community members even take responsibility for one another's mistakes and shortcomings.

Some people deny that genuine community of action is possible. If it required individual persons to subordinate themselves to a good proper to someone else—the false ideal of altruism—then genuine community would be impossible. However, persons can love one another unselfishly if they are united in pursuit of values in which each person sees a fair promise of his own fulfillment, but which all together see as important enough to demand and to deserve frequent sacrifices of individual satisfactions.

Many people fear community. They are afraid that their own individuality might be more and more absorbed in another or in the others. However, true community takes nothing from individuality. The closer persons come together in dedicated love, the more they differentiate and fulfill themselves as individuals. Each can give as much as possible only by realizing his highest individual potentialities. Absorption follows, not from community, but from the abuse of a relationship which should be community and has become exploitation.

79

The community of persons in objective culture is so obvious that little explanation of it is needed. Men have a common language; no one can have a private language. Language exists only in the use of things to communicate. Yet each person uses the common language in a personal and special way. Each person can make a contribution to the common linguistic stock by creatively expressing himself in language.

Men share a common technology. No single person can understand the complex machinery well enough to make it work. All together men can do so.

One could cite many other examples of community in objective culture. One of the best is a fine orchestra. No one person can play a great symphony. The whole orchestra must work together to make beautiful music.

A good family exemplifies all aspects of a true human community. The members share the same flesh and blood. Husband and wife are one flesh; the babies are nourished from their mother's body. The members of the family think and learn together. They gain knowledge by conversation in which they share their experiences and insights. All fulfill themselves by serving and caring for one another. All share the same home and use the same property. Each contributes according to his ability; each receives according to his need.

Communities are mysterious. Social theories vainly try to reduce human community to one of the four orders. They cannot succeed, for persons complete one another in community in all of the four orders. Moreover, the mysteriousness of community is rooted in the mysteriousness of the person. As the unity of the person is immediately present to us, yet beyond rational discursive explanation, so in the unity of community there is an ultimate common ground: we are fellow creatures who together make up the creator's self-expression in a way impossible for any of us alone. The human family was regarded as an image of the creator by believers who said: "In the name of the Father..."

(pp. 353-356)

Life and Death

The governing body of a political society at least claims
legitimacy--that is, a status of right to rule which makes its
power have the character of authority rather than of mere brute
force. The claim of legitimacy implies that laws are proposed
as rules which deserve respect and obedience. Every government
claims that its laws have a reasonable basis which makes them
worthy of moral respect in a way that arbitrary orders backed up
by threats never can be--even though the prudent person respects
terrorist threats. The latter respect is pragmatic and prudential,
not moral. In claiming legitimacy a government claims that
virtuous citizens will respect its authority.

To the extent that Americans think of their government as
legitimate, then, they think of the laws as making a moral claim
upon their minds and hearts. What do they suppose to be the
basis of this moral claim?

They do not consider the moral claim of the law to be
analogous to the moral claim of rules laid down by parents for
the guidance of their children. Parents are naturally in a better
position to direct their children than are the children themselves. Children ought to obey because parents know better and
because, presumably, they have their children's interests in
view when directions are given.

But among competent adults insofar as they function as
members of a political society, none are naturally the superiors
of others. This point provides a basis for understanding the
principle of equality enunciated by the Declaration of
Independence: All men are created equal. The equality asserted
is not in natural endowments, in possessions, in achievements,
or in virtue, but solely in political competency: No one is
naturally a ruler, no one is naturally a subject, and there are
no natural slaves.

If these positions are accepted--that is, if one agrees that
the legitimacy of government is not analogous to parental
authority and is not a function of the prerogatives of innately
superior individuals--then the original question stands. What
is the basis for the legitimacy of government according to the
American conception of it?

The American proposition suggests the answer: Governments
obtain legitimacy from the consent of the governed. We believe
that this position can be understood in such a way that it is
defensible as the right answer to the question. But there are
many ways to misunderstand "consent of the governed." To avoid

these misunderstandings, we must say something about consent. In particular we must consider briefly four points: (1) the scope of consent; (2) the normative element involved in consent which gives legitimacy; (3) those whose consent is required; and (4) the mode of voluntary acceptance which counts as consent.

First, the view that the legitimacy of a government depends upon the consent of the governed should not be taken to imply that each and every act of government requires consent of the people. If such were the case, a nation would be no more than a group of people acting together only when and just so long as each member of the group saw fit to participate. Political society would have no more stability than a group of children playing voluntarily together in a park.

Thus, when particular acts of government are in question, one does not determine their legitimacy by asking whether they directly have the consent of the people. One rather asks whether these acts are lawful. And ultimately questions about the lawfulness of the government's own acts must be resolved by appeal to the supreme law of the land: the Constitution. The consent which makes a legitimate democratic government is consent to the constitutional system, which provides the basic political organization of society, lays down basic rules and procedures, defines the most important and permanent offices, and determines how power is to be allocated and legally checked.

Thus the Preamble to the Constitution of the United States makes fully explicit the dependence of this basic law upon consent, and also makes clear the locus and the effect of this consent: "We the People of the United States...do ordain and establish this Constitution for the United States of America."

Second, the consent of the people to a constitution which gives a government legitimacy--that is, moral authority--cannot arise from the mere fact that people do accept it; the acceptance also must have a certain moral quality. An agreement such as a mere social contract, adopted under a threat of one sort or another, could determine what a group of people will do together. But such an agreement of itself could not give legitimacy to the government and its laws. One cannot derive an "ought" from an "is." The mere fact of consent, if it is a fact without some inherent moral force, would not turn power into just power, into authority.

Consent given by someone who is not competent, by someone acting on the basis of ignorance or error concerning what is being approved, or by someone acting under psychological coercion is valueless. Such consent provides no moral basis for government. Moreover, if one consents to something to which one ought not to consent—for example, to do something wrong in itself—the consent, even if wholly voluntary, gives no color of morality to what is effected. So the consent which gives legitimacy to government is only such personal compliance as members of the society ought to give and do voluntarily give.

Many people comply with the demands of the law because they fear punishment. And many people accept a constitutional arrangement because they want for themselves protection of certain goods, such as life, liberty, and what Jefferson called "the pursuit of happiness." (This latter can be understood, in accord with the dictum that happiness means different things to different people, as the doing of those things by any individual which that individual considers to be inherently worthwhile.) People want protection of these goods against the behavior of others—other people in the society and other powers outside it—which would render them insecure. In other words, many people accept a constitutional arrangement because they do not want to be killed, raped, enslaved, beaten, deprived of their possessions, and so on.

The vulnerability of most persons, even of those who are personally very strong, to harm by other individuals or groups, together with the limits of the ability of the strong to protect those for whom they care, makes clear why most people do consent to a constitution. Almost any government is better than none at all. But these facts do not show that people ought to consent. And, as we have argued, legitimacy does not depend on the fact alone, but only on the fact of consent together with its quality as a morally justified act.

The moral justification for consent begins to appear if one notices that there is nothing irresponsible or arbitrary in the concern of people for basic goods such as life, liberty, and the pursuit of happiness. Security in such goods is no mere subjective demand. It is a requirement entailed by reasonable care about them, not only as they pertain to oneself but also as they can be shared in by others—including in "others" both those for whom one specially cares, as one's family and friends, and also those for whom one has no more but also no less than the respect for any fellow human being from whom one would wish a like respect towards oneself.

Thus as soon as the focus shifts from the fact that people want certain things to the inherent goodness of some of the things which are wanted, the claims of reasonableness come into play. Concern for the basic goods is a response to their inherent appeal. Thus, the concerned person can give a justification for his or her concern; consent to government is not a brute fact.

"Why do you consent to a constitution?" Not merely "Because I want protection," but "Because my responsibility for my own life and other goods, and for the security of others for whom I care, demands that I obtain protection."

If consent is justified in this way, the principle of one's concern extends to all others who can enjoy these goods and who need security in them. Human life and the other basic goods are no less exigent in whomever they happen to be at stake than they are in oneself and in those to whom one is specially attached. This is the point we meant to suggest by saying that reasonable care about goods must extend to those whom one merely recognizes as fellows in the community of mutual human respect for the dignity which attaches to every person as such.

Thus, justified consent which provides the basis for legitimate government arises not merely from a coincidence of individuals' concerns about their own security and welfare (and that of those dear to them) but also from a truly common concern about goods recognized as having an inherent and common appeal to reasonable persons.

From the vantage point of this insight it is clear that the idea of fundamental rights and the idea that one's consent is necessary for the legitimacy of government are closely related. One ought to consent to government because it is more than a device for getting what one wants, more even than a common facility by which all living in a certain place can obtain together what they want individually. Government is required to secure rights. Rights are grounded in goods of persons which are prior to their to their merely factual desires—"prior" in the sense that the goods make the desires reasonable as well as stimulate them psychologically.

These goods deserve to be recognized, appreciated, respected, and promoted whether people are disposed to do so or not. Of course, all who are sane are disposed to do so when it comes to themselves, and to those for whom they specially care. But hardly anyone is consistently disposed to do so when it comes to others, to strangers or competitors. Then the inherent and common appeal to reasonable persons of life, liberty, and the pursuit of happiness takes on the exigence of a duty demanding respect for a right. Hence, the Declaration of Independence does not say that everyone wants security in life, liberty, and the pursuit of happiness. This factual premiss would be inadequate for the argument. The Declaration asserts that every person is endowed with an unalienable right to these goods.

The introduction of a normative element into the definition

of the consent which is required for the legitimacy of government implies that there can be constitutions which deserve consent and those which do not deserve it, constitutions which make a moral claim and those which fall short of making a claim or which make only a false claim to the moral approval of the people. It is clear that people can either consent or refuse consent to a constitution of either sort. Thus, there are four possible situations. There are constitutions worthy of consent which receive it; those worthy of consent which do not receive it; those unworthy of consent which nevertheless receive it; and those unworthy of consent which do not receive it.

In our view it is only in the first of these cases that there is a morally legitimate government which is established by the constitution in respect to those people who do consent to it. This situation alone determines a central, paradigmatic sense for "government," "political authority," "law," and "rule of law." All of these expressions, of course, are used in ordinary language of regimes which fall short of morally legitimate government. But the American proposition is that valid laws must meet the test of constitutionality, and that the constitution must be such that it deserves and receives the consent of the governed, which alone gives government legitimacy.

The introduction of a normative aspect into the consent which is required to make government legitimate raises at once the third of the questions we listed above: Whose consent is necessary? In any society there are two classes of people who are not likely to consent to a just constitution insofar as it is such.

First, there are those who are not competent for such a voluntary act: children, the severely retarded, and so on. These present no serious problem for a theory of legitimate government. They can be treated as if they were citizens in the fullest sense by an extension to them of the rights and duties of which they are capable, but government acts toward them in a quasi-parental fashion rather than in a fully political fashion.

Second, there are those who are competent to consent but do not choose to consent, even though the constitution is just. Such persons usually will acquiesce in the operation of the constitution and comply to a great extent with the laws. But they do so out of self-interest. They do not respect law; they do not distinguish between just power and mere force.

The question is: Does a government lack legitimacy because it does not have the consent of such persons? In our view the lack of the moral support of those who care little or nothing about morality in no way detracts from the legitimacy of government. It is the consent of those, the upright, who care about justice and are interested in the issue of the government's legitimacy which is decisive. In the fullest sense only they are governed by laws; only they are directed by lawful authority. Citizens whose involvement in political matters is based on self-interest rather than on justice are governed by law only in a derivative and imperfect sense. The lack of their consent is irrelevant to the moral claim of the law upon the minds and hearts of persons who are responsive to moral claims.

Morally speaking, persons who acquiesce in the operation of the constitution and conform to the laws out of mere self-interest are aliens to the political society. If they live in it with the status of citizens, they nevertheless function as if they were not committed to the rights which true citizens respect because of their response to the appeal of basic common goods, such as life, liberty, and the pursuit of happiness.

The Common Good

In what we have said thus far, little has been said about the coercive power of the state. Yet as a matter of fact, every political society uses force to back up its regime, whether or not this regime is a legitimate government. So much is this the case that—as we mentioned above—a monopoly on coercive power is often considered to be the defining characteristic of the state. On our account this characteristic is less important.

Yet is is not insignificant. Governments are instituted to protect unalienable rights—life, liberty, and the pursuit of happiness. In a world in which there always are domestic outlaws and foreign enemies prepared to violate these rights, an important function of the state is to protect them not only by the rule of law but also by force. If government is legitimate, force is used lawfully in the service of justice. It is certainly part of the American proposition that it is the business of government to establish justice and to provide for the common defense, by using proportionate force when necessary to protect rights against outlaws and enemies.

But it also is clear that there is consent to government for the sake of promoting and protecting a wider range of goods than those which fall within the narrow boundaries of security. The phrasing of the Declaration which refers to a right to the "pursuit of happiness" —a positive if personalized set of goods and activities—already suggests this. And the Preamble to the Constitution mentions the promotion of the general welfare as

86

one of the purposes for which the fundamental law is established.

Some have held that it is unjust to use governmental authority beyond the minimum ends of guaranteeing peace and security, law and order—protecting life, bodily integrity, physical liberty, and property. But no such suggestion ever has been seriously entertained by the American people or by the people of any other modern, democratic state. Indeed, the very concern for political equality which entails the demand that government be by consent of the governed also tends to generate a demand for the extension of government into those areas of social and economic relationship where exploitation of the weak by the strong is likely to occur—even without overt violence— if the state does not foster institutions more responsive to a fair sharing of human goods than to the mere satisfaction of selfish or arbitrary demands.

For Americans, then, the common good or the public interest is not limited to protection against overt violence and security in possessions. Our common political purposes comprise other goals than these, and so we consent to a government with authority to promote wider purposes. These purposes are a set of goods which Americans do in fact reasonably care about and do not believe capable of being promoted effectively except by means of the apparatus of the state, under direct control of the government.

The various goods which comprise the common good include some which are considered to be inherently worthwhile by many members of the society. The protection of human life is one such good; education is another. Yet some, perhaps increasingly many, members of society consider these goods to be in themselves of merely instrumental value. There are other goods included in the common good which are universally considered merely instrumental. For example, the provision of public roads, of a system of weights and measures, of a postal service, of a monetary system, of a legal form of bequest—all these are in the purely instrumental category.

Thus, an important part of the general welfare is the facility provided by law for members of the political society to carry out their private purposes in ways which the authority of government will recognize and its power, if need be, support. Besides legal facilities for contract and bequest, civil law provides a whole apparatus for private transactions, for holding and using property, for settling private disputes peacefully and impartially, and so on. And material facilities which are provided by government to promote the general welfare are not limited to economic and fiscal ones; public hospitals also are such a facility, and even amenities such as public parks and museums are developed and maintained for the sake of the general welfare.

From the preceding considerations it is clear that the common good of American society is not made up of an invariable set of intrinsic and instrumental goods. The human condition clearly requires that considerations of security and protection against violence remain a basic purpose of political society, and therefore that the power of government be used or available for use for this purpose. Certain less fundamental purposes also are likely to remain constant: for example, provision of a monetary system. But the commitment of American society to other goods has varied in the past and can vary in the future. Our nation has been less committed than it now is to promoting health, education, and welfare; one can imagine a future in which it will be less committed to these purposes than it is at present.

However, such changes in the goods which political society pursues do not change the fundamental character of the American proposition. We did not become a new nation when the Social Security Act was passed; enactment of a thoroughgoing program of socialized medicine would not radically alter the basic law of the land. Likewise, citizens who consent to the constitution do not alter their consent each time the government concerns itself with some new area of public interest.

In short, the actual content of the common good has varied to some extent and could vary much more. Such variation does not alter the nature of the state or affect the consent which the people give to the constitutional system. This conclusion raises two questions. First, are there any limits to what might be regarded as pertaining to the common good or the public interest? Second, if the particular goods which comprise the over-all purpose of the state do not themselves serve as the object of consent--that is, are not themselves that to which the people make the common commitment which knits them into a unified political society--then what is the object of consent?

The answer to the first of these questions is that there are some limits as to what may be rightly considered to be part of the public interest or common good--and thus part of what people consent to when they consent to the regime as just, and in this way give it the legitimacy of a government which exercises just powers with the consent of the governed.

The very notion of a common good or of a public interest suggests that there is a contrasting category of goods which are individual or private. The Declaration of Independence listed liberty as one of the goods to which men have a right, and also listed the pursuit of happiness, which can hardly be understood except in a way which leaves room for a plurality of individual life-styles and private conceptions of what is intrinsically worthwhile. The Preamble to the Constitution likewise takes as one of the fundamental purposes of government to "secure the Blessings of Liberty to ourselves and our Posterity." If all goods were included in the common good, if all interests could be absorbed within the public interest, it would be hard to make sense of such a purpose.

In the Federalist Papers Hamilton explained that bills of rights usually are required in a state to make clear the privileges of subjects which are not to be infringed by the ruler. He maintained that such a statement of rights really is unnecessary in a constitution founded by the people themselves, precisely ordained by them to preserve liberty.

Later, Madison argued for the amendments which became the Bill of Rights of the United States Constitution, but he did not deny Hamilton's libertarian argument and its assumptions. In fact, he admitted the force of the argument against the proposed amendments that by enumerating certain rights it might seem that others were disparaged. Madison sought to obviate this difficulty by means of a provision which became the Ninth Amendment: "The enumeration in the Constitution, of certain rights, shall not be construed to deny or disparage others retained by the people."

The most notable example of the exclusion of certain purposes from the concerns of government, whereby these purposes are reserved in the domain of liberty for individual pursuit and for cooperative pursuit in nonpolitical, voluntary associations, is in the First Amendment: "Congress shall make no law respecting an establishment of religion, or prohibiting the free exercise thereof..." While this protection of liberty originally applied only to the federal government, not to the States, it has been extended to the latter, and this exemplifies well the concern of Americans that their government be limited.

Reflection upon reasons for excluding religion from the domain of governmental concerns will suggest why the public interest must be limited, not only in this but in other matters as well. We noted above that the common good includes goods which the political society as such can effectively pursue; religion clearly is not one of these. Experience had shown that the coercive power of government cannot effectively promote sincere religious faith, and that attempts to promote religion by state action lead to formalism as well as to strife, rather than to piety together with peace and security for all.

Furthermore, religion seems to be one of those goods which is inherently suited to pursuit by private, fully voluntary associations rather than by public institutions. The privilege of pursuing one's own ultimate destiny in one's own way, immune from public interference, seems to be a central element in each person's pursuit of happiness. Governmental interference in this area is regarded by Americans as an unjust infringement upon a basic zone of liberty.

It should be noted that some Americans favor what is said in the First Amendment about religion because it is a necessary implication of their own religious beliefs or disbeliefs. For example, some religious persons hold that religion is so much a personal and private affair, an encounter between the individual conscience and God, that no human agent can be anything but an obstruction. They thus reject government involvement because they reject anything like an institutional church. Some non-religious persons hold that religion is so pernicious that the government must keep clear of it, or so much a matter of mere subjective feelings that there is no rational way to deliberate and decide about it—that anyone's religion is fine for him or her. On this basis, such people give their own theological—or should we say, "atheological"?—twist to the First Amendment.

Those who personally hold such beliefs and disbeliefs are, of course, entitled as Americans to do so, and they are free to favor the American system for their own religious reasons. But to insist upon any such reason as the necessary significance of the First Amendment would be, paradoxically, to read into it precisely the establishment of religion which it was intended to forbid. And any consistent juridical interpretation of the First Amendment in accord with the perspective of one or another specific theology or atheology would certainly lead to decisions which would inhibit the free exercise of alternative forms of belief, which the First Amendment was intended to protect.

Thus a nontheological—and nonatheological—understanding of the limitation placed upon government by the First Amendment is essential if it is to fulfill its own purpose consistently. The principle underlying American respect for freedom of religion is a very general one, a principle very basic to the American conception of political life. The principle can be stated as follows. The public interest extends only to those goods the cooperative pursuit of which gives political society the unity which it has. Since the common pursuit of goods in political society does not encompass all the goods which men and women can pursue and wish to pursue, there is a wide sphere of individual and social activity which lies outside political society, and thus outside the legitimate concern of government and direct regulation by law.

The exclusion of religion from the concerns of government both in the beginning and today is sufficiently explained and justified by the fact that many people who are ready to share in American political society reject religious faith, and many hold diverse faiths which cannot be rendered compatible without unacceptable compromise. Moreover, cooperation in political society for other purposes is possible--as proved by the American experience--without religious unity. Thus, government based upon consent cannot infringe upon religious liberty. Analagous arguments will make clear why there are other fundamental liberties which Americans consider nearly as inviolable as freedom of religion.

It follows from the preceding argument that it is a serious mistake to regard the public interest as the sum of all the private interests of those who make up the political society, the common good as the sum of all the individual goods of the members of the community. Private interests and individual goods account for diversity within American society. Such interests distinguish a variety of life-styles without necessarily throwing them into opposition with one another, that is, without making them political opponents and compelling them to organize political parties on religious or ideological lines.

Thus, by its very nature the public interest or the common good does not embrace all the goods pursued by members of the political society. It embraces only those goods to which they have a common commitment precisely insofar as they are all citizens of the same nation, members of the American polity.

Any attempt to extend the public interest or the common good to include activities which are properly private would lead to an unjust governmental infringement upon the liberty of members of the political society. This injustice is one which would never be consented to by upright members of any political society; it is one which Americans do not consent to.

In this way we reach the answer to the first of the questions posed above: Are there any limits to what may rightly be regarded as pertaining to the public interest or the common good? There are limits. The limits ultimately are drawn by the principle that all members of the political society should at all times be at liberty in all areas of life concerned with purposes which are not effectively pursued through the common activities of the political society. There will of course be dispute about the application of this principle. But where it applies, violation of it always will be gravely unjust and will detract from the legitimacy of government, which extends no further than the consent of the governed.

These same principles--liberty and justice--provide the basis for answering the second of the questions posed above: What is the object of consent--to what is it that Americans commit themselves together in a way which forges them into a single polity?

Since the particular goods which comprise the public interest are variable, it is the justice of the constitutional framework itself to which the members of a political society based upon consent of the governed primarily give their consent. Moreover, this very quality of the constitutional framework--the justice which alone makes it worthy of consent--demands that the liberty of the members of the political society be respected. To understand the thesis that according to the American proposition liberty and justice are the basic principles of legitimate government, we now consider the nature of liberty and justice, and the relationship between them.

Justice as the Chief Common Good

The conception of justice which is relevant here is justice as fairness. As we noted above, the reasonableness of pursuing common objectives by public means and governmental authority requires that the benefits of the pursuit be fairly distributed, and that the burdens of the effort also be fairly allocated. The normative element in the consent of the governed is based upon the distinction between merely wanting certain goods such as security and respecting these as goods which are as exigent for others--whom one merely regards as fellow humans with the respect one wishes from them--as for oneself and those close to oneself. Thus, laws get moral force from the common good only if they articulate a system of cooperation which, besides being effective, also is a fair system. Government may not pursue the common good by every expedient means, even by destroying some members of the polity for the sake of greater benefits to others. Such an approach would be unfair.

This point, of course, raises the question what "fairness" means. It is tempting to suggest that "fairness" means "sameness" in the sense that all should be treated alike. But treating everyone the same would, if taken in all strictness, destroy the order of society in which different persons with different needs, abilities, tasks, contributions, merits, and risks cooperate together in one effort precisely by making the most of their diversity and complementing one another's limitations. The very differences among people are not negligible from the point of view of justice; it belongs to equal dignity that individual characteristics be appreciated and respected. This appreciation and respect is a most important part of the American proposition. It distinguishes the ideal of American polity from that of any society which loves liberty less than a form of equality which demands uniformity and conformity and forgoes the uniqueness of individuals for the sake of an egalitarian ideal of justice.

Thus, like "sameness," "equality" also is too easily assumed to be a helpful notion in understanding fairness. Actually, in political society the quantitative implications of equality generally are irrelevant. When the concept suggests anything very definite, it is likely to suggest something which is an impossible goal and a questionable ideal. Of course, Jefferson assumes the principle that all men are created equal in the Declaration, but this principle must be understood as the exclusion of inequality—— the inequality which obtains in a polity in which the constitution assumes natural castes, so that some are naturally rulers and others naturally subjects.

The concept of fairness which determines the consent of Americans to their basic law, the constitutional framework, can be clarified by considering a small private association or club. In such an association——assuming it to be voluntary at least in the way in which consent of the governed must be voluntary——it is easy to see what would be fair. Even if such an association were organized for immoral purposes, one could see that some ways of organizing it would be fair and others unfair to the members. Such a club will have its constitution and rules, even if these are not expressly formulated and written down. If these rules and procedures were understood, one would be able to tell at once whether the club was fair or unfair.

Would one who shared the commitment to the common purpose around which the organization was formed be willing to belong to it, accepting whatever role and responsibilities in it for which one was fitted? Would one be willing to have someone for whom one cared deeply——such as one's dear child——cooperate in the club (assuming there to be no objection to its purpose), accepting any position in it, abiding by its rules, dealt with by its procedures, to the extent of the reach of its constituting purpose? Considering the organization coolly and as a nonparticipant, would one who came to know and sympathize with each member be content with that member's lot in the club? If the answer to these questions is affirmative, the association has a fair constitution. But if the answer is negative, then the organization in some way lacks basic fairness.

Thus the fairness of a constitution means that the procedures and the rules and the limits of political society are such that reasonable participants would not feel exploited if they were in any role in the society, and they would be willing to have others with whom they identified by ties of affection or sympathy in any role in it. By "reasonable participant" here we mean one who is genuinely concerned about the common good—not one who uses the political process without commitment to the common purpose of political society. A reasonable participant, thus, is one who is neither motivated merely by self-interest nor by laudable desire to minimize evil in a bad situation, one whose motive is the intent which does to others as one would be done by, and which thus is able to confer authority and form community with all those who agree in working for and seeking to enjoy together these same goods.

Another way of articulating the point we have just made is that the fairness which constitutes a political society in justice is no more and no less than equality in human dignity and mutual respect which is dictated by the golden rule or principle of universalizibility. The difference between particular acts of individuals shaped by this moral principle and the justice of a constitution is that the latter systematically institutionalizes the principle, and thus presents an embodiment of it which can itself be understood as a good which is promoted, respected, shared, and enjoyed by the members of a polity who find their political association not merely useful but inherently good, personally fulfilling, gratifying to their personal need for harmony between their individual identities and social solidarity.

From the vantage point of this account of justice as fairness, one can understand and appreciate both the force and the limitations of other more specific principles which often are proposed in an attempt to define the demands of justice.

Does fairness demand that in an ongoing process of interpersonal relationship between two or more persons the interrelationship be equalized so that the benefits and burdens, the advantages and disadvantages, to each participant balance out? Often this is the case, for in many relationships, such as those involving contracts and torts, only such a balance provides a rule which reasonable persons will accept for themselves and so seek to impose on others. But in other relationships, such as the care provided by the strong and healthy for the weak and sickly, such equalization is out of the question and is not demanded by justice, since one would wish oneself, one's dear child, or any person for whom one felt sympathy to receive at least some support and assistance which could never be balanced by an equal repayment.

Does fairness then demand that each member of society contribute according to capacity and receive according to need?

Again, especially when one thinks of the basic necessities of life and provision for them, fairness does.seem to require equality defined by proportionality to principles of capacity and need. Yet there must be limits to the demand for contribution according to capacity or there will be nothing of an individual's own which can be used with liberty for the pursuit of happiness. And needs which go beyond the basic necessities, needs which are generated by the self-indulgence and self-destructiveness of some members of society, needs which are artificially created—the needs for the latest toys—are needs that cannot expect the same respect as needs for minimally adequate diet, basic health care, shelter, clothing, elementary education, and the like.

Does fairness demand that members of the political society who contribute more than others to its well-being receive proportionately in recompense? Up to a point, certainly. Veterans programs for those who have risked their lives in a shooting war are seldom criticized. Yet perhaps certain civil officers contribute more than other citizens to the well-being of political society by making considerable personal sacrifices to enter and remain in public service. Still, it is not necessarily unjust if such persons are not rewarded as well for services rendered as the presidents of many large corporations or even as some star athletes.

Finally in the allocation of the costs and losses of the common pursuit of political society some members forsee and accept avoidable risks for the sake of the common good, while other members have no opportunity to forsee and avoid (or at least insure against) these risks. Does fairness demand recognition of this willingness to contribute and to serve? In many cases an affirmative answer no doubt is indicated; those who volunteer for extremely hazardous duty in wartime, for instance, deserve something from their compatriots that others do not. Yet this principle cannot, any more than the others, be elevated into an absolute criterion of justice. Often members of society do not forsee risks only because they lack intelligence or information. If such persons accept the responsibilities which fall to them, they seem hardly less deserving than those who make similar contributions with greater foresight, which would have permitted them to avoid the risks they accept with greater voluntariness.

In short, a reasonable participant in political society, considering its basic law in the light of the moral principle of the golden rule (or universalizibility principle), will sometimes think in terms of one, sometimes in terms of another, criterion in specifying just balance or proportion. And the selection and application of these specifying criteria, as well as their mutual limitation, is a work solely for the fair-mindedness of a person who respects others with the respect he or she wishes from them.

Such a person also is prepared to give a public account of judgments in terms which will deserve and can be expected to receive approval as reasonable by other reasonable participants in the society.

If one understands fairness as we have explained it, one can readily understand why fairness often demands procedures which limit the government's effort to maintain law and order. Limitations on search and seizure, the requirement that a person be indicted, and the conduct of a trial with many protections for the accused (who is presumed innocent until proven guilty)--these provisions do not make for maximum efficiency in the process of criminal justice. They do not promote law and order if this is understood merely as a state of affairs providing the maximum level of security for almost all citizens. But these protections contribute greatly to the fairness of criminal procedure as an aspect of justice, as part of the object of the reasonable consent which gives government legitimacy and makes the legal process an exercise of lawful authority rather than of mere repressive power.

Fairness in legal procedure and in the administrative procedure of government is essential, but it does not by itself constitute the fairness which legitimates just laws. Within limits, at least, one can imagine laws unfair as to their substantive provisions fairly administered and enforced. Thus, the laws themselves also must be fair. The purpose of any particular law-- the mischief it is to remedy or the good it is to promote-- dictates what classifications of persons may be made without arbitrary discrimination by which some are benefited or burdened unfairly in comparison with other members of the society. And, of course, if a law is to be fair, its very purpose cannot be discriminatory.

Fairness in the laws themselves is part, at least, of what is meant by "the equal protection of the laws." If this phrase is considered not only as a legal standard to be applied by judges but also as a political standard to be respected by responsible legislators, equal protection also demands that the variety of projects undertaken by political society and the level of public commitment to various projects mandated by government power reach a balance which will be generally acceptable to reasonable participants in the society.

No single project undertaken by government makes equal demands or provides equal benefits to all. But a fair political process, with checks and balances working properly, limiting the power of majorities and the great influence of powerful minorities, should result in a mix of public activities satisfactory enough that reasonable participants in all the various roles in the society will find the whole package satisfactory. None will feel singled out for extraordinary burdens or ignored in the distribution of benefits, at least not in the long run, in a manner which would amount to being "picked on"--unfairly treated in comparison with society's "pets."

The Relationship Between Justice and Liberty

But even the addition of the fairness required by equal protection of the laws to the fairness required by due process is not enough for the fairness needed to justify the laws of a polity which is based upon the consent of the governed. Another condition is necessary. As we have noted above, it is an injustice if government injects itself into matters which lie outside the common good. Such infringement is an unfair violation of the liberty of members of the polity. On this basis, the Fourteenth Amendment to the Constitution of the United States forbids every state to "make or enforce any law which shall abridge the privileges or immunities of citizens of the United States." And the Ninth Amendment, as we have already mentioned, recognizes the rights retained by the people, the zone of liberty which lies outside the common good.

This aspect of constitutional fairness has several important implications in addition to the proscription of treating as public those matters which are properly private.

The first of these implications is that a fair regard for the liberty of persons forbids government to coerce citizens into cooperating in programs not essential to the common good which they sincerely and reasonably believe to be seriously wrong.

We have inserted "not essential to the common good" in the preceding sentence because there are cases in which conscientious objections of some citizens must be overridden to prevent unjust harm to what all agree to be included in the common good. For example, defensive wars must be fought despite the objections of pacifists, and their participation cannot be altogether avoided to the extent that they remain members of the society whose resources and institutions are being employed for purposes which they deplore.

But when there is no such overriding public necessity, the liberty of citizens is at stake if the government embarks upon projects which offend the consciences of citizens. They should be able to remain good citizens without having infringed their liberty to stand aloof from what they detest as evil, and they cannot stand aloof if government wantonly disregards their misgivings, since these limit their consent, while they are drawn along willy-nilly with public policies and acts which they deplore.

A second implication of the libertarian aspect of the requirements for justice is that unless it is essential for the common good, government should not try to prevent citizens from doing those things which they regard as transcendently important. For example, deeply held conscientious convictions about what is ultimately true and good often are believed to carry with them an obligation to communicate these beliefs to others. On this basis, it seems to us, the First Amendment is sound in closely linking freedom of religion with liberty of speech and of the press, with the right to assemble peacefully and to petition for the redress of grievances. All of these guarantees protect the rights of conscience insofar as conscience is not only a standard of private morality for one's individual life but also a standard of one's personally responsible participation in various relationships with others, including the relationships of political society.

It also is worth noticing that respect for liberty of conscience is important for the effectiveness of a free polity. When many participants in a society regard themselves as conscience bound to do certain things, especially to communicate their deeply held convictions to others even at a grave risk to their own peace and security, then any attempt by governmental power to prevent such communication is likely to be self-defeating. While the liberties which are guaranteed by the First Amendment sometimes appear in the short run to have a disturbing effect upon American society, on the whole and in the long run respect for these liberties not only contributes very importantly to justice but also promotes stability in a practical way, by avoiding the unstabiliz- ing effects of conscientiously motivated subversive activities.

A few additional remarks will help to clarify the relation- ship between justice and liberty.

First, it is not only the case that liberty must be protected by just laws; it also is the case that the formation and function- ing of political society itself is a most important exercise of the liberty of its members. The consent of the members of the polity to the constitutional framework, their acceptance of par- ticular laws, their participation in the political process by voting and accepting office, by protest and petition, and so on-- all these are exercises of liberty. The real participation of citizens in the political process as an exercise of liberty gives meaning to the formulation of Lincoln that American government not only is of the people (as is any government) and for the people (as is any just government) but also is by the people.

Nevertheless, although justice and liberty mutually depend upon one another, they are not identical. Indeed, they are quite distinct.

Justice is an attribute of the polity insofar as it is a unity organized by its constitution, laws, and procedures, a unity formed by common consent in response to the common demand of the common good. Justice characterizes the single social order primarily and all its parts and aspects secondarily and derivatively insofar as the political order of society is founded upon the moral principle of universalizability—which dictates equal dignity and mutual respect—and not on mere power.

Liberty is a relation of individuals and groups within political society insofar as they are not subject to lawful authority. Liberty exercised for the common good becomes the working of political society, the activity of the people as governing rather than as governed. Liberty to act or to refrain from acting for other purposes is the scope for personal and social flourishing which is privileged against the demands of political society and immune from the coercive sanctions which government legitimately uses to protect justice when it is at stake.

(pp. 26-46)

6: LESS PLAUSIBLE THEORIES OF ETHICS

Background for Chapter 6, "We Don't Always Know What Is Good For Us"

Before exposing the heart of his theory, Grisez touches upon a number of the many approaches to dealing with moral matters, both systematic and unsystematic. But he focuses particularly upon relativism, for American culture, political and ethical thinking are permeated with a relativistic mentality.

The opening four sentences of Chapter 6 provide a precise guide to determine where Grisez differs from relativism. Simple-looking as they are, they provide the basis for rejecting all forms of relativism.

"We are free to choose what we will do. But we are not free to make whatever we choose right.

We must follow our best judgment concerning what we ought to do. But our best judgment can be mistaken."

Sixth Plank: Ethical relativism is false. Therefore...must be standards....

Life and Death

Why Ethical Reflection Remains Necessary

Legal standards direct and regulate society and provide means by which members of society can pursue their purposes in orderly and recognized ways. Moral standards are primarily sought by persons to shape their own activities. It is a mistake to think of moral norms as if they formed an additional legal code. Upright persons undertake ethical reflection about moral questions not so much to settle controversies with others as to make sure that their own lives will meet the test of reasonableness, will be examined lives worth living by persons conscious of and grateful for the human capacity for rational reflection and self-criticism. Thus the question "Who is making these rules, and why should I accept them?" which always is appropriate when one is confronted with laws is out of place when one is seeking moral standards. A serious person regards any proposed moral standard as an appeal to reason and accepts it if no more reasonable alternative can be found.

There are a number of reasons why moral guidelines are necessary and legal standards by themselves are insufficient.

As we explained in chapter two, section H, not all of morality can be legislated. Thus law necessarily leaves open to individuals a more or less broad set of options, some of which are questionable from a moral point of view. Upright persons will wish to know which of the legally permissible acts are morally acceptable and thus to be seriously considered.

Moreover, upright persons tend to extend their ethical reflection to the law itself. The fact that laws are in force is no guarantee that they are just. Anyone who is concerned about moral goodness will wish to know whether present laws—or any proposed laws, including our proposals—are morally worthy of wholehearted support.

Some Less Plausible Theories of Ethics

Before we criticize the consequentialist method of ethical reasoning, we consider briefly some other current approaches to moral questions. These approaches are generally considered less plausible than consequentialism, and the difficulties inherent in them lend consequentialism much of the plausibility it has.

Very often those who deal with difficult moral questions, including professional philosophers and others considered to have expertise in critical reflection, proceed in an unsystematic and ad hoc way. They do not raise the question: What method of ethical judgment is sound? Instead they deal directly with the moral issues and proceed from assumptions which they expect readers or listeners to grant.

One very simple way to do this is to argue by analogy. A real or imaginary case which seems simple and clear is taken as a premiss, and the extent to which people's moral judgments about the case coincide is used as another premiss. The conclusion is then drawn that the same moral judgment should hold for a somewhat similar but less simple and clear case, concerning which moral judgments have diverged.

The analogy proposed by Judith Jarvis Thomson, which we criticized in chapter seven, section F, between abortion and disconnecting oneself from the violinist, is an example of this way of arguing. Our criticism of her argument makes clear why arguments of this sort are weak. If the instances which are compared are not alike in all relevant ways, then the analogy, although persuasive, loses its appearance of rational cogency. If the instances which are compared are alike in all relevant ways, the

moral standard implicit in the judgment of the clearer case also
will apply to the less clear one. But such arguments will be
effective only when the principle itself is not in question. However, the issues considered in this book concern principles, not
merely the application of standards to cases, and the same is
generally true of important arguments about public policy issues.
Thus, arguments by analogy cannot provide a rational ground for
settling the issues in dispute.

Another approach to moral issues which avoids the problems of
ethical theory is casuistry. Casuistry is a method of moral reasoning by which one applies an accepted set of principles to difficult cases by clarifying the peculiar features of these cases,
making explicit all the principles which might be relevant, and
comparing the difficult cases to simpler cases determined by each
of the relevant principles. In law casuistry is indispensable,
and it also will be used by anyone or any moral community which
holds and develops a complex set of moral standards. But casuistry has its limitations. Like argument by analogy, it assumes
that there are principles which are not in doubt. The application
might refine or qualify an accepted standard but will not so
radically alter it as to dictate contradictory decisions concerning cases previously decided by the standard.

Therefore, any adequate approach to the issues treated in
this book must confront the problems of ethical theory and provide
an account of the way in which moral standards themselves can be
critically defended--that is, how one can rationally prefer one
to another candidate for the status of moral norm when the candi-
dates are incompatible with each other directly, not merely in
tension with each other in application to difficult cases.

One of the simplest ethical theories compares the source of
moral judgments to the sources of factual and scientific judgments.
Just as one knows factual truths by observation or experience and
develops science on the basis of particular factual truths, so
it is suggested one knows moral truths by experience with the
moral data and develops moral principles by generalization from
such experience. On this theory one might say that conscience is
a moral sense by which one intuitively perceives moral truths.

A slightly different version of intuitionism suggests that
general moral norms are grasped directly, somewhat as self-evident
principles--for example, of mathematics--are believed by some to
be grasped. Intuitionist theories of this second sort account for
the universality and necessity which many people believe to belong
to moral norms.

However, appealing as intuitionism is, moral judgments do
not seem to be either like matters of fact or like self-evident

general principles of any theoretical discipline. Moral judgments and moral standards are normative, not theoretical. They say what ought to be, not what happens to be or what necessarily is. Whether one thinks of intuition on the analogy of sense perception or on the analogy of insight into some sort of necessary principles of the order of things, it is difficult, to say the least, to understand how one could intuit what might or might not be, but ought to be.

Furthermore, both particular moral judgments and proposals of general moral norms conflict. This conflict, as we have just explained, is what gives rise to the need for ethical theory. Intuitionism seems to suggest that there really should be no more conflict here than there is about matters of fact or self-evident principles. But the conflict remains, and no one who holds an intuitionist theory is in a position to explain the fact of conflict or to suggest a rational method for resolving it. Intuitionists thus are reduced to what seems a bare and unsupported assertion of conflicting moral claims. Those who do not accept such claims are called "morally blind" or "morally muddled," but when such charges are laid mutually, discussion is at a standstill.

The failure of intuitionism has led many modern, especially twentieth century, philosophers to doubt that there is any rational way to vindicate any moral norm or judgment. Certainly, if claims to truth in the moral domain are mistaken—if there is no truth or falsity to be had in this domain—then moral norms and particular moral judgments will not be able to be vindicated rationally.

In this case moral judgments often are regarded as the expression of the feelings or attitudes or commitments of individuals or groups: Such things have a function in generating and shaping behavior but are themselves simply facts about persons or societies, not normative truths. The theory that moral judgments are facts of this sort is called "subjectivism"; as applied to societies and cultures, it sometimes is called "relativism." We shall simply say "subjectivism" to cover all forms of this theory.

Certain facts make subjectivism appealing. For one thing, some who are confident that they know the truth about morality are tempted to fanaticism; they may be harsh and intolerant toward others who disagree or who fall short of the standard of true morality. Another point is that people who hold differing moral views, provided that they are sincere, generally are considered morally upright only if they follow their own best judgment, so that different people are morally good in following conflicting moral judgments. Another point is that morality seems to be a matter of a person's free decision; if there were an objective truth in moral norms, then such freedom would seem to be excluded. Again, subjectivism gains some plausibility from the fact that very often people use moral language to do no more than express their feelings, attitudes, or commitments. Thus, often those who do not like a public policy say it is "unjust," because this is a very emphatic way of expressing one's negative feelings or attitudes or one's preference for some alternative approach.

However, intolerance does not follow necessarily from the belief that there is moral truth, nor does tolerance follow from subjectivism.

One can hold that there is moral truth but that it leaves room for a certain range of life-styles which ought to be tolerated whether one likes them or not. One also can hold that forms of behavior one considers incompatible with true moral standards ought to be tolerated for the sake of various human goods, such as liberty and justice.

Moreover, it is obvious that persons of sincere good will can disagree irreconcilably in regard to ethical questions and can consider themselves bound to follow courses of action which lead to tragic conflict with one another. Those finding themselves in such conflicts need not, and often do not, condemn as vicious those with whom they are in conflict.

Furthermore, one can embrace subjectivism and have completely intolerant feelings, attitudes, and commitments. And if one is a consistent subjectivist, one will consider such intolerance beyond criticism or reproach from any source. Those who embrace subjectivism must confront moral disagreement as a matter of fact to be dealt with according to their own feelings, attitudes, and commitments. Such persons might forbear to do all they would like, but not out of any respect for objectively valid principles of liberty and justice—for there can be no moral foundations for such values. Their validity extends no further than their effectiveness if subjectivism is correct. A subjectivist involved in a moral conflict cannot think an opponent sincere but mistaken, for there is no moral truth about which one can be mistaken.

The desire for tolerance surely is worthy, but it does not require subjectivism. Rather it requires a distinction between the viciousness or guilt of one who acts and the wrongness or evil of what is done, between the virtue or good will of one who acts and the rightness or goodness of what is done. People of good will can do what is evil by mistake or through weakness, and it also is possible for vicious people to do good despite their worst efforts.

All persons must follow their own consciences, for one's conscience is one's best judgment as to what one ought to do. Nobody is morally guilty who does his or her best to find out what is right and then acts according to this best judgment. But such a judgment, for all its sincerity, can be mistaken--that is, can be in error (if, contrary to subjectivism, there is moral truth). Thus, if one finds certain practices of others ethically indefensible, one need not pass a judgment of moral condemnation upon those who engage in or defend such practices. Tolerance of those who disagree with one's judgment, compassion for those who do what one judges to be evil (often in circumstances in which one might oneself do far worse evil), are fully compatible with a firm judgment that the practice one rejects is truly immoral, not merely inconsonant with one's own feelings, attitudes, or commitments.

Other facts which at first glance make subjectivism appealing also fail on closer examination to lend it rational support.

The suggestion that moral freedom entails subjectivism depends upon a confusion--one which is very widespread--between moral judgment and moral choice. Moral life, obviously, is not a matter of given facts. In the moral domain a person is no mere puppet moved by natural forces. Rather, as a moral agent, one determines oneself, writes one's own autobiography, creates one's own history. A person can say "No" to the world which presents itself and with that "No" can undertake to make a world more in accord with a moral vision. Thus moral life is the sphere in which men and women are superior to what is given in advance. How, then, can one submit to moral standards which do not reflect one's own decisions?

The answer is that moral decision is twofold. One is the choice of what one will do; the other is the judgment as to what one should do. Due to this ambiguity it makes perfectly good sense to say, "He decided that he would be doing something wrong if he killed his defective child, but he decided to kill the child to end the suffering of everyone concerned, including himself." The first "decided" refers to judgment, the second to choice. In neither sense is decision a fact of nature. But decision as judgment can have an objectivity as an expression of moral truth-- if subjectivism is mistaken--which decision as choice cannot have.

If this were not so, there would be no morally wrong acts; the very fact that one decided to do something would make one's choice be right. If subjectivism were correct, there would hardly be room for immorality; immorality would at most be dissonance between one's actions and one's own feelings, attitudes, and commitments--a dissonance one always could remedy by changing one's feelings, attitudes, and commitments as well as by changing one's behavior. In any case, inasmuch as feelings, attitudes, and commitments are themselves merely one set of facts among others, a subjectivist theory does not account for the sense that moral life involves transcendence to the given. Rather, it renders this sense of transcendence inexplicable. A theory which leaves room for moral truth but distinguishes it as normative from the truths of fact and self-evident principle which are the model for intuitionist ethical theories will avoid the difficulties of intuitionism without falling into subjectivism.

Finally, it can be granted the subjectivist that people often do use moral language without intending by it to express more than their own feelings, attitudes, and commitments in a particularly forceful way. Some children call anything they dislike "unfair." This use of moral language is accounted for by the subjectivist theory, just to the extent that truth is no concern of those who talk this way.

But even here the subjectivist theory does not fully explain what is going on. Moral language as subjective expression has something which makes it preferable to a straightforward expression of one's feelings, attitudes, and commitments. Moral language makes an appeal to the reasonableness of others, while a merely subjective expression could at most appeal to sympathy. This special feature of moral language is understandable if, in fact, the cases in which it is used in a subjectivist way are parasitic upon standard uses in which something more is being expressed: a moral truth which deserves attention and respect as well as sympathy for the person—a fellow member of a moral community—who utters it.

In short, subjectivism is inadequate as an ethical theory. It puts an end to rational discourse about morality as surely as intuitionism does. It precludes justification of basic moral principles and reduces them to the status of facts. And it renders unintelligible the fact that one can be mistaken in one's moral judgments and be in need of correction. Moreover, subjectivism makes it very difficult to understand how anyone can do what is morally wrong, since immorality will merely be a matter of inconsistency which sufficiently energetic and ingenious persons always can try to remove by altering themselves or their culture rather than by conforming action to existing standards—which are only facts to be dealt with efficiently like any other obstacle to doing as one wishes.

Although few if any who engage in the euthanasia debate profess either intuitionism or subjectivism as an ethical theory, many popular discussions of these issues seem to presuppose an intuitionist or a subjectivist theory of morality.

More and more people try to support their diverse and incompatible moral views by an appeal to "experience," as if experience were a final and unanswerable argument. Actually it is no argument at all. People who appeal to experience often imply an intuitionist theory. This is so if they think that they discern moral truth in their experience. Otherwise they imply a subjectivist theory if all they mean is that their experience has contributed to their peculiar feelings, attitudes, and commitments, which are what they are, and neither need nor can have any more justification than any other fact, such as feeling depressed, liking Bach, or being committed to one's country right or wrong.

Again, polls showing changing public attitudes often are cited as if they indicated that traditional moral standards are surpassed and no longer valid. But mass public opinion—even if it reflects something more worthy of respect than the effectiveness of the opinion-making media—does not settle morality unless subjectivism is correct. And if it is, the new morality is no more true than the old one, and there can be no more justification for accepting the latest opinion than for holding to traditional opinions.

The history of twentieth-century ethical theory, apart from the articulation of various versions of subjectivism, is largely a series of attempts to find a way of getting beyond intuitionism and subjectivism. If these views are untenable, most philosophers think, there must be some rational way to criticize and justify moral norms, even the most basic of them. How can one do this?

Many religious persons would answer that moral judgments are true simply because God has given his commandments to humankind, and these commandments can be reflected in human moral judgments, which thus conform to a standard which cannot be wrong.

Philosophers generally will not accept this account, partly because it depends upon religious faith and partly because it is difficult to discern the practical implications for difficult questions of the commandments traditionally believed to come directly from God. Thus some argue that euthanasia must be excluded as forbidden killing; others that it must be permitted as compassion toward a suffering neighbor.

However, a more basic problem with divine-command theory of morality is that it seems to be another form of subjectivism, but one with God as the sole subject whose determinations constitute morality. Of course, on this account the norms are not truths and cannot be rationally defended. If one attempts to avoid this conclusion by providing reasons why God's commands ought to be accepted and followed in practice, then one appeals to a moral

108

norm which claims respect apart from the fact that God commands anything.

Thus even those who hold that God does give certain commands which transcend human understanding and that these commands ought to be accepted in faith--a position we ourselves hold--preserve the possibility of rational defensibility for religious morality only if they can explain why one ought to believe and live one's faith. If one abandons the possibility of rational defensibility for religious morality, one forgoes the possibility of proposing faith with any sort of moral appeal. The alternative is to propose it as something either with no appeal or with an appeal to nonmoral interests.

One way to try to supply reasons why divine commands ought to be accepted is to appeal to human nature. Presumably, various kinds of action comport well or badly with human nature, considered as a whole.

The difficulty with this theory is that all possible human acts are consistent with human nature if this nature is considered as something which is given. Thus, viewed in this way, human nature provides no norm by which one can separate good from bad acts. However, if nature is considered not merely as a given but as a normative ideal, then naturalness is equivalent to what human persons ought to be. The appeal to nature thus becomes an appeal to intuition, or a merely question-begging attempt to articulate this intuition.

The ethical theory of Immanuel Kant is an attempt to find a moral norm in the nature of human persons themselves, while it excludes as immoral much of what men and women actually do. Kant argues that goodness attends one's actions to the extent that it issues from principles which can pass reason's test of perfect self-consistency; evil attends one's action to the extent that it is elicited by one's given needs and interests, desires and fears, in a way which escapes or evades control by the rule of reason.

Kant surely has located a necessary condition of moral goodness. A person who is uninterested in principle, who is willing to make special exceptions in particular cases for no reason at all, clearly is unconcerned about morality. But it is not clear that Kant has located a sufficient condition of moral goodness. It seems possible for anyone to achieve rational consistency if he or she is ingenious enough at making distinctions.

Moreover, if as Kant suggests immorality attends action which flows from impulse unregulated by reason, then moral failings seem rather to be something a person suffers than something a person does. But while people do fail morally through weakness, such failings seem less seriously immoral than those acts in which reason seems to play a larger role. In short, Kant does not show how a person, precisely as a rational agent, can be immoral (and in the moral sense "unreasonable"). The violation of rational principles such as the laws of logic leads to the total breakdown of rational functioning; the violation of moral norms does not but rather represents a peculiar perversion which is only maximally possible if there is no breakdown in rational functioning. One of the data from which ethics begins is that there is a distinction between being immoral and being mentally ill. Kant cannot account for this distinction.

The challenge to go beyond intuitionism and subjectivism, which is not adequately answered by the theories discussed thus far, is met more plausibly by those ethical theories which are called "teleological." A teleological theory also begins from some truths which are considered to be too basic to demonstrate-- truths which are claimed to be self-evident or known by intuition after a reflective clarification. But these truths themselves are not proposed as moral norms. Rather, a teleological theory maintains that moral obligations are determined by what promotes human well-being or human flourishing. The basis for moral norms thus includes two kinds of propositions. One of them characterizes certain goods--"goods" not in a moral sense but merely in the sense of things desired for their own sake-- as constituents of human well-being or flourishing. The other kind of proposition specifies the manner in which human acts must be related to these human goods if the acts are to be morally right.

Teleological theories have considerable initial appeal. Morality does seem to be for persons, for their full development and true well-being. It seems mistaken to think that moral rules are mere restraints upon human desires and actions, mere limits which would prevent people from being all that they might become.

Moreover, the proposition that human well-being is to be promoted does seem to be self-evident. In arguments about what is to be done the disagreement is always about what will promote well-being, in what it consists, whether an action or policy which seems to promote it really--perhaps in the long run--does not do so. Thomas Aquinas, for example, argues that the first principle of practical reasoning is: Good is to be done and pursued, evil is to be avoided. And he holds this principle to be self-evident. Moreover, "good" here signifies, not moral goodness, but rather what contributes to human well-being.

(pp. 336-345)

Background for Chapter 10, "The Ethics of Love"

Grisez refers to consequentialism as a plausible but inadequate theory. But he feels compelled to confront and challenge consequentialism more vigorously than any other approach. It has become extremely popular and influential. Although utilitarianism is a crude form of consequentialism, other more subtle forms are employed in situation ethics and in the dominant positions of recent Catholic moral thinking.

Many Catholic moral theologians have arrived at a consequentialist approach to moral issues starting from their changed stance toward contraception. Some twenty years ago most Catholic moral theologians held: 1) that contraception is morally wrong; 2) that there are intrinsically evil acts; 3) that it is never right to do evil to achieve good. Compassion seems to have led many to acknowledge that contraception is not intrinsically evil but that certain situations render contraception morally justifiable. Such a position is recognized as more plausible if it is denied that there are any intrinsically evil acts. But then the traditional natural law approach with insistence that the nature of the act is an essential constituent of morality must be suppressed. Hence the adoption of subtle forms of consequentialism.

Grisez for years has been challenging this shift of approach. He is genuinely concerned about the influence of consequentialism. He views it not only as meaningless but as dangerous nonsense. When Richard McCormick chides him for a "nervous fear" of consequences he replies, "I think my attitude is not one of nervous fear.... Rather it is an attitude of reasonable terror. For, as I see it, consequentialism is not merely a meaningless theory, it also is a pernicious method of rationalization." ("Against Consequentialism," p. 67)

Sixth Plank: ....   Utilitarianism..."dead-end"...nonviable theory.

Consequentialism: A Plausible but Inadequate Theory

For the moment we put aside the question of what constitutes human well-being or flourishing. This question, concerning what goods are basic to morality, we shall consider shortly. But first we wish to consider the theory of the method of ethical reasoning which we call "consequentialism." This theory has become extremely popular in modern times, both among professional moralists and among others who discuss moral and public policy questions. The influence of consequentialism upon the issues discussed in this book has been enormous.

According to the simplest consequentialist theory of moral reasoning the moral good or evil of human acts is determined by the results (consequences) of these acts. If an act has good consequences, then that act will be good; if it has bad consequences, it will be bad. Of course, most acts have consequences which are partly good and partly bad, and moral judgment is necessary only when one must compare alternative courses of action, among which one might choose, to determine what one ought to do. Consequentialism holds that the morally good act will be the one which on the whole gives the best results. All the alternatives, including not acting and delaying action, must be compared. If one can add up the good results expected of each possible course of action and subtract in each case the expected bad results from the good, then according to the simplest form of consequentialism the morally right choice is that alternative which will yield the greatest net good--or, in an unfavorable situation, the least net harm.

In other words, the consequentialist wishes one to think about what one might do in terms of its impact upon human persons --the extent to which it will benefit or harm them. The right thing to do will maximize benefits and minimize harms. Only the one best act will be morally good, and it will be obligatory. Other possible courses of action will be immoral, more or less seriously so depending upon the extent to which they are less beneficial or more harmful to someone than the morally right act.

A consequentialist theory of moral reasoning seems implicit in the ethical and political theories of a great many modern thinkers. Machiavelli and Hobbes, for example, seem to argue in this way for proposals which seemed radical in their day. Marx, when he justifies revolutionary action, seems to do so by pointing to its necessity to overcome alienation and attain a new level of human life, much better than the dehumanized existence in which humankind has suffered until now. Even many contemporary

Christian thinkers seem to offer consequentialist arguments, sometimes based upon an otherworldly conception of human flourishing, for their moral teachings. But more than any others in the English-speaking world, the utilitarian thinkers, including Jeremy Bentham and John Stuart Mill, explicated and defended consequentialism as a method of ethical reasoning. The consequentialist formulation which they made popular is: The right act is that which brings about the greatest happiness for the greatest number.

The utilitarians joined consequentialism with a theory of human well-being which was more or less frankly hedonistic. Hedonism equates what is intrinsically good for persons with pleasure or enjoyable experience, what is bad for persons with pain or undesirable states of consciousness. The utilitarian theory thus proposes that the morality of actions be judged by the extent to which they cause enjoyment and minimize misery. Obviously, consequentialism need not be tied to hedonistic value theory; consequentialism itself perhaps is more plausible than this or that theory of value with which it has been connected.

Still, consequentialism with a more or less strong component of hedonism underlies many proposals for altering public policies and laws in ways which diverge from traditional morality. Justifications for mercy killing, for example, which invoke quality-of-life considerations generally evaluate quality in terms of the enjoyable activities and experiences an individual is likely to have in comparison with the pain and suffering the individual must undergo if life continues. Considerations of the interests of the family and society bring into account the relative costs and benefits to others, in accord with the utilitarian injunction to consider the good of all concerned. When it seems that the benefits of continued life for the individual and for others are overbalanced by the harms of suffering and burdens, then it is presumed such killing would be kindly and that it is morally permissible and even obligatory.

There are many different forms of consequentialism. We have described the simplest form.

It is direct. It locates the preponderance of value which determines the moral worth of each particular action in the particular state of affairs brought about in and through that action. More complex versions of consequentialism are indirect. They look to the overall state of affairs which will be brought about if one accepts a certain rule or other principle, and then the moral significance of particular acts is judged by their conformity to that rule or other principle.

Again, some versions of consequentialism are pure. They admit no moral value which cannot be judged by consequentialist considerations alone. Other versions of consequentialism are mixed. They hold that some or all moral values can be judged only if consequentialist considerations are supplemented in appropriate ways by nonconsequentialist ones--for example, by the limiting requirements of justice.

Act consequentialism and rule consequentialism do not seem to us to differ as much as is sometimes supposed. Act consequentialism admits that if a judgment is right in any particular case, then the same judgment should be made and followed by anyone who faces a similar set of alternatives with a like balance of good and bad consequences. Thus the judgment of the particular act, just insofar as it is a rational appraisal, is really universal and thus is a rule. And a rule consequentialist, when pressed, does not insist that rules must be maintained if on the whole and in the long run change in them would be for the better. Thus rules are qualified to permit all reasonable exceptions, and reasonableness is judged by the consequences of acts.

Rule consequentialists sometimes argue that their position takes account of situations in which it is harmless to the community and advantageous for each individual to act in a certain way but disastrous for all if everyone acts in that way. However, act consequentialism can justify making and enforcing rules--since the making of a rule is itself a particular act--to restrain everyone from contributing to a situation when the cumulative effect would result in a common disadvantage. Among the consequences of an individual act are the implications it has for the actions of others and the consequences it will have when joined with the predictable acts of others. Thus act and rule consequentialism seem to yield the same results.

Even if some forms of consequentialism are not reducible to the simplest sort, every kind of consequentialism involves a common feature: They all require the weighing of values implicit in various alternatives, whether these alternatives be courses of action, rules, life-styles, or something else. We hold that precisely because of this feature, shared in common by all forms of consequentialism, it is an unworkable theory of moral reasoning. It cannot do the job for which it is intended by its proponents.

In recent years many philosophers have criticized consequentialism. Many of these criticisms have tried to show that consequentialism would yield moral judgments at odds with the considered moral opinions of most morally serious people. For example, it is often pointed out that consequentialism cannot justify common moral judgments about justice, because a consequentialist is concerned about the maximizing of the total benefit and has no way to assure fair distribution of goods.

But a consequentialist has two ways to respond to objections of this sort. First, it can be argued that fairness itself is important because unfairness causes a great deal of misery and leads to conflict which breeds even more misery. If strict fairness is not required to avoid bad consequences and if some inequality in distributing benefits is beneficial on the whole, then the consequentialist will argue that it is fanatical to insist upon strict fairness.

Second, consequentialists can-and often do--regard their theory as a revisionist approach to moral dilemmas, as a new morality. If it does not account for prevailing moral opinions, that might be because these opinions are corrupted by the prejudices of ancient traditions. The consequentialist will urge that this new approach be adopted to put moral judgment, at last, on a rational basis, a basis similar to that adopted by science and other advanced forms of human thinking.

Our own critique of consequentialism does not depend upon an appeal to moral intuition for counterexamples to consequentialist judgments. Our position is, not that consequentialism gives wrong answers, but that it cannot rationally justify any moral judgment, because it is an altogether unworkable way to proceed from an appreciation of the basic human goods involved in human well-being or flourishing to judgments on the moral quality of human acts, humanly approved rules, or the like. The subject matter upon which consequentialists try to bring their theory to bear, we maintain, is such that no one can reason about it in the way consequentialism urges.

Consequentialism is a calculative method. It suggests that the good and bad effects of each alternative be tallied, that the total bad effects be subtracted from the total good effects of each alternative, and that the net results of each computation be compared with the others. The alternative which gets the best--or least bad--score is the one to be accepted.

This calculation simply cannot be done unless the values of the various outcomes are such that they can be measured against one another. But the good effects of one alternative--in the simplest case of one action--often seem to be simply different in kind from its bad effects. Moreover, the good and bad effects of each alternative often appear simply incommensurable with the good and bad effects of the other possibilities.

The appearance of incommensurability between various goods which are components of human well-being is revealed clearly by examples. A young woman has a choice whether to be a physician or a lawyer. Assuming that the decision is not settled by an existing resolution to take up the career which will probably yield a better income or something of the sort, the young woman will see that each profession is humanly worthy in its own way. A physician can help to promote health, cure disease, and comfort the dying. A lawyer can help people cooperate together, promote public order, and protect justice. One simply cannot add up the pro and con features of these ways of life and assess the worth of each. There simply is no neutral scale on which she might weigh in homogeneous units the good and bad aspects of the two professions.

Of course, if one assumes a prior commitment to some further good, a commitment which is not allowed to be put in question while considering these possibilities, then the comparison may be carried out with a definitive result. For example, if a young man is determined to follow that career into which he can enter with fewer years of time and fewer dollars for schooling, then a simple comparison will tell him to favor the law and avoid medicine. If he has made up his mind to follow as lucrative a career as possible, a study of his own talents and of the market situation will indicate, at least with a certain degree of probability, which alternative to accept.

But moral choices are not simply selections of the most efficient ways of reaching some antecedently established goal. Rather, moral choices are made in a context in which one recognizes multiple goals, accepts the possibility that some of these may be called into question, and does not preclude the need to accept constraints on the pursuit of some goals.

The incommensurability which appears in choices like the one just described also appears in choices which most people would consider paradigmatic cases of moral decision, as moral dilemmas very difficult to resolve. For example, if one must decide whether to undergo chemotherapy for cancer, one must consider the pain, disruption, expense, psychological repugnance of the treatment and its effects. One also must consider the obligations which would go unfulfilled if one dies sooner than necessary, the various activities and experiences one will miss out on. It is hard to see how any of these items could be rationally weighed against one another. The same thing is true in other cases. How, for example, is the value of the life of a severely defective infant to be weighed against the costs of treatment, the burdens to the child's parents and to society, and so on?

When consequentialists propose their theory, it seems overwhelmingly sensible. Choose the course of action which will yield the greatest net benefit to all concerned. If one disagrees, the challenge is: Do you mean that one ought to prefer an alternative which brings about more misery on the whole? Clearly, one cannot prefer this if it is really the alternative. But now we have shown, on closer inspection, that the comparison of alternatives does not appear to present one with instances in which any alternative is clearly and unambiguously likely to bring about either a greater net benefit or more misery on the whole. Rather, all of the morally interesting alternatives seem to embody incommensurable goods.

We hold that this appearance of incommensurability of the goods in the alternatives between which one must choose is veridical: The appearance is reality and cannot be overturned. These goods are either means to or components in human flourishing. That these human goods are incommensurable is implied by the fact that human individuals can make free choices. One can make a free choice only between options which embody incommensurable goods. If possibilities which initially seemed to offer significant alternatives turned out not to embody any incommensurable goods, then one's judgment would be determined and no choice would be necessary. Other possibilities simply would fall away in favor of the one which appeared best.

The point can be clarified in the following way. If goods were commensurable, then there would be no need for free choice, since in each case of deliberation between alternatives one could discover by calculation which possibility was the best. If one could discover which possibility was the best—using "best" in a single, uniform meaning—then it would be psychologically impossible not to take the alternative which one had discovered to be the best. Of course, if one were able to take what was known to be less good—using "good" in the comparison in a single, uniform sense—such a choice would be irrational. But the point we are making is even more basic. If one of the alternatives about which one deliberates were recognized to be determinately better than the other options, then it would be impossible to choose any of the others. Choice, after all, is for the sake of the good in what is chosen; choice of what is less good rather than of what is more good could not be for the sake of anything.

It is possible to choose unreasonably that which is less good than an alternative which one might choose—for instance, to choose unreasonably to do what is morally evil rather than what is morally required. But such unreasonableness is possible only because what is judged to be "best" is not discovered to have as much good--using "good" in a single, uniform sense--as any alternative and some more good besides. Rather, each eligible alternative is seen as having some special good--peculiar to itself and incommensurable with the good held out by the other possibilities--which will be attained only if that alternative is chosen and must be forgone if another alternative is taken instead.

If goods were commensurable as consequentialist calculation demands, then one of the options could be discovered to have as much good as the others and more good besides. The "as much" would replace or compensate for the good forgone in the alternatives not chosen; the "more besides" would make the best alternative irresistible. If goods were commensurable, there would be a common standard of goodness, and no alternative ever would hold out an appeal peculiar to itself. By the common standard one possibility would be found to have all the good, all the appeal, of any alternative possibility, and then some; the alternatives simply would not measure up.

The preceding, quite abstract argument can be confirmed by reflection upon experiences one has of making choices, particularly those choices of acts for which one feels morally responsible.

If we seek within our experience for the cause of the fact that we have actually done something for which we feel moral responsibility, we usually come back to a point at which we ourselves made a choice, at least a choice to "go along" with something. Prior to the choice itself we were aware of two or more possibilities, incompatible with each other and lying in the future before us. It seemed to us that none of these possibilities was bound to occur. We thought that only we ourselves could settle whether each possibility would or would not ever become real.

We therefore considered each alternative in turn by noting the pros and cons of each. These pros and cons were not altogether comparable. Although there may have been some common factors, we did not find that one alternative included all the pros and excluded all the cons of the other (or else they would not have appeared to be genuine alternatives). With some perplexity at the lack of any common standard by which to measure the various pros and cons, we acutely felt the need to settle the indeterminacy in the facts ourselves. In considering each of the alternatives from the point of view of the good and appeal peculiar to itself other possibilities seemed clearly inferior. But since every possibility seemed better after its own fashion, the quest for the altogether better was frustrated. The possibilities offered incommensurable goods; there simply was no way to measure the peculiar "better" of one alternative against the "better" of a diverse sort proper to another.

One's problem in choosing is like that of a person who is asked which is preferable, a dollar bill or a copper cent. So long as the credit of the government is good, the bill is worth more as money. But if one needs a bit of copper to bridge a gap in an electrical circuit, then a penny is preferable and the paper bill worthless. So it is when we choose: We must settle which of two or more possible "betters" we will realize.

Thus we determine ourselves by taking as a measure of good the standard by which one alternative will appear decisively better. And once we have chosen, the rejected alternatives seem to pale in appeal. No longer impartially considering all possibilities from the perspective of each of them in turn, we view the whole set of possibilities from the single viewpoint of the good proper to the one we have chosen.

Looking back on a choice already made, we always seem to have chosen the greater good—the alternative which appeared better—unless we have a change of heart, which happens, for example, when we repent of having done something immoral. Some argue from the retrospective experience of the superiority of what was chosen that we do not really determine ourselves but rather are determined by the facts to choose the greater good. They forget that before the choice was made, each alternative seemed better in its own way, and our perplexity in seeking the greater good was terminated only when we ourselves selected the single measure of good which we then applied to all the possibilities—a measure according to which one alternative only then became unambiguously better.

Consequentialism goes wrong by ignoring this fact: There is no "greatest net good" because goods are incommensurable. One's computer balks and says that this does not compute. Consequentialism logically must presuppose that while deliberation is going on, the choice already is made, the value standard already settled, so that there will be no self-determination. But in this assumption a consequentialist must ignore the facts of experience. We do determine ourselves, not by computation, as if there were commensurable goods, but by accepting one way of being satisfied rather than another as the standard by which we shall proceed in a given case.

Of course, the consequentialist can accept the conclusion that free choice entails the incommensurability of goods and try to escape the implication that consequentialism is unworkable in principle by denying that human persons make free choices. As a matter of historical fact most consequentialists have embraced some form of determinism. Those in the English-speaking tradition have usually held the form of determinism which is called "soft determinism," or "compatibilism." According to this view human acts are determined in a way which is compatible with their being imputed to the people who do them, for human agents remain free in the sense of being uncoerced even though their acts are neither uncaused nor self-determined but rather are determined by a cause. Often compatibilists are psychological determinists who maintain that one necessarily chooses that alternative which seems best.

A consequentialist who accepts a deterministic account of human choice and action, however, merely relocates the difficulty which we have already pointed out in the consequentialist position.

If the factors which cause choices are nonconscious ones, then the effort of thinking about moral questions is futile, since one will choose as one is nonconsciously determined to choose.

If the factors which cause choices are consciously grasped reasons--that is, if psychological determinism is accepted--then a consequentialist ought logically to identify the sufficient condition of the choice with the result of the consequentialist calculus. In other words, what seems best will be what is discovered by calculation to promise the greatest net good. But this leads to a conclusion which the consequentialist cannot accept: What one ought to do will be identical with what one will do. This conclusion cannot be accepted because it is a fact, always taken for granted by ethical theory, that one can do what is wrong, that one can violate the requirements of morality.

A consequentialist might argue that even on a consequentialist theory which accepts psychological determinism a person still might fail by ignorance or miscalculation to discover what is right. Thus the objective norm will be established by consequentialist calculation properly carried out, the subjective choice will be determined, and the choice will be divergent from the norm. The consequentialist thus would be urging that there is one sovereign norm of morality: Calculate carefully! But to say that one ought to calculate carefully so that one's choices and acts will be determined by the greatest net good simply moves the question about freedom and morality to a different level of choice and action. Either one is free to calculate and not to calculate, and this choice is not determined and so not controlled by consequentialist considerations. Or one is determined to calculate and will do it as one is determined to do it--if consequentialism is relevant at all in precisely the way that one ought to do it.

Thus, whether persons can make free choices or not, consequentialism cannot provide guidance for morally significant choices. On the one hand, the commensurability of goods which consequentialism requires is incompatible with free choice, so if persons do make free choices, goods are incommensurable and consequentialism is not workable as a method of judging what the choices ought to be. On the other hand, if persons do not make free choices, they are determined to choose an act either in accord with or at odds with the consequentialist judgment. If at odds, then it is senseless to say that people ought to do what the consequentialist judgment says, for they cannot. If people are determined to act in accord with the consequentialist judgment, then it does not make sense to consider their choices and actions morally significant, for they cannot do other than they ought.

The consequentialist, therefore, must either accept the unworkability of his theory because of the incommensurability of goods, or admit the pointlessness of moral reflection because of the impossibility that one choose and act as one ought when one is otherwise determined, or deny a fact which all ethical theory presupposes: that people sometimes do what is morally wrong. We condlude, therefore, that consequentialism fails as a theory of moral reasoning.

If the foregoing refutation of consequentialism is correct, any ethical theory which involves it fails just to the extent that the theory does involve it. Someone might object that it is hard to believe that so many serious philosophers and others hold a theory as bad as this. After all, the subject matter is not esoteric but is the making of moral choices, which everyone directly experiences. Our reply is that the very failure of consequentialism helps its proponents to feel that it is an important ethical theory well grounded in their own experience.

When consequentialists argue for the moral permissibility of certain kinds of action—for example, the permissibility of killing those whom they think would be better off dead—the possibilities are examined in the light of the consequentialist's own prior commitments. These prior commitments need not have involved personally adopting a proposal to kill anyone but might have involved condoning the acts of others. Moreover, the prior commitments need not have had to do with the specific kind of act under consideration provided that they had enough bearing on the goods at stake in the kind of act for which the consequentialist argues and the kinds of act alternative to it in the situation the discussion envisages.

Enough bearing for what? Enough bearing so that the consequentialist does not perceive the incommensurability of the goods, but perceives them according to a uniform standard, which allows the calculation consequentialism requires to be carried out after the manner of an intuitive estimate. One who has approved abortion, for example, might consider the case of a severely defective infant in terms of the good preferred to human life in the approval of abortion and on this consideration judge that life with defects is of such poor quality that the child would be better off dead.

Thus the consequentialist feels confident that "greater good" or "greatest net good" has a very clear and definite meaning. But these expressions, as consequentialists use them, mean no more than "the good which anyone with my commitments would prefer." Still, consequentialists want their judgment to be accepted as a moral judgment; they claim that their judgment expresses a standard which any reasonable person ought to accept. So consequentialists project their personal commitments upon the objective possibilities and then read off this projected set of preferences as if they were an objective description which any reasonable person would perceive.

In other words, although consequentialism is wholly unworkable as an ethical theory, it is quite serviceable both as a method of rationalization and as a form of persuasive discourse, by which one can commend one's personal preferences and prejudices in terms which suggest moral objectivity.

As a method of rationalization consequentialism is sufficiently subtle that it can be accepted by persons of fairly subtle intelligence who have a theoretical interest in moral questions and who are conscious enough of more vulgar methods of rationalization to find their arbitariness unacceptable. As a form of persuasive discourse consequentialism provides a great deal of material which subjectivist theorists analyze quite accurately, only to miss the fact that like other parasitic uses of moral language, consequentialism is rhetorically effective only because there are standard, nonsubjectivist ways of using the language of moral evaluation.

Someone familiar with recent analytic ethics is likely to object that there is nothing unreasonable in the effort to combine arbitrariness and the willingness to universalize in the formation of an ethical theory. Such a strategy, after all, is that explicitly adopted by R.M. Hare and other prescriptivists. However, we think Hare is attempting to do what is rationally impossible— namely, to derive the moral "ought" from the premoral "is" of a combination of facts: facts about premoral desires, facts about linguistic usage, and facts about decisions. The interested reader is referred to a lengthier examination of Hare's approach published elsewhere.

(pp. 346-355)

"Against Consequentialism"

Utilitarian impartiality also appears less attractive if one considers the imaginary counterexamples philosophers propose against utilitarianism. These are usually drawn from the fields of justice and personal integrity. Would it be right to secure the greatest happiness for the greatest number by isolating one innocent person in a perpetual life of horrible torture? Would it be right to save a dozen suspects from a lynch mob by offering one other—not more probably guilty than the dozen—as victim to the mob's wrath? As John Rawls points out, utilitarianism does not take seriously enough the distinction between persons; it merges the benefits and harms to everyone into a totality:

> Thus there is no reason in principle why the greater gains of some should not compensate for the lesser losses of others; or more importantly, why the violation of the liberty of a few might not be made right by the greater good shared by many.

Consequentialism implies that there are no intrinsically evil acts. This view can seem attractive if one considers kinds of acts one holds to be morally acceptable. Most college students today easily accept consequentialism in the field of sexual ethics. But consider: Would it ever be right for a professor to assign grades in a course, not according to the work the students have done, but rather according to the extent to which they agree with him? Confronted with this question, students usually begin to see that acts of some kinds are always wrong.

My thesis is that consequentialism is rationally unacceptable because the phrase "greater good" as it is used in any consequentialist theory necessarily lacks reference. I do not reject consequentialism merely because I think it dangerous; I reject it because I think it dangerous nonsense—"nonsense" in the sense that inasmuch as expressions essential to the articulation of consequentialism necessarily lack reference, the theory is meaningless.

To speak of the "greater good" as consequentialists do is to imply that goods are measurable and commensurable. But goods cannot be measured unless there is an available standard applicable to them as goods, and they cannot be commensurable unless all of them are called "good" in one and the same sense, and one and the same measure can be applied to all of them. I deny that "good" said of the alternatives to be judged morally can have a single sense and in this sense signify anything which can be measured by a common standard.

In an extensive survey of work in utilitarianism from 1961-1971, Dan W. Brock points out that utilitarianism requires that

utility be calculable. After suggesting that there are obvious
difficulties in making such measurements, Brock adds:

> More important and perplexing, however, is how the
> necessary calculations can, even in principle, be
> made and whether the logical foundations necessary
> to the intelligibility of these calculations exist.
>
> Moral philosophers have paid surprisingly little
> attention to these two problems. Most discussions
> of utilitarianism in recent books and journals
> simply assume that it is possible to determine in any
> situation what is required by utility-maximization,
> and then go on to consider whether this always
> coincides with what is required by morality.

Brock's remarks might be discounted as the view of an unsympathetic
student of utilitarianism. But this would be a mistake.

J.J.C. Smart, a leading proponent of unrestricted, direct
utilitarianism, admitted in an article published in 1967 that because of obstacles to calculation

> ...the utilitarian is reduced to an intuitive
> weighing of various consequences with their
> probabilities. It is impossible to justify such
> intuitions rationally, and we have here a serious
> weakness in utilitarianism.

Similarly, A.J. Ayer, who defends a form of consequentialism with
respect to the formation of social policies, criticizes Bentham's
attempt to apply consequentialism to the moral judgment of individuals. Ayer concludes:

> In virtue of what standard of measurement can I set
> about adding the satisfaction of one person to that
> of another and subtracting the resultant quantity
> from the dissatisfaction of someone else? Clearly
> there is no such standard, and Bentham's process
> of "sober calculation" turns out to be a myth.

If "greater good" is to be meaningful in the formulation of
a criterion of morality, three conditions must be fulfilled:
1) "good" must have a single meaning; 2) what is good in this
unique sense must be measurable; and 3) the result of measurement
must settle moral issues either directly or indirectly.

Clearly, the necessary meaning of "good" cannot be specified
in moral terms. What Rawls says of utilitarianism is true of all
consequentialism: Its point is to define "good" independently of

"right" and to define "right" in terms of "good." And, in general, consequentialists see this requirement and try to meet it. If consequentialists said that ethical considerations determine what a good consequence is, they would either be going in a circle or setting off on an infinite regress.

If the single meaning of "good" which consequentialism needs cannot be specified by moral principles, how can it be specified?

Most philosophical consequentialists have been liberals. Instead of saying that all humans have the same goal, they have tried to define "good" univocally, to leave room for differing concrete goals, but to make them commensurable with one another. Many utilitarians, following Bentham, define "good" in terms of happiness. Others define "good" in terms of the maximum satisfaction of desires, less the minimum of unavoidable frustration. Since different people have different enjoyments and desires, either approach allows for differing goals. To ensure commensurability, those who take either approach must deny that any sort of pleasure or desire differs from any other sort in a way which would make their inherent goodness differ. Desire theorists, for example, often say that all human desires have the same initial claim to satisfaction.

If happiness is used to define "good" univocally, "happiness" itself must be used univocally. If it is, the theory becomes implausible. For example, if happiness is taken to be a certain quality of consciousness, how can one explain certain people's dedication to causes which are irreducible to states of consciousness. For them, happiness is participation in something bigger than themselves.

A consequentialist can use "happiness" in a very wide sense to allow for the diverse life styles people regard as intrinsically good. But if this maneuver makes it plausible to say that everyone desires happiness, "happiness" ceases to be univocal and thus becomes useless for the consequentialist. People not only get happiness by different means, but "happiness" as an end is different things to different people.

Attempts to define "good" univocally in terms of satisfaction of desire also fail.

Do all human desires really have the same initial claim to satisfaction? Some people desire sadistic pleasure. Many people desire death for criminals. Pornography sells better than the best literature; more people desire the former than the latter. Some people desire feminine deodorant spray. It sells. Most people have what some economists call "artificial desires." Keynes, for instance, distinguishes the needs people have of themselves from the needs they have insofar as they wish to get ahead of others. Galbraith talks of wants created by production and advertising. He points out that the desire for increased expenditure may be stronger than any need which can be satisfied by it. Are all these desires to be counted uncritically in calculating moral right and wrong?

Another difficulty with these theories of value is that enjoyments and desires differ in kind, not only in degree. As I said above, "happiness" means different things to different people. One can compare the enjoyment of drinking a Coke with that of eating a candy bar or the desire for the one with that for the other. But how many appetizing meals in a French restaurant give enjoyment comparable to that of a happy marriage? How many satisfactions of desires for particular objectives are comparable to the satisfaction of one's desire to be a good father, an excellent philosopher, or a faithful follower of Jesus?

Jeremy Bentham, who took calculation seriously, dealt with the problem of commensurability in a characteristically straightforward way:

> Money is the instrument for measuring the quantity of pain or pleasure. Those who are not satisfied with the accuracy of this instrument must find out some other that shall be more accurate, or bid adieu to Politics and Morals.
>
> Let no man therefore be either surprised or scandalized if he find me in the course of this work valuing every thing in money. Tis in this way only we can get aliquot parts to measure by. If we must not say of a pain or a pleasure that it is worth so much money, it is in vain, in point of quantity, to say anything at all about it, there is neither proportion nor disproportion between Punishments and Crimes.

Since one must calculate, one can. So "good" is reduced to pleasure and avoidance of pain, and these are reduced to money. Bentham's leap-of-faith is breathtaking. He is no cynic saying that every person has his or her price. He is a moralist saying that the best things in life simply cost more than a Coke or a candy bar.

The definition of "good" in terms of enjoyment faces another objection. Enjoyment is a conscious experience which normally arises but is distinct from some activity which extends beyond consciousness. Let us imagine a device which could record total experiences as they were being lived and then play them back in the brains of other persons. One might enjoy receiving such a recorded experience—for example, of one's favorite athlete winning one's favorite game. But would one wish to spend the rest of one's life receiving such recorded experiences, however enjoyable they might be? This thought-experiment isolates enjoyment as a conscious experience from the whole of real life which one enjoys. If one agrees that one would not wish to spend the rest of one's life receiving recorded enjoyable experiences, one can still value enjoyment, but only insofar as it is part of a real life in which goods transcending consciousness also are participated.

Why do so many intelligent and serious people think that all forms of desire are commensurable? I think the reason is that it seems obvious that each individual has a rational system of preferences. "Isn't it evident," a desire theorist might argue, "that any sane person faced with a choice can say which alternative he or she prefers? If so, one always knows what one wants more. Thus individuals, at least, somehow manage to make all their desires commensurate."

At the level of basic commitments, the economic model is useless. Here one comes to the goods which shape different styles of life. Many people are not dedicated to anything, but all who live their own lives must have a sense of identity, an idea of what their life is about. If a word like "commitment" connotes too formal and reflective an act for the way most people set the direction of their lives, one can say more modestly that all who live their own lives must think in terms of some concerns to which they are most deeply attached. These are goods in which one wishes to participate for themselves, not for anything ulterior. For these goods, one would give anything, yet money cannot buy them. This is as true of goods such as being contented, being somebody, and being liked—by which many people one would hardly call "committed" shape their lives—as it is of goods such as being a Christian, being a liberal, being a reformer, and being authentic by which some people quite consciously constitute their own identities.

The point of the preceding explanation can be made specific by considering the limits of cost-benefit analysis. The economic advantages and disadvantages of a proposed public project can be quantified. But people also want freedom of speech and of religion, equal protection of the laws, privacy, and other goods which block certain choices, yet which cannot be costed out. Cost-benefit analysis can tell one the most effective way of attaining certain objectives, assuming one accepts the objectives and has no concerns about the means and the side effects of the means required to attain them. But such analysis cannot tell one whether the objectives one seeks are objectives one ought to seek, or whether nonquantifiable factors should be ignored.

If a consequentialist admits that justice and theoretical truth, or any other two goods, are fundamental and incommensurable, then the consequentialist also admits that "greatest net good" is meaningless whenever one must choose between promoting and protecting or impeding and damaging these two goods in some participations. For if these goods really are incommensurable, one might as well try to sum up the quantity of the size of this page, the quantity of the number nineteen, and the quantity of the mass of the moon as to try to calculate with such incommensurable goods.

Different kinds of quantity do have something in common with each other. About all of them, one can ask: "How much?" Each can be measured using a measure homogeneous with itself. But different kinds of quantity are objectively incommensurable. One can relate them to one another only by adopting a system of weights and measures. Similarly, diverse modes of basic human goodness do have something in common with each other. About all of them, one can ask: "Is this something I would give anything for?" Participations of each good can be measured by an instance one accepts as a standard. But the many basic human goods are objectively incommensurable. One must adopt a personal hierarchy of values in order to relate them to each other.

Of course, goods which are not basic but derivative can be commensurable. Means or useful goods are measured by ends or intrinsic goods, because the former are subordinate to the latter. However, if one is dealing with basic goods, which are intrinsic to the full being of human persons, one cannot make them commensurable by relating them to something more basic.

The arguments in the preceding section showed that attempts by consequentialists to give "good" a univocal meaning have not succeeded. But those arguments were based upon assumptions—though ones I think a consequentialist would accept—which could be false. Moreover, an optimistic consequentialist always can hope that despite past failures someone eventually will show how the theory can be made to work. The argument I am about to state is based not on assumptions, but on facts and analysis. If this argument is sound, any reasonable person can learn from it that consequentialists never will be able to make their theory work. No one will show how to do the calculations consequentialism requires, because such calculations are impossible. "Greater good," as the consequentialist needs to use it, inevitably lacks reference, and so consequentialism is meaningless.

My criticism of consequentialism is that it is inconsistent to hold both that the goods involved in various alternatives are commensurable and that a person can deliberately adopt an alternative which promises a lesser good than the alternative which ought to have been adopted.

Therefore, the consequentialist must hold that one could purposely adopt a proposal which promises measurably less good than an alternative proposal which one should adopt. Nevertheless, as the data of deliberation already described establish, there never is any reason for choosing the alternative which one does choose except the good it promises. It follows that if one alternative promises a measurably greater good than another, one who is deliberating has all the reason for choosing the alternative which promises the measurably greater good which he or she has for choosing the other, and has the further reason for choosing the former provided by the greater good it promises.

Thus, given the commensurability required by the consequentialist's theory of judgment, no one can do what one ought not, since no one can deliberately prefer the lesser good. The reason for choosing the greater good—assuming the goods are commensurable—is not merely a good reason, it is a sufficient reason.

An analogy will help to make clear the force of this argument. If one were literally interested in nothing whatsoever except acquiring money, whenever one considered possible courses of action one would look for only a single thing: how much money one might acquire if one chose each course. When one saw that a certain possibility was not the best bet, one could not choose it. Likewise, since one who chooses can be interested in various possibilities only insofar as they promise good, whenever one deliberates one considers what good one can hope for by choosing each possibility. If one could see that a certain possibility promised measurably less good, one could not choose it.

Whenever one chooses, one determines whether one will be the sort of person for whom this or that potentially greater good shall be the greater good. The consequentialist assumes that the decision about the controlling value is a judgment of what is greater, not a choice of what shall be greater. But the ability to make a choice precisely is the prerogative to adopt the goodness of one alternative rather than the goodness of another as the principle by which one determines oneself and shapes the action which expresses oneself.

Once one has chosen, the alternatives which have not been chosen often seem to pale in significance. The viewpoint of the alternative which has been chosen tends in retrospect to alter the attractiveness of the others. Not long after having made a difficult choice, one often wonders what could possibly have appealed in alternatives which were not chosen.

Someone might object that not all morally significant action follows upon deliberation and conscious choice. For example, a morally good woman is inclined to help others; she sees someone in need of her help; she thinks of nothing but their need and what she can do to satisfy it; she acts spontaneously—without thinking, without consciously choosing. Surely, such an act is good; a sign of its goodness is that the woman might be praised for it, even more highly praised than less good persons who carefully considered their own interests before deliberately choosing to render assistance.

I admit that such spontaneous acts can be morally good. They do not follow upon deliberation and conscious choice. But my thesis is not that all morally good acts are deliberately chosen. Rather, it is that the acts which consequentialists seek to regulate by their purported criterion are thus chosen. Clearly, the consequentialist is not talking about spontaneous acts such as the one described, for in these spontaneous acts only one course of action is considered and it is done without choice. Commensuration cannot begin unless there is some deliberation.

If the foregoing criticism of consequentialism is correct, then consequentialism is not merely a theory with difficulties (a fact admitted by even the most earnest proponents of the theory), nor is it merely a theory which is false (the possibility generally envisaged by those who reject consequentialism), but it is one of those philosophical theories which is literally meaningless. The meaninglessness of consequentialism follows from the conclusion that the goods are not commensurable in the way the consequentialist requires, for this lack of commensurability eliminates all possibility of reference for the expression "greater good" as the consequentialist uses this expression.

If consequentialism is meaningless, it also follows that any ethical theory which admits it is defective to that extent. An ethical theory might be sound in other respects, but if it allows any role for consequentialism—for example, in the resolution of conflict cases—it is incoherent in this respect. Some moralists reject consequentialism and adopt a moral criterion based on personal relationship and covenant, yet maintain that in a world broken by sin, situations occur in which moral ideals must be compromised. In these cases, a lesser evil may be done to avoid a greater one. Such theories admit consequentialism without realizing it, and to this extent become incoherent.

The famous case of the careening trolley car provides another example. One is steering a trolley down a steep hill, notices that the brakes have failed, knows there is a switch at the bottom of the hill which will allow one to steer onto either of two tracks, and observes a few people on one track and a

large crowd of people on the other. If no other factor comes
into play, the larger group includes all the instances of good--
several human lives--included in the smaller and more. One has
no choice but to steer away from the larger group. But if one
sees only strangers in the larger group and members of one's own
family in the smaller, then friendship also is involved. The
goods are incommensurable. If one has time to deliberate, one
can choose.

What about cases in which one might be tempted to kill one
person to save two or more? Sometimes, what is involved is indirect killing, as in the example of the trolley car, in which
steering away from the larger group is causally but not morally
equivalent to steering toward the smaller. I find it hard to
think of any clear example in which the killing of one or of a
few certainly will save the lives of two or of many where the
killing and the saving occur in distinct actions related to
each other as means to end. Usually, the choice of certain death
renders the life-saving only probable. If there are cases in
which one has the choice of killing one person or some persons
for the ulterior purpose of saving two or more, the life or
lives one might choose to sacrifice are not counted among those
to be saved, even if one notes no objective difference except
in number between the two groups. For to choose to use some
for the benefit of others reduces those who are used to the status
of mere means. One has a choice precisely because one can regard
those who would be sacrificed as sharing in a priceless dignity,
which one should not subordinate to any purpose extrinsic to
themselves.

In politics, there is another use of "greatest good" which
is meaningful but useless to the consequentialist. One can say
that a public official is pursuing the greatest happiness of the
people if he tries to find out what they want and to give it to
them.

However, "the greatest happiness of the most people" as
defined by a census of their desires does not settle what is
morally right. I criticized the desire theory of value in section two. The majority often is unhappy with decisions upholding
minority rights; demagogic politicians often sacrifice minority
rights to majority prejudices. But the social covenant expressed
in the society's constitution can demand that the happiness of
the majority yield to justice for the minority.

It is reasonable enough to suppose that one does a morally
evil act if one chooses as a means an act which impedes or damages one or more basic human goods and which of itself does not
promote or protect any such good. But what about an act which
in itself has a good and a bad aspect, an act which does not

131

impede or damage a good for the sake of an <u>ulterior</u> good? In this case, the performance of the act itself--considered as a unit indivisible by the agent--impedes or damages some participation of a basic human good. But the very same act promotes or protects a good. Can it be morally right to choose such an act?

Such a choice is not excluded by the general principle that evil may not be done that good might follow therefrom, since in this case the good does not <u>follow</u> <u>from</u> the evil. Both are indivisibly joined in one act. A person intent upon the act's good aspect can choose it, not choosing the bad aspect as a means, but only accepting it as an unavoidable side effect. One steers the trolley <u>away</u> <u>from</u> the big crowd; it is incidental to one's intent that one steers <u>toward</u> the small group of people. In this case the so-called "principle of double effect" applies.

I have written elsewhere about double effect. In received formulations, it includes a requirement that there be a proportionately grave reason for doing an act which has a side effect which it would be wrong to seek as an end or choose as a means. I accept this requirement, and this leads Richard McCormick to say:

> But I agree with Stanley Hauerwas that ultimately Grisez cannot "avoid the kind of consequentialist reasoning that our human sensibilities seem to demand in such (conflict) cases" (note omitted). For if a good like life is simply incommensurable with other goods, what do we mean by a proportionate reason where death is, in Grisez's terms, indirect? Proportionate to what? If some goods are to be preferred to life itself, then we have compared life with these goods. And if this is proper, then life can be weighed up against other values too, even very basic values.

I admit that if an act has two aspects, one needs a proportionate reason for choosing it. I deny that "proportionate reason" can be specified by measuring life against other nonmoral values, or the goodness of some instances of life against the goodness of other instances of it. How, then, do I answer the question: "Proportionate to what?"

My own view--which I have not stated clearly enough in previous works--would be better expressed by saying one needs a "morally acceptable reason" than a "proportionate reason." My answer to McCormick is that one must have a morally acceptable reason for doing the good one is doing, considering the evil one is accepting as an unavoidable side effect. But is this not to admit that one measures the good against the evil? Yes and no. One can compare these if one has a moral standard. One cannot measure these against each other and reach any moral judgment if one considers them only as premoral values and disvalues.

In my view, a person considering an act having a twofold aspect and noting that the act is not excluded by the principle that the end does not justify the means, still ought to think about other moral grounds on which the act under consideration might be forbidden. I distinguish eight modes of responsibility, only the last of which dictates that one does not turn directly against a good. The first seven articulate other necessary conditions for moral judgment.

For example, my second mode of responsibility is a version of the universalizability criterion. A man who is considering putting poison around his garden to control the rabbits which are eating his lettuce ought to ask himself how he would react if he were in his neighbors' shoes. Perhaps the gardener has no children, there are no fences, and the children sometimes wander nonmaliciously into the gardener's yard. If he were in his neighbors' place, would he not be concerned enough about the safety of the children to exclude as too dangerous the use of poison to control the rabbits? If an honest answer to this question is that if it were his children and their lettuce, he would not be willing for the sake of rabbit control to endanger the children, then the reason is not morally acceptable—in traditional language, proportionately grave—when it is his lettuce and their children.

It would take too much space to go through all the modes of responsibility, illustrating how each of them can contribute meaning to "morally acceptable reason" or "proportionate reason" (if the latter, misleading expression is to be retained). However, the basic idea of my view of this condition of double effect should be clear from this one example. The good one is doing must be such as to justify the evil one is accepting as a side effect, not in the sense that premoral goods must be commensurable, which is meaningless, but in the sense that one's doing and one's accepting must be permissible according to every relevant moral criterion. Sometimes one is required not to permit a certain evil, though one does not directly do it.

In previous works I have urged that play and esthetic sensibility are basic human goods along with such other goods as theoretical truth and life itself. Many people disagree. The two former goods seem to them much less important. I think this reaction reflects most people's commitments, not any objective hierarchy of goods. A scholar is likely to think that theoretical truth is more important than play. But a fine musician can well believe that his or her art—which is a form of play—

and esthetic sensibility to it are more important than theoretical truth. This reversal of the scholar's priorities is not immoral. If one respects all the goods, one is morally free to commit oneself in a special way to some of them. In fact, one is morally obliged to do so.

Life itself can seem both more important and less noble than the other basic human goods. This view is not unreasonable, but it does not reflect objective commensuration. It reflects, on the one hand, the interest we mortal animals have in our own survival and, on the other, the rather low place human life as such has in most people's commitments. However, if one has devoted many years to promoting and protecting human life as such—for example, by writing and lecturing against abortion, capital punishment, and nuclear warfare—then one acquires a sense of the nobility of "mere" human life.

A Jew of Christian might object that between some basic human goods there is <u>an</u> <u>objective</u> hierarchy. Is not the good of religion, which is a harmonious relationship with God, infinitely more important than other basic human goods?

Some Christians have held that the ethical sphere as a whole must give way to the religious. I think this position arises from a confusion between the created, immanent human good of religion—which is neither more nor less absolute than other basic human goods—and the goodness of God Himself. The good of religion is a finite participation in divine goodness, but so are other basic human goods, and the latter are neither reducible to nor commensurable with the good of religion.

However, though there is no objective hierarchy which places religion above other basic human goods, it is reasonable to make one's religious commitment overarch one's whole existence. A commitment to the right sort of religion is an excellent principle by which to integrate one's identity. It gives ground to the highest hopes, yet at the same time allows wide scope to promote and protect other basic human goods.

Christians believe that all other basic human goods take on a new meaning from the existential integration of other goods with the basic Christian commitment. This commitment is to share in the redemptive work of Christ; the pursuit of other basic goods becomes an effort to build up the Body of Christ. Of course, nonchristians do not see things in this light, nor should they.

Moreover, Christians should not confuse the importance
religion has for them--because of their God-given, but freely
accepted, faith and hope--with the importance which religion has
as one basic human good among others. If these are confused,
one is on a short road to religious fanaticism.
(pp. 28-29; 43,44,46-48,51,56,60-61)

Eight Ultimate Goods--Inclusivistic/Exclusivistic Choosing--
Modes of Responsibility

Background for Chapters 7-9, "Purposes--Ulterior and
Otherwise," "'Ought' Points Toward Fullness of Being,"
"Two Ways of Choosing"
Background as well for Chapters 11-13 in which the modes of
responsibility are developed.

When I was assigned to teach ethics some years ago
Francis P. Molloy, S.J. shared his experience in this field
with me. Among his insights which have shaped my thinking
was the following division:

    Ethos (Customs)   Ethics   Metaethics

Common sense or sociology relates to Ethos and can identify
the customary practices of a community. Ethics refers to the
ethical principles which undergird or assess the customs.
Metaethics assesses specific ethical principles and
establishes the criterion of morality.

BNM is a textbook on the metaethical level. It proposes
an ethical theory which is genuinely beyond the new morality.
Like the new morality it insists upon individual freedom
and responsibility. But unlike the new morality it rejects
relativism root and branch. However it does not reiterate
traditional natural law ethics. Grisez has indeed drawn
inspiration from St. Thomas's treatment of natural law.
But he has reinterpreted Thomas's texts, going beyond customary, accepted interpretations, going beyond Thomas himself,
and he has incorporated valuable insights from modern thinking. The most valuable source to witness Grisez intensely
analyzing Thomas and to recognize the origin of his own
theory is "The First Principle of Practical Reason: A
Commentary on the Summa Theologiae, 1-2, Question 94, Article
2." It is too difficult an article for the Reader but the
ideas govern the presentation of his theory in the readings
actually chosen.

Grisez produced a significant work on contraception
(1964) before the Papal Commission on birth control was
appointed; he published (1970) a substantial study on abortion three years before the Supreme Court decision on that
issue; he has provided us with a monumental work on

euthanasia (1979) in the midst of growing awareness of
infanticide, "mercy killing," and proposals of "living
wills." In each of these books after impressive, scholarly
presentation of the issues from the side of law, customs
and positions of diverse communities he addresses the issues
from an ethical perspective. This requires that he expose
succinctly his general ethical theory. The three different
summaries should provide insight into his metaethical theory
of ethics. The timing of the publications indicates Grisez's
astute perception of important trends.

Seventh Plank: To be a complete person...provide for eight
  ultimate aspects of oneself. The eight...goods...provide for
  these...and are irreducible...incommensurable.

Eighth Plank: Moral good is not a ninth good...is choosing...
  inclusivistically.... Moral evil is choosing...
  exclusivistically.

Ninth Plank: Eight modes...specify the first, basic principle....

Life and Death

A Nonconsequentialist Theory: Human Goods

Consequentialism has achieved widespread acceptance. However,
because of its inherent unworkability it should not be accepted.
We have pointed out the essential reason why consequentialism is
not really a theory of moral reasoning. Many other philosophers
have shown that there are other unsolved problems for a consequentialist. We believe the preceding considerations make clear
that the problems not only are unsolved but are insoluble. Consequently a teleological approach to ethical theory must be nonconsequentialist if it is to be defensible. A defensible teleological
theory must take fully into account the fact of moral existence
revealed in our critique of consequentialism: the incommensurability of human goods. We begin an exposition of the theory we
consider sound by discussing first the question of the goods to
which teleological moral reasoning directs action.

Reflection on the motivations of human acts which are morally
significant—that is, those done by deliberation and choice—
reveals that some acts are done for their own sake. Play and
recreational activities often are done for no purpose beyond the
activities themselves. Such activities are not lacking in purpose and meaning; their purpose and meaning is within them. One
might say they are done "just for the fun of it." Thus, these
activities are considered inherently worthwhile. In saying they

are good one is not making a properly moral judgment. Rather, one is saying that such activities are part of human flourishing; they perfect and complete human persons and give their lives some of the meaning they can have.

The immediate reason why one chooses in a particular case, however, often is subordinate to an ulterior motive. If one asks a laborer why he labors, he might answer: "To make money." If one asks why he seeks money, he might reply: "To feed myself and my family, because we get hungry." If one tries to push the inquiry beyond this point, one might find oneself none too gently rebuffed, not because the laborer is ignorant of a further purpose, but because apart from satisfying the basic conditions to survive, there simply is no further purpose here. To try to question the self-sufficiency of a purpose which is in fact ultimate as motive is likely to seem to simple persons a way of ridiculing them.

Thus, play and recreation, while inherently worthwhile, are not the only things human beings recognize as giving meaning to their lives. Knowledge of truth and appreciation of beauty also are recognized as good. Those who consider knowledge and esthetic activities merely instrumental are rightly considered philistines who do not appreciate the full potential of their own human personalities. Such persons, if not considered immoral, are pitied as individuals somehow defective in personal capacity for a fully human life.

As our example of the laborer suggests, life itself also is a good which people wish to preserve and protect for its own sake. So also is health, the perfection of the living body precisely insofar as it is an organism. Like the other goods we have mentioned, life and health can have an instrumental importance as well as serving as motives by themselves for human acts. But life and health can, and often are, considered to be intrinsic aspects of human flourishing.

This point is clearer in respect to health, since people seek to be healthy not only because they can thereby do other things they value but also because they consider health itself desirable. The same seems to be true of staying alive. Much of humankind over its history has struggled to feed and clothe and shelter themselves and to continue the race through children.

However, some deny that human life has the intrinsic worth and dignity we attribute to it. They attribute to life a merely instrumental value. Since the intrinsic worth and dignity of life is pivotal for the ethical determination of the issues with which this book is concerned, we shall devote section H of the present chapter to an extended response to the view that life is not an intrinsic good of persons.

There are still other inherently worthwhile activities which contribute in their appropriate ways to human flourishing. Human beings strive to establish harmony between various aspects of their own personalities, harmony with other people, and harmony with God. Friendship among people obviously is a human good for itself, although friends also must have a common interest, which will shape their action toward some one or many other basic human goods. Likewise, for those who believe in the divine, friendship with God is considered good for its own sake. Many religious people regard prayer not merely as an instrumental activity but as a part of life which is important simply because it is a way of being with God.

Self-integration, similarly, is considered worthwhile. As in other societies which have reached a level of abundance at which mere survival is no longer the primary concern of most people, many people in our society regard self-integration as a central purpose of their lives. People want to "get themselves together," to "find themselves and establish their identities," to be "happy." For those who do not consider themselves self-integrated, or as well integrated as they wish to be, many acts can be chosen as means to the pursuit of this good.

But this good itself can be realized in acts which participate in it. Just as there must be some specifying common interest which unites friends in a relationship they consider good in itself, so in activities by which a person pursues other goods in an integrated way the person can be motivated by the inherent goodness of his or her acts insofar as they embody in harmony all aspects of the personality fully alive: bodily powers, dispositions, emotions, beliefs, commitments, and so on. Thus, one can choose to act for one's own self-integration and can regard other human goods for which one acts as providing opportunities for the enjoyment of self-integration. The conception that virtuous activity is its own end exemplifies this notion of self-integration as an intrinsic component of human flourishing.

We have listed the goods which seem to us to constitute human flourishing. Perhaps the list is not complete. We have made no attempt to establish a perfect classification. For the purposes of this book such precision is unnecessary. We only wish to make clear that there are several incommensurable human goods, that human flourishing has many intrinsic aspects. Each of these goods makes a peculiar and irreducible contribution to the complete well-being of persons. While every person loves some goods more than others, it simply would not make sense to say that participation in goods one prefers makes the forgoing of others no loss, no limitation to oneself. If the goods were commensurable, this would be so, but because they are not, every choice is at once self-realization and self-limitation.

Our list might appear to have one glaring omission: Pleasure is not included as a basic human good. The omission is intentional. Pleasure is an experience, and experiences are not actions, whereas human flourishing is constituted of acts. The human goods are not products of human acts or ideals at which actions aim. They are realized within human acts by the very doing of these acts--realized not exhaustively, but participated to a greater or lesser degree.

Of course, the performance of actions worthwhile in themselves often is a pleasant experience. But sometimes it is not pleasant to do good acts, and the enjoyment which good acts do bring is rather their _felt_ goodness than some separate good participated in by them. Thus the enjoyment involved in friendship or knowledge or healthful eating is not a good and motive apart from these goods but simply is their goodness consciously experienced.

How Morality Depends Upon The Human Goods

If what we have said thus far indicates the goods--or at least some of the goods--toward which human actions ought to be directed, nothing we have said thus far shows how one can reason from one's awareness of human goods to moral judgments concerning what one ought to do. To approach this question we recall that the method of moral reasoning we are articulating is teleological but not consequentialist. A teleological theory justifies moral judgments about right and wrong in terms of what is humanly good or worth while. Basing moral obligations on the well-being or flourishing of persons surely is intuitively plausible. We hold that it also is theoretically defensible.

When a person considers that an action is right, this consideration makes a demand upon the person: The action is regarded as one to be done. But no action can be done unless it can be chosen, and no action can be chosen unless it promises a good which makes it appealing. Unless the "is to be" of the normative judgment is a mere extrinsic compulsion, which might elicit servile obedience but no moral respect, the person who is called to respond by action must perceive the demand as an intrinsic appeal--in other words, as an expression of the goodness in the action which makes it interesting as a possibility.

Moreover, if choice is self-determination, then the goods one can choose must be considered as aspects of one's own identity. If follows that the rightness of moral choices must be based upon the well-being or flourishing of persons, for a moral agent can identify with this and find self-fulfillment in it. We do not deny that there are other principles of morality transcendent to human persons, but these principles must specify moral demands by way of human goods, for otherwise they would be alien impositions upon human flourishing, which would elicit resistance rather than respect from reasonable persons.

Thus we hold that the basic human goods are the principles which are in some fashion expressed as norms for action by moral judgments--in other words, that "oughts" arise from "goods," that what makes some acts right and some wrong must somehow derive from what makes all acts possible: the appeal of the goods which makes possibilities live options for a human agent. But this raises the question: How does this normativity work? Obviously not all acts which are possible are right. How can the very principle of the possibility of some actions (those which are morally excluded) require that these possible actions not be made actual? The nature of this normativity of human goods for human acts can be clarified by the following considerations.

In the first place, nothing is considered good unless it is thought of as having a basic reality which can be more or less developed and perfected. To be a good entity of a certain kind is to be an entity of a kind which can be more or less perfectly, and which in fact is more rather than less perfectly. The possibility of degrees of perfection depends upon potentiality in the entity; goodness is realization of potential. But not every realization of potentiality is good. Sometimes an entity which can be more or less fully what it is will be deprived of its fuller and fullest realization on the whole by realizing only one potentiality.

The point can be illustrated by considering living organisms simply as such. The perfection of an organism is health. Health is a disposition for the exercise of the functions of the organism so that its whole repertoire of possible life will be unfolded. In this respect a healthy organism is one which is realizing its potentialities. But growing cancerously also is within the potential of an organism. This realization of potentiality is not good. The trouble with it is that it deprives the organism of its fuller and fullest realization on the whole. Hence, the good of an organism is a fulfillment of life potentialities which leads to further fulfillment and more abundant life. What is bad for an organism is a realization of some potentialities in its vital processes which tend to deprive it of continuing and more abundant life.

The same thing is true, analogously, in other realms. To think in ways that are inconsistent, muddled, unsure, and unsystematic is one way of realizing the human power of thought. But this actualization of potentiality is bad, not good. What is good is thinking which is consistent, clear, sure, and organized into schemes of explanation. Such thinking is good because it makes knowing flourish and expand. Bad thinking is self-limiting. Likewise, in the realm of fine art creativity is good because it is expansive of the realm of artistic entities. And in the technical sphere efficiency is a value because it is getting the most one can out of what one has.

Human goods are the principles of the possibility of all human acts. They establish moral norms insofar as acts flow from deliberation and choice. Every choice is both self-realizing and self-limiting. Insofar as any choice is self-realizing, the good which makes it interesting renders the choice possible for a person who is rational, not blindly or insanely driven to act. The good appeals to intelligence, not merely presenting itself as possible, but offering itself as a possibility to be realized through action. Thus there is a direct, normative appeal in every human good.

However, the direct, normative appeal of each human good is not yet moral normativity. Deliberation about the possibilities of self-realization through a morally evil act and choice of such an act also responds to this direct appeal. Indeed, the normative appeal of the good which is held out by a possible morally evil act is the content of the experience of temptation. Every teleological theorist recognizes that the pursuit of particular goods through particular acts can be immoral.

Still, although no single good provides a moral norm, the normativity of all the basic human goods together does give rise to a moral norm. For the goodness of the person as a human agent through deliberation and choice lies in realizing, not all potentialities for action, but rather in realizing those which are conducive to fuller and the fullest self-realization. Or, in other words, while every choice has an aspect of self-limitation, some choices are self-limiting in a way that others are not. Choices which are restrictive of the very principles upon which one can act humanly tend to stunt and constrict the person rather than make the person flourish. Thus such choices are morally bad. They are ones which, although possible because of their responsiveness to the appeal of some basic human good, are unnecessarily self-limiting because they are

143

incompatible with a realistic appreciation of other goods and openness toward the possibilities these other goods hold out.

Of course, the moral normativity of all the human goods together cannot require that one simultaneously act for all of them or actively oppose all that threatens them. One can only do so much. Choices must be made; these will necessarily involve self-limitation in fact. Individuals and communities must commit themselves to something and forgo other possibilities. Yet one can forgo a possibility without altering one's appreciation of the good which gave rise to it. To alter one's appreciation of a good is to reject its normativity. An act whose choice involves this is morally evil.

Thus, the basic requirement of morality is that one choose and act for some human goods, while at the same time one maintain one's appreciation, openness, and respect for the goods one is not now acting for. A strong basic requirement which would demand something more specific is impossible in view of the plurality and incommensurability of the goods, and the limitations of human powers and opportunities, which together make choice necessary.

The preceding explanation of the basic requirement of morality is, we realize, very abstract. And a clear understanding of the relationship between the morality of acts and the basic human goods, which are aspects composing human flourishing, is central to ethical theory. Therefore, we are going to explain the same relationship again in a somewhat different way.

Any sound teleological ethical theory must be consistent with the fact that not every choice is morally evil, yet every choice responds to the appeal of the human goods promised by one possible course of action and leaves unanswered the appeal of the equally basic and incommensurable goods promised by one or more alternatives. That each of these goods is to be realized and protected is a starting point for deliberation about possibilities which would bear upon it. Such a starting point is a principle for practical reasoning about what to choose and to do. Corresponding to the whole set of basic human goods is the whole set of principles of practical reasoning.

This whole set of principles directs that all the goods be realized and protected. But even bad acts depend upon and respond to some of these principles. Therefore, none of the principles of practical reasoning is a moral norm merely by being a practical principle. The underlying assumption that human life ought to be preserved and respected, for example, does not of itself dictate that no one ought ever to be killed.

The distinction between moral good and evil according to the theory we put forth is primarily a distinction between ways in which proposed courses of action are related to all of the principles of practical thinking. Some proposals are consistent with all of these principles, although they hold out the promise of participation in only some of the basic human goods toward which these principles direct human interest and action. Other proposals are consistent with some of the principles of practical thinking—those which direct action to the goods promised by these proposals—but inconsistent with at least one principle of practical thinking. Proposals of the former sort are morally good, while those of the latter sort are morally bad.

Thus, for example, if a physician is considering whether to treat a certain patient or not, and to treat the patient in one way or another, the proposed courses of action about which he is deliberating can be related in two different ways to the whole set of principles of practical thinking which express the claims of the whole set of basic human goods. On the one hand, as the alternatives are understood, all the various forms of treatment might promise a benefit for the patient's health, and none of them might seem inconsistent with any other basic human good. On the other hand, as the alternatives are understood, while all of them promise a benefit to the patient's health, some of them might be rejected by the patient on grounds of conscience—for example, by a Jehovah's Witness who will not accept blood transfusions. Assuming that patients cannot justly be treated against their will, the physician must consider alternatives rejected by the patient differently than those the patient accepts.

Those rejected by the patient, while equally or even more conducive to health, are inconsistent with another principle of practical thinking: The liberty of patients must be respected. A consequentialist might argue that the greater benefit to health which is promised by the treatment involving transfusions outweighs the violation of the patient's liberty. We have shown, however, that consequentialism is not workable; a physician who reasoned in this way would merely be rationalizing the imposition of his own preferences on the patient. According to our view alternatives which are consistent with all the principles of practical reasoning will be morally acceptable; those incompatible with any principle of practical thinking will be morally wrong. Thus, if the liberty of others must be respected and if a certain treatment cannot be given without violating this principle, then the giving of such a treatment is morally excluded.

A morally evil proposed course of action is intelligible
and interesting because of the good it promises. It can be
adopted if one is prepared to regard the good with which it is
inconsistent as a lesser good than the good it promises. It is
possible to regard one basic human good as a lesser good than
another precisely because the goods are incommensurable, and so
any of them can appear to be lesser goods if they are judged by
a standard of goodness specified by another mode of goodness.

However, it also is unreasonable to regard any basic human
good as a lesser good than another simply because the goods are
incommensurable. If one cares about all of them precisely insofar as they are goods, not insofar as they are particular modes
of goodness toward which one has a special bias, then one will
never judge any human good by a standard specified by one or
more other human goods.

One who is about to choose in a morally right way respects
equally all of the basic goods and listens equally to all of the
appeals they make through the principles of practical thinking.
Because of the incompatibility of practical alternatives—since
one cannot do everything at once—choice is necessary. No single
good, nothing promised by any one possible course of action,
exhausts human possibilities and realizes the whole potentiality
for humankind's flourishing. But just as two propositions
having no common terms cannot be inconsistent with each other,
so a proposed course of action is consistent with those principles of practical thinking to which it is merely irrelevant.

Thus, one can choose one possibility which promises certain
goods and is irrelevant to other goods promised by an alternative
without violating the practical principle which directs action
to these other goods. In this case one remains open to these
other goods. One does not adopt a restrictive standard of
goodness. One's understanding of the various human goods, one's
appreciation of their special potential contribution to the
flourishing of persons, remains the same after the choice as
before.

One who is about to choose in a morally wrong way does not
respect equally all of the basic human goods and does not listen
equally to all of the appeals they make through the principles
of practical thinking. The proposal which one is about to adopt
involves detriment to some human good. One is tempted to accept
this detriment for the sake of the realization of another good
which will thereby become possible. Such a proposed course of
action is responsive to at least one principle of practical
thinking, and it might be merely irrelevant to—and thus consistent with—some others, but it is both relevant to and in-

consistent with the principle which directs one to promote and respect that good to which the action will be detrimental. Yet the principle which is to be violated is as basic as the one on which the proposed course of action is based; the good which is to be realized is no more an aspect of the flourishing of persons than the one which is going to be harmed.

A person in adopting such a proposal cannot remain open to the good promised by morally acceptable alternatives, for this good is going to be violated. In choosing to accept this violation one implicitly adopts a restrictive standard of human goodness. One's understanding of the various goods is affected by the choice. The good which is violated is no longer considered equally basic and incommensurable with the good to which it is sacrificed. The good which is violated now becomes a "lesser good," and the good for which it is violated becomes a "greater good." The choice, which is partially irrational insofar as it conflicts with some principle of practical thinking, is rationalized by reducing to the extent necessary a basic human good from its status as an intrinsic component of human flourishing to the status of a mere means.

If the preceding explanation of the relationship between the morality of acts and basic human goods is correct, still there remain two serious questions to be considered. First, is not moral good and evil something more personal and interpersonal than the relationship between human acts and their principles which we have been discussing? Does not moral evil involve a violation of the good of others? From a religious viewpoint must it not be seen as sin, as alienation from God and rejection of his love? Second, how does the basic requirement of morality take shape in concrete moral obligations to do or to avoid specific acts?

The answer to the first question is this: The central locus of the distinction between moral good and evil is in the relationship between choices and human goods, which we have been explaining. But the impact of morality and the reason for its importance is by no means limited to this relationship. It affects one's relationship to other persons, to God, and to one's own fulfillment.

If I choose with the attitude that my choices define and limit the good, I shall lack the detachment to appreciate the possibilities of others' lives, which would complement my own by realizing the values that I cannot. Their good, which I do not choose, will become for me at best a nongood, something to which I shall remain indifferent.

Egoism can decrease only to the extent that I remain open to the embrace of all the goods, those as well as these, yours as well as mine. The attitude of immorality is an unreasonable attempt to reorganize the personal and interpersonal universe, so that the center is not the whole range of possibilities in which humankind can share, but the goods I want and actually pursue through my actions. Instead of community immoral choices generate alienation. The conflict of competing immoralities is reflected by incompatible personal rationalizations and social ideologies, each of which seeks to remake the moral universe in accord with its own bias.

Those who understand immorality in religious terms cannot be expected to find any merely philosophical account completely satisfying. But the philosophical account we have proposed might coincide, so far as it goes, with a religious view. It certainly is impossible to maintain a fully open attitude toward all human goods, irreducibly diverse and incommmensurable as they are, unless one accepts the reference of human conceptions of goodness to a real unifying source of goodness which is beyond human comprehension.

For if the goods which humans comprehend--which constitute a unified field for human choice and action--are not diverse participations in a unity beyond all of them, then they must be unified by reference to one another. In that case what one chooses will appropriate an absolute priority to which what one rejects must be subordinated--if it is to be regarded as good in any sense at all. However, if one accepts the reference of human conceptions of goodness to a reality beyond human comprehension, then openness to that goodness can count as love of it, although one does not make it by itself the objective of any particular action.

Such love of the good can be interpreted in a religious context as at least compatible with a response of human love to God's love. And if the goodness in question is identified with God, respect and openness to all human goods can be understood as human fulfillment by participation in a goodness which first of all is God's. An immoral attitude, by contrast, would exclude a real goodness beyond the goods humans can know and choose; immorality would refuse to seek human fulfillment as a realization by participation in God's own goodness. From a religious point of view any morally evil act, in which the good chosen is made more absolute than it is, will be an instance of implicit idolatry.

The principle of morality which we have articulated also can be seen as a basis of a personalistic morality aimed at

personal fulfillment. The basic human goods against which one
ought not to act are not impersonal; the moral norms forbidding
violation of these goods are not mere legalistic rules. These
goods each make their intrinsic and irreducible contribution to
the flourishing of human persons. They do not transcend persons
by subordinating their good to some higher, nonhuman purpose.
The various goods only transcend persons as they are by drawing
them toward what they are not yet but still can come to be by
their creative efforts.

How the Principle of Morality Shapes Obligations

As we have pointed out, the fundamental moral requirement is
that one respect and remain open to all of the basic goods. To
respect a good is to treat it always as a good. Even when one
does not pursue a good, as we have explained, one can acknowledge
its special contribution to human life. At the very minimum this
acknowledgement requires that one not direct one's action against
any of the basic goods. This ethical principle articulates the
classical maxim that evil may not be done that good might follow
therefrom. It also is expressed, more loosely, in the saying
that the end does not justify the means. Thus there are absolute
prohibitions of certain types of choice--that is, those which are
directed against one of the basic goods. For example, one may
not choose to kill innocent persons as a means to overthrowing an
unjust ruler, since this action would be directed against the
good of life.

The absolute negative norms which demand unconditional respect for the basic human goods are, not restrictions imposed to
limit the flourishing of persons, but rather exclusions of arbitrary limits which would be placed on the principles of human
good. To diminish in no way the full scope of these basic principles is to maintain an indispensable condition for human flourishing, for it is to preserve the possibility of all actions
which might promote this flourishing.

Beyond one's immediate objectives there always remains an
unlimited and unforeseeable possibility of something more, of
human goods to be realized in oneself and in other persons. This
something more will unfold as it might only if people in choosing
remain creatively faithful to it, and such faithfulness demands
respect for the goods which ground its very possibility.

A consequentialist, observing that any choice is relevant
to two or more human goods, proposes that morality be determined
by reference to all of the goods involved. However, consequentialism focuses upon the goods only as they are concretized in

limited, prospective good results and confines the person within the limits of measurable goods, reduced to unity by the standard arbitrarily adopted for the occasion. The consequentialist might assert that morality must be for human fulfillment, but this theory demands that human fulfillment be like the perfection of a product which at some point is completed and no longer open to being more abundantly. Consequentialism thus not only demotes the "lesser good" from its proper status as an intrinsic component of human flourishing to the status of a mere means; it also demotes the "greater good" from its proper status as an inexhaustible aspect of the potential flourishing of human persons in always new and richer ways to the status of an attainable goal, an objective to be reached and then replaced by some new objective.

The ethical theory which we have articulated, no less than consequentialism, holds that morality is determined by reference to all of the intrinsic aspects of human flourishing. But this ethical theory, unlike consequentialism, reflects the complexity and richness of human flourishing and maintains openness to personal fulfillments beyond any measure even conceivable at a given moment in a person's life or in the life of humankind.

We have now indicated one way in which the basic requirement of morality takes shape in concrete moral obligations to avoid specific acts. Respect for all the basic human goods demands that one never act directly against any of them, that one never adopt a proposal to realize some good by acting in a way detrimental to one or more of these goods, which are aspects of potential human flourishing. It follows that every kind of action which could be justified only on the basis that if evil might be done that good would follow is morally excluded.

But the basic requirement of morality generates other forms of responsibility, many of them more affirmative than negative in the direction they give to one's action. Several of these forms of responsibility are especially important for the problems considered in this book. They are ones which bear upon one person's treatment of others.

First of all, human beings, if they respect all that contributes to human flourishing, will be ready to cooperate with other persons in the realization of human goods. A person who loves what is humanly good, and is not fixated upon his or her individual participation in and enjoyment of good, will not stand idle while others starve, suffer, and die. Such a person will find intolerable the exploitation of others and will do what is possible to help them.

This form of responsibility has important implications for

the treatment of dying patients. Persons who are morally good not only will refuse to make choices directed against human life but also will extend themselves to care for a dying person and to protect what goods one who is dying still can enjoy, even if they happen to have no contractual or other well-defined duty to such a person.

Second, persons who respect all that is good will never make themselves a special case. Morally good persons will recognize as a form of responsibility which must shape every choice the golden rule or principle of universalizability. Such persons do not regard themselves and those with whom they have special, close ties as "more equal" or more worthy of respect than other persons. Persons who act in accord with this form of responsibility will try to identify with other persons' concerns and will not fail to ask what they would want if the roles were reversed.

Such attempts to put oneself or those for whom one especially cares in the positions of persons who will be affected by one's acts will be very important in dealing with the senile, the defective, the insane, the comatose. In such cases there is no more direct way to determine one's obligations, which in other cases would depend on the patient's consent. There is a temptation to separate oneself from those in so different a condition, to begin to think of them as mere objects or organisms, as vegetables or non-persons. This norm excludes all such ways of thinking about patients. It also excludes letting patients die of starvation and thirst. Who would wish themselves to be treated in such a way? Similarly, there are excesses of treatment which are excluded: those to which no one in the patient's place would consent.

Finally, all who respect all of the basic human goods recognize many specific duties to other persons. The readiness to promote and respect all the goods of persons leads to cooperative activity, to organized efforts by communities of people. The work is divided, the activity shared, and thus roles created and duties defined. Not everyone has the same obligations, since no two persons belong to all the same communities or have similar roles in the communities to which they do belong. But no one who is morally good can avoid making genuine commitments to many communities. These commitments are the proximate moral principle of the many specific moral obligations which are defined by one's duties. Thus, morally good persons regard their involvement in social roles not merely as a way of fulfilling themselves but as a way of responding to the appeal of human goods by working with others for common fulfillment, by serving others who cannot take care of themselves.

Moral obligations which stem directly from the requirement to respect and promote basic human goods do not depend upon common commitments. They hold regardless of any special relationships among persons. For example, if human life must be respected, then possible courses of action which involve killing people for the sake of ulterior goods are morally excluded, regardless of who these people are and how one is related to them. And if one has a strict moral obligation not to kill someone, that person's life is morally protected; he or she might be said to have an unalienable right to life.

By contrast, moral obligations which stem from common commitments make special demands on members of the community toward one another. Those to whose role it pertains to do or to refrain from doing something have duties to fulfill which their roles require. Other members of the society, who would be affected in one way or another by nonfulfillment of the requirements of a role, have rights or entitlements that the role be fulfilled. Rights and duties of this sort are moral responsibilities, yet they are not absolute, for changes in the community and its definition of roles can alter one's duties or rights. Thus a patient whose right not to be killed is unalienable has only a conditional and perhaps alterable right to the care of a particular physician or hospital.

Still, it is very important to keep in mind that rights and duties which arise from community are not mere social conventions. They are mediated by a common commitment but are ultimately grounded in the normativity of the human goods which are the principles of morality. Hence, most of the moral requirements of a person's daily life are located in the claims which other members of the community have upon one's responsible service.

Thus, parents, having undertaken to generate children, have a duty to provide and to care for them, even if they are defective. Physicians have a duty to care for their patients, even if the patients in many cases are not pleasant, interesting, and rewarding.

In sum, we have articulated four forms of responsibility or modes of moral obligation by which the basic requirement of morality begins to take shape in specific moral judgments. The four are: never to act directly against any basic human good, to help others when possible, to consider impartially actions which will affect others, and to respect the rights of those to whom one has duties. These four modes of obligation are normative principles for the more specific moral norms concerning various kinds of action. Using these modes of obligation, we shall argue in chapter twelve for certain moral positions relevant to the problems considered in this book.

Before proceeding to this matter, however, we must keep a promise made earlier: to reply more carefully to the objection of those who hold that human life is not one of the intrinsic aspects of human flourishing but is only a means, of great but merely instrumental value, to the properly personal goods of human individuals.

(pp. 358-371)

Contraception and the Natural Law

This more adequate theory of moral law is to be found in the later works of Thomas Aquinas. However, I do not wish to present my sketch as a historical study nor do I commend this theory because it happens to be that of a much commended author. Rather, I present the theory for consideration on its own rational merits, confident it can meet that test.

The most characteristic feature of this theory of moral law is its notion of practical reason. Reason does not become practical merely by its subject matter, nor by being moved by will or inclination. Rather reason is practical by nature just as really as it is theoretical by nature. And just as theoretical thought is by its very nature is-thinking, so practical thought is by its very nature ought-thinking.

In this characterization we must notice that "ought" does not refer exclusively to legal duty or to strict obligation. Practical reason controls the entire domain of free action, not by directing or censoring it from without, but by creating its structure from within. Obligation-thinking occurs in extreme cases of moral judgment, the case in which there happens to be only one good way of acting or the case in which we are interested in determining the least good way of acting that is open to us.

Hence practical reason must consider what is to be pursued and done whether that "is to be" refers to the minimum good of strict obligation or to the more adequate good which usually is possible and always is well to do. Obligation and counsel do not differ from one another as if the one really is to be done and the other not. Instead they are merely different modes in which the prescriptive force of practical reason is expressed.

Once we have grasped these points we will not be surprised to discover that according to our theory the circle of free acts and that of morally significant acts are one and the same. Every deliberate act must be either good or evil. The reason is that deliberation is the work of practical reason—which can think only in modes of is-to-be—and that the degree of our control over deliberation is precisely the degree of our freedom.

Unlike conventional natural-law theory, our theory is not compelled to reserve an enclave for freedom. The moral norm of practical reason need not treat freedom as something alien, because this moral norm works from within and respects the special conditions required by its place of work. It does not try to impose imperatives formed outside and based on merely formal aspects of reality.

Yet practical reason proceeds from principles. These principles are neither theoretical truths, nor facts of nature, nor are they imperatives whose rational force depends on an assumption laid down by authority. Instead they are fundamental prescriptions--basic formulations in the mode is-to-be--which practical reason itself forms for its own starting point. Because the principles of practical reason are its own, it need not try to derive them by any illicit inference from facts nor need it accept them from any extrarational decree of will.

Just what are these principles of practical reason and how does practical reason form them?

To begin with, since practical reason shapes action from within, it must require the minimum conditions without which action is not possible at all. The least condition for human action is that it have some intelligible object toward which it can be directed. One cannot act deliberately without orientation; one cannot commit himself to action without some sense of what the action is to achieve.

The objective need not be a definite goal. A man can give his all for love, but even then he must have some sense of what his action means precisely in terms of its attainment of the ideal of love. The objective which practical reason requires, therefore, need only be some form of intelligible good.

Consequently, the first prescription of practical reason is that good should be pursued and that actions appropriate in that pursuit should be done, and also that actions which are not helpful in pursuit of the good or which interfere with it should be avoided.

Of itself, this general norm excludes no value accessible to man. The general norm of practical reason is completely liberal and altogether open to every value that can give direction to action under the auspices of intelligence. All ethical theories take this general norm for granted. It does not conflict with any of the goods in which they may specialize.

In fact, so liberal is the general norm of practical reason that no human action can violate it directly. Only insofar as some actions violate subordinate principles are they in an indirect way opposed to its sense. Thus the good referred to in the general norm is not only moral goodness, the immanent perfection of human actions as such. Rather it is every good that man can attain by using his wits and his freedom.

We must be absolutely clear that this general norm of practical reason and the other basic prescriptions we shall consider shortly are not in any sense imperatives received from without. They express the necessities which reason must determine for itself if intelligent action is to be possible. Good is to be done not because God wills it, but because one must do something good if he is to act intelligently at all.

Of course, metaphysics can show that the human mind has been created, and that its practical reason and the primary principles it necessarily forms are a participation in divine intelligence. God has made man able to govern his own life by his own intelligence just as God by His wisdom governs the universe as a whole.

This first principle is perfectly acceptable, a reader might think, but toward what definite goods can practical reason direct human action? The first principle by itself obviously provides no direction and tell us nothing about what to do.

This question is hopelessly muddled at the outset if one tries to draw up a list of approved goods while rejecting others as unworthy of human concern. Just that sort of arbitrary selection has led to all the ethical systems which fill a philosopher's library, some of which we referred to while discussing situationism.

The proper way to understand the question rather is this. What in fact are all the goods which man can seek? What goods define the totality of human opportunity? What are all the goods which offer possibilities to human effort?

This question must be answered in such a way that no arbitrary exclusions narrow the gamut of human possibilities, precisely because it belongs to man to be open to indefinite development and to determine the course of this development by his own intelligence and freedom. The basic principles of practical reason make this openness possible, hence they cannot also restrict it.

The answer to the question, therefore, is to be found only by examining all of man's basic tendencies. These prefigure everything man can achieve. It is impossible to act for anything without having an interest in it and it is impossible to become attracted to anything, and so to develop an interest in it, except to the extent that it falls within the scope of some inclination already present within oneself.

The task of discovering all of man's basic inclinations may seem impossible of fulfillment. Indeed it is not easy, but it is by no means as difficult as the theoretical confusion in ethics might lead one to suppose.

Since we are interested in the primary principles of practical reason, our question about the natural inclinations can be viewed in two distinct ways. One is the way of theoretical reflection in which we are now engaged. The other is the way of practical insight itself.

Let us first consider the theoretical question. What are all the inclinations with which man is endowed prior to acculturation or any choice of his own?

This question requires and can be settled only by empirical inquiry. Fortunately, psychologists, despite their theoretical disagreements, have come to a remarkable consensus that human motivation presupposes a number of basic inclinations.

Although these inclinations are classified and named in different ways by different authors, they tend to form a list which can be summarized as follows. Man's fundamental inclinations are: the tendency to preserve life, especially by food-seeking and by self-defensive behavior; the tendency to mate and to raise his children; the tendency to seek certain experiences which are enjoyed for their own sake; the tendency to develop skills and to exercise them in play and the fine arts; the tendency to explore and to question; the tendency to seek out the company of other men and to try to gain their approval; the tendency to try to establish good relationships with unknown higher powers; and the tendency to use intelligence in guiding action.

Anthropological investigation only confirms what psychology states. In fact, these basic motives are the topics according to which anthropological investigations commonly are conducted. This is so precisely because these motives are the principles which collectively define whatever human life might be.

The basic human inclinations, of whose existence and place theoretical reflection thus assures us, become the source of the primary principles of practical reason not by theoretical reflection but by practical insight. The act of practical insight itself cannot be performed discursively or communicated linguistically. However, we can reflect upon that act in an attempt to understand the precise relationship between the basic inclinations and the principles of practical reason.

The inclinations, simply as psychic facts, are not themselves principles of practical reason. Although these are facts which might move us to action whether we reason or not, they are of themselves no more reasons for action than any other facts. It is very important that we be careful here not to commit the usual error of proceeding from a preferred set of facts to an illicit conclusion that those facts imply obligation.

If, however, we do not suppose that the inclinations themselves are the principles we are seeking, what role do they play in the formation of the primary principles of practical reason? Their role in the formation of the principles is this, that our understanding grasps in the inclinations the possibilities to which they point. Since understanding is determined by the general norm which we discussed previously to direct action in pursuit of the good, intelligence prescribes every one of these objects of natural inclination.

Thus we form, naturally and without reflection, the basic principles of practical reasoning. An example is the rational principle of self-preservation. Life is a good whose requirements are to be served; actions which promote it should be done; what is opposed to it should be avoided.

All of these basic principles are affirmative. Each of them prescribes that one of the goods indicated by one of our basic inclinations is to be accepted as a guide for our action.

In thus deriving practical principles from given inclinations, our practical intelligence is operating neither rationally nor irrationally. It simply is working intelligently—that is, intuitively—using experience as a point of departure for forming its own fundamental insight. The principles are practical intelligence's interpretation of experience.

The principles go beyond experience in a certain way. Indeed, interpretation always goes beyond its data. But because these are practical interpretations of human sources of motivation, the way in which they go beyond the inclinations is precisely by becoming principles of practical reason rather than by becoming mere facts about the given inclinations.

It is because they go beyond experience that these basic principles have the mode of ought-thinking even though they depend upon the given content of experience. The principles of practical reason cannot be mere forces moving one to act. They must be reasons for acting. "Is-to-be" in their statement marks the work of practical reason. Just as being is intelligible objectivity, oughtness is intelligible motivation.

It is also because the principles go beyond experience that every one of the goods prescribed in one of them takes on an intelligible form and characteristics. The felt need for food refers only to oneself and only to the concrete food one requires to satisfy hunger. But food as an object—rather, as something included in the object—of a primary practical principle is grasped as an ideal.

The food which is to be obtained and eaten is a human good, not merely my good. Hence the principle concerns every man's food and eating as well as my own. It concerns the food for unborn generations which is worrying the demographers. It concerns the food to which a good chef devotes his career. It concerns the food a glutton loves too well.

This last point is interesting, because although the glutton behaves in a repulsive fashion, his very behavior reveals most clearly what status food has as a principle of human action. It is not merely a definite good sufficiently cared for in the most efficient way by limited means. Food shows itself to be an ideal by the very fact that when a person commits himself exclusively to it he can build his whole life around it.

But how do these primary practical principles actually establish definite obligations? Do they not underlie everything that we might do, no matter what? Certainly, they seem to open the doors too liberally, for they begin from every possible basic human good and they endorse every one of these goods indiscriminately. Or perhaps it is better to say that the effect of practical reason interpreting experience in such a way as to form all of these primary affirmative principles is to invent the possibility of all human goods.

However that may be, the endorsement does seem indiscriminate, since every act ever performed for any reason at all, including every immoral act, had a good reason in these primary practical principles. If there were no good reason, an act never could be performed deliberately. Then it would not be a human act and there could be nothing moral about it. In fact, we can diagnose insanity by observing that a person's action has no intelligible reference to any basic human good at all.

The problem cannot be solved by suggesting that we restrict ourselves to natural goods. All of these basic goods are equally natural and whatever we derive from them is equally a product of our ingenuity. That is why the categories of anthropology always are being filled with diverse concrete content.

Neither can the problem be solved by appealing to the general norm, because that only requires us to act for an intelligible good, and all of these principles qualify. In each of the primary principles of practical reason the general norm is present in a diverse special mode. Hence the general norm does not commend any one of the essential goods more than another to us, although it does commend each of them in a peculiarly different way, since "good" is predicated analogously of all the basic human goods.

At this point situationist theories arbitrarily prefer some of these goods to others. Some of the basic goods, we notice, are substantive values which can be achieved in definite material embodiments—human life and health, procreation, and certain others. Another group of the basic goods are what we might call "reflexive" values. These are specifically human and are specified by some aspect of man's subjectivity itself. These include human association, the use of reason to direct action, and others. The situationist subordinates material goods to some reflexive value despite the fact that practical reason depends equally on both.

This preference at least can appear reasonable. After all, that is how one would choose if he were in a position to make a choice, since the reflexive values considered in themselves must in some way be superior to the material ones. However, the situationist is not arbitrary only in this respect. He also arbitrarily prefers one reflexive value to all others and treats his preferred value alone as an ideal.

Even such nonmaterial but substantive values as truth, which is the object of the basic inclination we call "wonder," are regarded by a situationist as mere conditions for his ideal, because truth transcends the human and makes objective demands which could conflict with situationist subjectivism.

It might seem, then, as if there is no way to derive any definite obligations from our series of primary principles. There they stand, opening the way to all human possibilities. But they do not tell us what to do. The solution to our perplexity will be at hand when we stop looking to these principles for a set of directions. They simply are not a crowd of guides able to tell us the best way to do life in one day.

The primary principles of practical reason determine action from within by shaping our experience into categories relevant to human interests, by making it possible for us to recognize that we have problems, and by stimulating us to reach intelligent solutions to our problems. They have their effect only by serving as points of departure for the development of interests, interests which lead to choices.

That is all very well, a critic might complain, but why call such a liberal set of principles a moral law? These principles are at the origin of all human actions and there is no rational way to mediate between them or to establish operational priorities among them. Even if they provide some vague positive direction, how do they exclude any moral evil?

In one sense, of course, the primary principles of practical reason do not exclude evil, since one or another of them always is available as a good reason for whatever a man deliberately does. But why should we want exclusion? Is it not enough that man be what he can be?

Certainly it is enough, and the principles demand only that the human possibilities they establish should be maintained. All they ask of us is that we make no arbitrary selection among them, for that would be to spurn something of human value. Of course, this mild and reasonable demand itself is a certain exclusion. It means that in all of our practical reasoning each of the primary principles must be maintained and allowed to exercise its influence.

From freedom, to which the primary principles of practical reason contribute the possibility of meaningfulness, they require only a decent respect. In the will, where the principles also work, each of them demands respect from its co-workers and from the will itself. None of them is servile, and every one of them requires that its peculiar contribution to human goodness be respected.

What the basic principles of practical reason exclude, in other words, is any action <u>against</u> one undertaken in order <u>to maximize</u> another. No one of these values is absolute, but none of them is so relative that it does not resist submergence.

If he wishes man can choose one value over against the others. He always has the value he chooses as a sufficient reason for doing so, yet such choices are made at the expense of rationality, because the prescription which is degraded also is primary, underived, self-evident. It has equally valid claims upon our interest, because it has precisely the claims it gets by being represented in a primary principle.

We shall explain in greater detail in the next chapter the various ways in which basic affirmative principles of practical reason cause definite obligations. For the present, however, it is enough to grasp in general the way in which this is possible. Whenever it happens that an attitude of nonarbitrariness toward the basic human goods requires us to have a certain intention, and that intention requires a certain action or omission, then we have a definite obligation.

The point will be clearer, perhaps, if it is approached negatively. We violate a definite obligation whenever our action is not in accordance with the kind of intention that we must maintain if our intention is not to imply an irrational preference of one value over others. The insane man's action has little or no intelligible relationship to any of the essential human goods. The immoral man's action has an intelligible relationship to some of the goods but not to others. The virtuous man's action has an intelligible relationsip to all of the goods.

Act in accord with reason expresses the meaning of virtue just to the extent that it tells us to hold fast to all the primary principles of practical intelligence, which we spontaneously form as the origin for all our rational deliberation.

The theory of moral law which we have been considering has very definite advantages over situationism.

Our theory explains what situationist theories assume—namely, how practical reasoning begins. There is no need to invoke will at the beginning or at the end of a sound ethical theory. Only unsound ones must find a way of making facts, which are not intelligible motives, play a role in grounding obligations that they cannot really fulfill.

Our theory also has an advantage over situationism in being able to provide a starting point from which really significant guidance for life can be derived. The situationist's key value becomes contentless and meaningless because situationism separates a reflexive value from substantive goods, completely subordinating the latter, especially if they are material.

Our theory keeps all of these primary values in the first rank of practical principles. Hence substantive values give definite meaning to reflexive ones, material values give psychological force to spiritual ones, and reflexive values give status as ideals to substantive ones by including them as co-aspects in the immanent perfection of human life.

Finally, our theory, unlike situationism, does not make impossible demands on man's ability to know. For the goodness of
action, even action affecting material values, it is enough that
our intentions and choices be good; actual results are not demanded by the ideals.

Of course, this does not mean that one can disregard the
facts which he can and should consider nor that action is justified by partially good intentions. If all the intentions underlying an action are sound, that can be only because the agent is
guided by love of all the essential human goods.

It is obvious also that our theory of moral law is superior
to conventional natural-law theory. The point that our theory
explains the origin of ought-thinking has been stressed sufficiently. Our theory also eliminates legalism from the notion of
obligation, although legal obligations and imperatives have a
place insofar as they express in certain domains the requirements
of essential human goods.

The negative emphasis of conventional natural-law theory
also is eliminated. We begin with a series of primary principles
all of which are affirmative. Our method of excluding moral evil
is not basic but derivative--the exclusion of irrational preference among essential human goods all of which hold a primary
place in the proceedings of practical reason.

But what kind of account can our theory give of the end of
man? How are the essential human goods to be related to it?
Will the relationship be closer than the sanction of conventional natural-law theory? The answer to this question is too complex to permit adequate treatment here. However, a sketch is
possible.

None of the goods to which the basic principles of practical
reason direct us is sufficient to satisfy man's potentiality for
goodness as such. Precisely for this reason man can disregard
the prescriptions of reason and, as it were, gamble his existence
on an identification of one of the goods with goodness itself.
What reason requires is that all of the goods be maintained in
their irreducible but not absolute positions.

In fact, it is only possible for man to love all of the
goods properly if he considers each of them a participant in
perfect goodness. Only in this way can he keep all of them separate from perfect goodness but irreducible to any other particular value, for only in this way will he see that each good
uniquely represents the perfect good itself without ever encom-
passing its absolute goodness.

This complex orientation and delicate balance could provide man with a basis for establishing orderly direction in his life. Although the unity would not be monistic and although the actual achievement of goods could not be definitive, a man's love of all proportionate human goods as participations in pure goodness could guide him toward an existence both full and open.

The end of man, according to this theory, would be to achieve, insofar as possible, the goods accessible to man, and to maintain permanent openness for an even greater achievement. To this end moral action is naturally proportionate, simply because that action is morally good which is as proportioned to this end as human wits and freedom can manage.

Thus far philosophy. If the teaching of the Christian faith be considered, a further complexity is introduced. Faith teaches that the immanent value of human goods, insofar as they are obtained by human actions, can be preserved and simultaneously infinitely transformed through divine loving-kindness. Human action and its naturally suitable objects thus become divine in their value.

The result is that the perfect Good which man must love if he is to love anything well becomes actually attainable not only in Its participations but even in Itself. In this way the openness of human nature is fulfilled without any restriction. But man's natural values also are completely respected, for the Good Itself is not opposed to any of Its participations.

According to the theory of moral law which I outlined in the previous chapter, there is a fundamental affirmative precept of moral law corresponding to each of man's basic natural inclinations. All of these precepts together provide the foundation for all practical reasoning. These precepts make the demand never to be violated directly by the will. Of course, man can choose to act against them, but he does so at the price of sacrificing part of the very source of the rationality of his free action.

(pp. 60-72; 76)

Abortion

Therefore, it is in this sense, as self-determination, that freedom is a necessary principle of morality. Freedom is the beginning of every moral act, for whether or not we act to realize any particular possibility is a matter of our own choice. And where there is no choice, there is no morality, no question of right and wrong. We do not hold animals and infants responsible in the moral sense, because we do not see evidence of

163

deliberation and self-determination. They may be good or bad by instinct or by training, but though we call a dog "vicious" by analogy, we do not call a good dog "virtuous." If we punish and reward animals, it is not that we consider their acts right or wrong, but that we believe our treatment can determine their behavior as we wish.

Still, even though we find the source of the fact of moral action in our self-determination, this freedom does not explain the meaning or purpose of what we do. That we act depends on our choice alone; what our act is, depends on our understanding of what we are doing, of what good gives meaning to our action.

Moreover, the moral question--what we ought to do--is merely one factor we consider in deliberating about diverse goods and making choices. We can conceive intelligible alternatives to what we ought to do and we can choose an alternative contrary to our own moral judgment against it. If this were not so, we could never experience moral guilt, for we would never knowingly do what we believe wrong. In fact, we do. We are free to act against morality, but we are not free to make our immorality right, as everyone knows whenever he suffers from a bad conscience.

The source of the meaning or purpose of what we do is revealed when we ask: "Why did I choose that?" The answer must be given in terms of the good we saw in the possibility we chose. Although that good was not compelling to the exclusion of alternative possibilities which carried their own incommensurable goods, the good proper to the alternative we chose was a necessary condition for our choice of it and was a sufficient reason to make that choice intelligible (even if immoral). Thus the freedom of self-determination is not irrational, as if we could act with no reason at all. Rather, freedom is possible because each alternative that is open to us presents itself with a reason adequate to render its selection intelligible.

The immediate reason why we choose in a particular case often is subordinate to an ulterior motive. If we ask a laborer why he is working, he may answer: "To make money." If we ask why he wants to make money, he may reply: "To feed myself and my family, because we get hungry, and to get other necessaries to stay alive." If we try to press the inquiry beyond this point, we may find oursleves none too gently rebuffed, not because the person we are questioning is ignorant of a motive beyond the one stated, but because there is no further purpose. To attempt to question the self-sufficiency of a purpose that is in fact ultimate will seem to a simple person evidence that we are ridiculing him.

Considering the ultimate motives for which we act from a psychological point of view, we discern various categories of basic human needs. These are broader than the specific objects of physiological drives which in other animals are satisfied by instinctive behavior. We are interested, for example, not only in satisfying hunger and thirst, in avoiding immediate physical threats, and so on, but in preserving our lives, maintaining physical and mental health, and attaining a condition of safety and security.

If we consider the basic human needs in this broad fashion, we will find the categories of good for which we can act. For we can act only for that which engages our interest, and nothing engages our interest unless it corresponds to some fundamental inclination within ourselves or to an interest derived from such an inclination. The objects of such inclinations are what we mean by basic human needs, understood broadly as explained above.

The technique of questioning, both by reflection on our own purposes and by discussion with others, can be joined to a survey of psychological literature and a comparison with the categories of human activity found by anthropologists to be useful to interpret the facts of life in any culture.

Each of these approaches has its own limitations. The question technique sometimes terminates not in any objective basic need, but rather in an emotional motivation that reflects an unarticulated need only in its impact on feeling. For example, a child may say he plays ball "for fun"; he does not articulate his interest in terms of the value he achieves in the performance itself. The psychologists emphasize physiology and hence they distinguish drives--e.g., hunger and thirst--which subserve a unified intelligible motive--e.g., the preservation of life and health. The anthropologists sometimes include categories of activity which correspond not to basic needs, but to intermediate goods which are only means to more basic needs--e.g., warfare, property, and the form of economy.

A thorough, critical study of all of these approaches would be desirable; however, it would be a major undertaking in itself. I think that such a study would lend empirical support to the following list of fundamental human goods:

1) Life itself, including physical and mental health and safety.
2) Activities engaged in for their own sake (e.g., games and hobbies) including those which also serve an ulterior purpose (e.g., work performed as self-expression and self-fulfillment, which also has a useful and

165

economically significant result).

3) Experiences sought for their own sake (e.g., esthetic experiences and watching professional athletic competitions).
4) Knowledge pursued for its own sake (e.g., theoretical science and speculative philosophy).
5) Interior integrity—harmony or peace among the various components of the self.
6) Genuineness—conformity between one's inner self and his outward behavior.
7) Justice and friendship—peace and cooperation among men.
8) Worship and holiness—the reconciliation of mankind to God.

The first four of these groups of goods are understandable without introducing the notion of self-determination in their very meanings. Their achievement depends on human action but their meaning does not. The latter four, by contrast, cannot be understood without including the idea of self-determination. The first four embrace the perfections of a human being according to his specific nature: the exercise of natural functions, physical activity, psychic receptivity, and cognitive reflection. The latter four embrace the perfections of human beings according to their capacity to reflect and to live self-conscious lives: unity achieved by reflection and self-determination at each level on which alienation is experienced or believed to exist.

These categories of goods easily can be defined in such a way that the division is logically exhaustive. However, that procedure would only raise a question concerning the adequacy of the description of each member of the division. A more convincing test of the adequacy of this classification is to try to find basic human goods that cannot be located in it. I think that if the considerations mentioned above in respect to the limitations of various approaches are borne in mind, no purpose of human action that is really final will be found in addition to those listed.

In any case, it will be sufficient for our present purpose to note that any list of basic human goods would have to include life itself. Many people spend the greatest part of their time and effort for no other purpose, and simply staying alive generally is regarded as a good even when other goods cannot be achieved.

We are conscious of these basic goods in two distinct ways. By experience, we are aware of our own inclinations and of what satisfies them; our own longings and delights are facts of our conscious life that we discover as we discover other facts. At the same time, by understanding we interpret these facts in a special way; our intelligence is not merely a spectator of the dynamics of our own action, but becomes involved as a molder and director. Understanding grasps in our inclinations the possibilities toward which they point and understanding becomes practical by proposing these possibilities as goals toward which we might act.

Thus we understand, prior to any choice or reasoning effort, that the basic human goods are possible purposes for our action. To the extent that any action requires some purpose, the basic goods present themselves as purposes-to-be-realized, not merely as objective possibilities. We understand the preservation of our own lives, the pursuit of knowledge, the cultivation of friendship, and the rest as goods-to-be-sought by us.

Their appeal to us for realization is not conditioned upon some prior wish, but rather is the basis for the possibility of all our rational desires. In this respect, the goods are non-hypothetical principles of practical reason such as Kant wished to discover. But they differ from Kant's basic principles in having a content derived from inclination. Kant mistakenly believed that rational principles could be unconditional only by being purely rational. He overlooked the possibility that intelligence can form principles for practical reason by insight into the possibilities opened to our interest by our basic needs.

The practical principles thus express not what _is_ so, but what is-to-be through our own action. Practical reason is "ought" thinking just as theoretical reason is "is" thinking. But "ought" here does not necessarily express moral obligation; that is a special form of "ought." Not only are we inclined by appetite to eat when we are hungry, but we know we _ought_ to do so. This "ought" expresses the judgment of practical reason ("common sense"), but it need not have the force of moral obligation.

One important point to notice is that practical reason controls the whole area of free action by shaping it from within, rather than by imposing rules from without. If moral obligation is a special form of "ought," it too is an inner requirement of practical reason, not a demand imposed, as if by some external authority. The basic human goods are to be pursued in our actions not because God imposes pursuit of them on us, but because we must pursue some good if rationally guided action—which alone is caused by self-determination—is to be possible at all.

As expressions of what is-to-be, the practical principles present basic human needs as fundamental goods, as ideals. But the ideal character of these goods does not mean that they are wholly apart from man and his real life. The ideals are human ideals, realized in human persons and in human community. They do not transcend man by subordinating his good to any non-human purpose, but only by going beyond what man already is toward that which he is not yet but still may be. It will always be possible for us to discern more clearly in what such goods as health, knowledge, and friendship concretely consist; it will always be possible for us to seek to realize new dimensions of such inexhaustible possibilities.

Protestant situationists who have adopted a theory of objective values as an explanation of the source of moral obligation presuppose principles similar to those just described, although they do not explain the genesis of these principles by reference to basic needs. More important than this defect of analysis is their too hasty leap from the appeal of the values for realization--that is, from the modality of "is-to-be" in which practical intelligence formulates ideals--to moral obligation. They overlook the fact that if the immediate appeal of each value is translated directly into a moral obligation to respond, then every choice will violate moral requirements. For the very nature of choice is to respond to the appeal of some good at the cost of not responding to some other. If we could have both simultaneously, no choice would ever be needed.

But it is clear that choice is necessary and it is absurd to say that every choice is necessarily evil simply because it is a choice. Clearly, then, the appeal of the goods cannot be taken as the direct determinant of moral obligation. Everything we can do becomes possible only in virtue of these goods; no human act, good or evil, fails to respond to one or more of them, or succeeds in responding in every possible way to all of them. If the basic human goods, which are principles of practical reason, clarify the possibility of every choice, they cannot of themselves determine why some choices are morally good and others morally evil.

What does make this difference? What divides moral good from moral evil? The answer is that moral goodness and evil depend upon the attitude with which we choose. Not that any and every choice would be good if only it were made with the proper attitude, for some choices cannot be made with the right attitude. But if we have the right attitude, we make good choices; if we have the wrong attitude, we make evil ones.

But what is the right attitude? It is realistic, in the sense that it conforms fully with reality. To choose a particular good with an appreciation of its genuine but limited possibility and its objectively human character is to choose it with an attitude of realism. Such choice does not attempt to transform and belittle the goodness of what is not chosen, but only to realize what is chosen.

The attitude which leads to immoral choices, by contrast, narrows the good to the possibilities one chooses to realize. The good is not appreciated in its objectively human character, simply as a good, but as this good of such a sort to be achieved by me. Instead of conforming to the real amplitude of human possibility, such an attitude transforms that possibility by restriction. Immoral choice forecloses possibilities merely because they are not chosen; rather than merely realizing some goods while leaving others unrealized, such choice presumes to negate what it does not embrace in order to exalt what it chooses. Goods equally ultimate are reduced to the status of mere means for maximizing preferred possibilities; principles of practical reason as fundamental as those that make the choice possible are brushed aside as if they wholly lacked validity.

No single good, nothing that can be embraced in the object of any single choice, is sufficient to exhaust human good, to fulfill all of the possibilities open before man. If we choose with an attitude of openness to goods not chosen, the good is not restricted. We respect the possibility we cannot realize through this choice. But if we restrict our perspective by redefining what is good according to our particular choice, we are attempting to negate the meaningfulness of what we reject and to absolutize what we prefer.

A proper attitude respects equally all of the basic goods and listens equally to all of the appeals they express through principles of practical reason. Because of the incompatibility of actual alternatives, a choice is necessary. But a right attitude does not seek to subvert some principles of practical reason by an appeal to others. An immoral attitude involves such irrationality, for while the evil choice depends upon the principles of practical reason, it seeks to invalidate the claims of those principles which would have grounded an alternate choice.

If the principle that distinguishes moral good from evil is an attitude such as we have just described, still two serious questions must be considered. First, is not moral evil something more interpersonal than the unrealistic and narrow attitude just described? Does not moral evil involve the violation of the good of others? From a religious viewpoint, must it not be seen as alienation from God—a rejection of his love? Second, how does an open attitude such as we have described shape itself into concrete moral obligations to do or avoid specific acts?

169

The answer to the first question is easy. The principle of moral evil can be located in the unrealistic attitude described, but the impact or significance of such evil is by no means limited to oneself.

If I choose with the attitude that my commitment defines and delimits the good, I shall lack the detachment to appreciate the possibilities of others' lives, which could complement my own by realizing the values I cannot. Their good, which I do not choose, will become for me at best a non-good, something to which I shall remain indifferent. Egoism can decrease only to the extent that I am open to the embrace of all goods, those as well as these, yours as well as mine. The attitude of immorality is an irrational attempt to reorganize the moral universe, so that the center is not the whole range of human possibilities in which we can all share, but the goods I can actually pursue through my actions. Instead of community, immorality generates alienation, and the conflict of competing immoralities is reflected by incompatible personal rationalizations and social ideologies, each of which seeks to remake the entire moral universe in conformity with its own fundamental bias.

Those who understand immorality in religious terms of course cannot be expected to find any merely philosophic account entirely satisfactory. But the philosophic account proposed here might coincide with a religious view. It certainly is impossible to maintain a fully open attitude toward all human goods, irreducibly diverse and incommensurable as they are, unless we accept the reference of our conception of goodness to a reality we do not yet understand.

For if the goods we do know--which constitute a unified field for our choices--are not diverse participations in a unity beyond all of them, they must be unified by reference to one another. In that case, what we choose will appropriate the priority of an absolute to which what we reject will be subordinated--if it is regarded as good in any sense at all. However, if we accept the reference of our conception of goodness to a reality we do not yet understand, our openness to that goodness may count as love of it, although it is not an intelligible objective of any particular action.

Such love of the good can be interpreted in a religious context as at least compatible with a response of love to God's love. And if the goodness in question is identified with God, respect and openness to all human goods may be interpreted as man's fulfillment by participation in a good which first belongs to God. An immoral attitude, by contrast, would exclude a real goodness beyond the goods we know and choose; immorality would

refuse to seek human fulfillment as a realization by participation in God's own goodness. From a religious viewpoint, any
morally evil act, in which the good chosen is made to define
goodness itself, really is an instance of covert idolatry.

The second question--how a morally right attitude can shape
itself into specific obligations--is extremely important for
ethical theory.

The solution almost automatically taken for granted in
most contemporary discussions is that openness to all human goods
requires a moral judgment in accord with the utilitarian maxim:
the greatest good for the greatest number. However, as we have
seen, utilitarianism is incoherent, because the goods are many
and incommensurable, and there is no single standard or least
common denominator by which the "greatest good" could be
measured. In fact, self-determination is possible only because
the "greatest good" cannot be determined by calculation; utilitarianism is actually incompatible with freedom.

Of course, once a definite goal has been determined, it is
possible for us to calculate the efficient means to it. If we
take an immoral attitude toward the goods we choose, utilitarianism may seem a suitable method for rationalizing our prejudice. (Not everyone who theorizes as if utilitarianism were
a moral system practices what he teaches.)

Ideally, the discernment of specific moral obligations
would require neither calculation nor even reflection. If one's
moral attitude were right and his whole personality were perfectly integrated with that moral attitude, then his own sense
of appropriateness, his own spontaneous judgments, would be the
surest index of moral good and evil. This is what St Augustine
meant when he said (in religious terms): "Love God, and then do
what you wish."

However, when we have a moral question, obviously our
moral sensibility has failed us. At this point it is useless
to say: "Act by your own right will," because the question would
never have arisen but for the conflict within ourselves. "What
we wish" is not decisive because we wish one thing with one part
of ourself and another thing with another part.

Then too, when it comes to explaining our moral evaluation
to others, our moral sensibility is not helpful, because it is
incommunicable. At such a juncture, articulate reasons are
essential. We must ask what our moral judgments would be if we
were perfectly integrated in accord with a right moral attitude.

171

First, if we were open to all of the goods, we would at least take them into account in our deliberations. We would never make a choice by which one of the goods was seriously affected without considering our action in that light. Thus, we would never choose to act in a way that caused anyone's death without being aware of the impact of what we were doing. In this respect, Protestant situationism reveals moral sensitivity that seems missing from some utilitarian theories.

Second, if we had a right moral attitude we would avoid ways of acting that inhibit the realization of any one of the goods and prefer ways of acting that contribute to each one, other things being equal. One who has a positive attitude toward human life certainly makes a presumption in its favor and does not gratuitously negate this good (or any other).

Third, if we had a truly realistic appreciation of the entire ambit of human goods, we would not hesitate to contribute our effort to their realization in others, when our help is needed urgently, merely because no particular benefit accrued to ourselves. True enough, we have primary obligations to realize human goods in ourselves and in those near us, for we can do in ourselves what no one else can. But we should be more interested in the good than in our good. Therefore, we reveal an immoral attitude if we prefer our own good merely because it is ours, when our help is urgently needed by others. For this reason, one who had a morally right attitude certainly would prefer another's life to his own comfort, or to other goods to which he would prefer his own life.

Fourth, if we had a right moral attitude, we would fulfill our role in any cooperative venture into which we enter not only to the extent necessary to get out of it what we seek for ourselves but to the full extent needed to achieve the good whose concrete possibility depends on the common effort. This principle does not preclude the criticism of institutions or the reformation of structures, but it does rule out attempts to revise social relationships simply to make them more favorable to ourselves, even at the expense of the common good. Thus we cannot rightly seek to preserve and protect our own lives by institutions, such as criminal law, which we refuse to apply equally to the rights of others. Equality before the law is a moral principle as well as a legal one.

Fifth, if we were fully integrated toward the goods, we would carry out our engagements with them. As our life progresses, we make commitments, such as choice of career, which preclude the pursuit of many other possibilities. If these commitments are made in view of the real good we can achieve, we will not set them aside merely because we encounter difficulties.

A genuine respect for the goods we do not choose to pursue will make us doubly dedicated to the realization of those on which we concentrate our efforts.

The teacher who is cynical about education, the corrupt politician, the careless physician, the slipshod craftsman--all show a lack of faithful dedication to what they have chosen as their own share of man's effort to achieve the goods open to us. Parents and physicians both are especially engaged in the good of human life in the helpless and dependent. Therefore, failure on their part to protect and promote this good is an abdication of responsibility that reveals an improper moral attitude.

All of the preceding ways in which concrete moral obligations take shape reveal something about the reason why human life, which is one of the basic goods, must be respected. Yet none of these forms of obligation would require an unexceptionable respect for life. Not even the parent and physician need always act to preserve and promote life, for sometimes other goods also are very pressing. A proper moral attitude is compatible with the omission of action that would realize a good, provided that omission itself is essential to realize another good (or the same generic good in another instance).

However, there is still another mode of moral obligation which binds us with greater strictness. If we had a right moral attitude, which means a truly realistic appreciation of each human good, we would never act directly against the realization of any basic good and we would never act in a way directly destructive of a realiztion of any of the basic goods. To act directly against a good is to subordinate that good to whatever leads us to choose such a course of action. We treat an end as if it were a mere means; we treat an aspect of the person as if it were an object of measurable and calculable worth. Yet each of the principles of practical reason is as basic as the others and each of them must be respected by us equally if we are not to narrow and foreshorten human goodness to conform to our choices.

Of course, each of the basic human goods may be inhibited or interfered with when we act for any good. But it is one thing for inhibition or interference with other goods to occur as unsought but unavoidable side-effects of an effort to pursue a good, and it is quite another thing directly to choose to inhibit or destroy a realization of a basic human good. To reluctantly accept the adverse aspects of one's action is one thing; to purposely determine ourselves to an action that is of its very character against a basic good is quite another matter.

It is only possible for us to do this insofar as a direct attack on a good can be useful to some ulterior good consequence, the end rationalizes the means. But, against utilitarian theories, I think we must maintain that the end which rationalizes the means cannot justify the means when the means in question involves turning against a good equally basic, equally an end, equally a principle of rational action as the good consequence sought to be achieved.

Here, I believe, we arrive at the reason why we consider actions which kill human beings to be generally immoral. Human life is a basic good and it is intrinsic to the person, not extrinsic as property is. To choose directly to destroy a human life is to turn against this fundamental human good. We can make such a choice only by regarding life as a measurable value, one that can be compared to other values and calculated to be of less worth. To attempt such a rationalization is to reduce an end to the status of mere means. Whatever good is achieved by such a means could not have been chosen except by a pretense that the good of the life which is destroyed is not really an irreplaceable human possibility. Undoubtedly, it is for this reason that those who seek to justify direct abortion and other direct attacks on human life strive to deny the humanity and/or personality of the intended victims.

Two sorts of objections are likely to be raised against this conclusion. First, it will be argued that a single act of killing--for example, the single choice to abort an infant--should not be isolated from the whole context of a person's life. Second, it will be objected that almost every moral system has recognized some cases in which killing is justifiable: for example, in self defense, as capital punishment, in warfare, and, in the case of abortion, to save the mother's life. This second objection demands a careful treatment, and the next section will be devoted to it. But the first objection can be disposed of at once.

Each single act is an engagement of one's freedom, a determination of one's self by one's self. A particular choice against human life therefore has a moral significance in itself, for that choice either squares or not with a right moral orientation. Of course, one who performs an isolated immoral act is not damaged in moral character so badly as one who habitually chooses or approves such acts. But a little immorality is still immorality.

Actually, I think, those who ask us to consider the act of killing within the whole context of a person's life are assuming that "circumstances" or "other values" that are present "in the situation" will offset the disvalue of the act and so justify it. Such an argument really amounts to a covert form of utilitarianism.

Situations do not present themselves to us ready made.
They take their shape and find their limits because of our interests. Once we have chosen, a situation has been finally settled.
Before choice we always are able to extend our reflection so as
to enlarge the situation and even to transform it by taking into
account what our initial interest did not require us to notice.
Moral judgments, good or bad, delimit human situations; potentially our human situation is unlimited. For this reason it is a
mistake to look to the situation for the meaning of the act.

Nevertheless, Protestant situation ethics is not pointless.
There are cases in which there seems to be a genuine conflict of
obligations, so that one would appear unable to avoid falling into
some moral evil. Undoubtedly, the number of such apparent conflict cases would be greatly reduced if all the possible courses
of action were considered instead of some being excluded in advance because they would involve difficulty or hardship which
we all to easily decide is "impossiblity." Again, apparent conflict cases would be lessened if we kept clearly in mind that
there is no moral obligation to choose all possible goods, including incompatible ones. It is not immoral to leave some good
undone providing that good is appreciated and respected and some
other good is done.

Yet there remain conflict cases such as those in which
most moral systems have admitted the justifiability of killing
human beings. To such cases we must now turn our attention.
(pp. 311-321)

"Unqualified Values and Ethical Decisions"

If there are, literally, as you urge, "unqualified values"
it would seem that the pursuit of them would justify any act.
This is not your position, but how then do you argue from the
occurrence of an unqualified value to the justification of an
act?

For me, what is morally vital is not how much good or evil
one causes, but how one is disposed toward the values that constitute human persons. The principle of moral goodness is an
attitude of openness toward all of the unqualified values and
respect for them as principles that our choices cannot alter.
A good man has an integrated disposition to appreciate and to
serve these values; a bad man has an integrated disposition to
do as he pleases and to get what he wants out of life.

To go from this basic principle to the moral evaluation of
particular acts requires normative principles at two levels.
First there must be a set of generative principles which hold

175

irrespective of particular content, and which guide us in exercising our freedom to act toward unqualified values as such. Second, there must be moral rules with specific content, which can be formed or criticized by the generative principles, in the light of our insight into various values and the general conditions of life.

For ethical theory, the first sort of principles are the more important. I call such generative principles "modes of obligation." Among modes of obligation I would include at least the following eight.

First, one should shape one's life by a set of commitments to the various unqualified values. This set of commitments should be arranged in such a way that they can lead to a harmonious life style.

Second, the moral rules of all of one's actions should be universalizable; preferences not justified by reasons must be excluded.

Third, one should be open to cooperation with others since the goods to be realized constitute the <u>human</u> person, who is by nature social.

Fourth, one should not regard any particular participation in a value as if it were the value itself.

Fifth, commitment to a value cannot be arbitrarily limited; the values themselves have an openendedness that goes beyond any and all of their participations.

Sixth, when one is dealing with participations in a value and measurement is possible—in other words, in the domain of technique—one should prefer the greater good; efficiency is a virtue.

Seventh, to the extent that one's duties are defined by a fair set of institutions in a basically just society, one ought to do one's duties unless they conflict, in which case one should at least do one of the conflicting duties.

Eighth, one should not act directly against any of the unqualified values in any of its participations; the end does not justify the means!

Students of the history of ethics will note that the various modes of obligation I list have been proposed by diverse philosophers as fundamental principles of morality. Many ethical theories have got hold of part of the truth. Most, unfortunately, take the part for the whole and therefore propose inadequate criteria for forming or criticizing moral rules.

Assuming that the life of unborn human individuals is human life and that the life of human beings is an unqualified value, the eighth mode of obligation leads to a moral rule excluding direct abortion. But what about cases in which abortion is not directly sought as a means to some ulterior good? Here, other modes of obligation come into play. A rather extensive treatment of this problem will be found in my book, Abortion: the Myths, the Realities, and the Arguments.

Many affirmative moral rules are concerned with duties. If one reflects on the seventh mode of obligation, it is clear why such rules must have a good many built-in exceptions.

A particular act is justified if and only if the following conditions are fulfilled: (1) all the modes of obligation are used to form and/or criticize moral rules relevant to that act; (2) the values that would be participated or excluded by the act are considered; (3) the concrete circumstances of the act are considered; and (4) one can find no reason for thinking it probable that performance of the act would violate a relevant moral rule that has been properly formed and/or criticized.

Background for Chapter 14, "When Action Is Ambiguous"

Is it ever morally right to directly do evil to achieve good? The less plausible theories and consequentialism say 'yes.' Grisez says 'never.' For some centuries many moral thinkers proposed the principle of double effect to cope with situations in which doing good might permit a side evil effect. Contemporary Catholic consequentialists seem to interpret this principle as really claiming that evil may be directly chosen to achieve good. Grisez rejects this interpretation, insisting it is never right to go against a human good. The selections deal with one of the most subtle and difficult problems in moral reasoning and present some of Grisez's most profound reflections.

Tenth Plank: Resolving the ambiguous case:

A. If the action is an indivisible unity and if it directly realizes a human good, persons performing the act for the sake of the good need not be wrongly disposed toward the good which is simultaneously damaged.

B. If the two aspects of an action are related as means to end (the good result is attained in an act distinct from that in which the bad is caused), it is immoral to perform the action because it is never right to do evil to achieve good.

Life and Death

This clarification of what is involved in choosing enables us to state more clearly precisely what people are committing themselves to when they choose to do something. If one always chooses for the sake of the good one hopes to realize, it follows that one chooses to carry out a certain performance insofar as the performance is a way of realizing the hoped-for good. This good might be in the state of affairs which is the performance itself, or it might be in some ulterior act. Thus one in choosing is committing oneself to bringing about the state of affairs only insofar as it either embodies or is a necessary condition for ulteriorly realizing the good in which one is interested.

The good in which one is interested is much more limited than the entire state of affairs which one actually causes. For example, if two boys play a game of catch, the good in which they are interested is the playing of the game itself. Their play might unexpectedly call their parents' attention to the fact that they have leisure and thus lead to their being given some chores to do. Not thought of, this possible consequence is no part of that to which they are committed. Perhaps they have been told not to play catch, and they foresee that they will be caught and punished for having been disobedient. This consequence of playing catch, although understood to be part of the state of affairs their behavior will bring about, is not precisely what they are committed to.

It might be thought that the foreseen consequence lies outside the precise boundaries of their choice only because it is something which follows by parental fiat rather than by natural consequence from what they are doing. But this would be a mistake. If the boys are thoughtful, they also realize that in playing they are wearing out their ball and their gloves. Sometime in the future new equipment will have to be purchased. Even if they consider this natural consequence of using their equipment, it is no part of that to which they commit themselves when they decide to play. They are interested in the good of play, not in the wear and tear on equipment which is inseparable from this good.

Similarly, if a girl accepts jobs baby-sitting in order to earn money, not because she particularly likes to take care of children, she commits herself to the work just to the extent that she must in order to obtain the money she wants. Her commitment does not extend to the unforeseen effect that she will be away from home while the rest of her family enjoys a midnight snack. Her missing out on the treat is a consequence of her choice but no part of her action. But even if she knows that her family will enjoy a midnight snack and that she will miss out on it if she is busy elsewhere, she commits herself by choice to what is required to earn money, not to foregoing other satisfactions she might enjoy if she did not accept the work.

In general, if a person chooses to do something because the very action is a way of participating in a human good, this person brings about a very extensive state of affairs but only does that by which the good is participated in. And if a person chooses to do something as a means to an ulterior end, this person also brings about many consequences but only does that which is instrumental to the desired end. Deliberation concerns proposals for action. The proposals are shaped by hoped for goods. Action is expected to realize potential goods directly or indirectly. Thus, to choose to do something is to adopt a

proposal by which one commits oneself to trying to realize a
state of affairs just insofar as this state of affairs will
embody a hoped for good.

If "what one does" is defined narrowly by what one chooses,
what one in fact brings about is always much wider than what one
does. One brings about an indeterminate and indeterminable sequence of processes and events, many of them unforeseeable, some
which only could be guessed at, and comparatively few which could
be predicted with confidence are included in the proposal one
adopts, since much of what one foresees is incidental and perhaps
unwanted in relation to what one does. One is only committed to
a small part of what one brings about in acting—namely, to the
carrying out of the proposal one has adopted and to what is necessarily included in this. The entirety of what one brings about
cannot define what one is doing, since the whole sequence of processes and events considered together lacks the character of something worthwhile or useful, and without this character one cannot
wish to bring into reality the possibility one envisions in
deliberation.

If human acts are defined by what one does in the sense we
have explained, then it is possible to distinguish a person's acts
from the consequences of these acts. A person's acts, what he or
she does, consist precisely in the execution of proposals the person has adopted. The consequences of a person's acts include all
the processes and events which the person in any way causes in
acting, apart from the acts themselves.

Thus the boys' act is playing catch; the consequences include
being punished for disobedience, wearing out their equipment,
making thumping noises, frightening birds from the path of the
ball, displacing a certain amount of air, and so on and on. The
girl's act is taking care of the children in the manner necessary
to earn her fee; the consequences include missing out on treats
at home, having to change the baby's diaper, wearing the carpet
slightly when she walks the infant, learning by practical experience how to care for babies, and so on and on.

Someone is likely to object that in making the distinction
between human acts and their consequences as we do, we are drawing
a morally irrelevant line and perhaps distracting attention from
a morally more relevant line. Precisely what one wishes to accomplish can be distinguished from all that one in fact causes,
but—the objector will insist—one voluntarily brings about more
than what one wishes to accomplish. If they realize that they
may be punished, the boys not only voluntarily play catch but also
voluntarily disobey and run the risk of punishment; if she realizes she may miss out on a treat at home, the girl not only voluntarily baby sits and earns income but also voluntarily forgoes

the treat she might enjoy at home. Since at least the foreseen
consequences of one's acts--at a very minimum those foreseen with
high probability or practical certainty--are voluntarily brought
about, one cannot consider oneself wholly without responsibility
for them.

This objection is based upon an undeniable truth. One does
voluntarily bring about the foreseen consequences of one's acts.
Although they are not part of one's proposal, such consequences
are within one's awareness as one deliberates and chooses. One
might not want them, but one does accept them. Thus in executing
one's proposal one also causes consequences which have been willingly accepted. To this extent the objection makes a sound point.
But the objection also depends for its force upon a false assump-
tion--namely, that what is included in the proposal one has adopted and what is outside the proposal and merely accepted are
both voluntary in the same way. Thus the objection concludes
that responsibility for acts and for their consequences arises in
the very same way.

We grant that persons are not wholly without responsibility
for the consequences of their acts, even if these consequences
are unwanted. But we hold that certain basic truths about human
choice and about morality in making choices require that differences in the voluntariness of acts and their consequences be recognized and borne in mind, and that these differences will mark
out different grounds of responsibility for what one does and for
the rest of what one brings about. As it will become clear, we
are not saying that one's responsibility for what one merely accepts is necessarily any less grave than is one's responsibility
for what one really wishes to accomplish. But there is an important distinction between the two, which we shall now try to
clarify.

As we have explained, the practical reasoning and existential
attitude of a person involved in deliberation and choice relate
in different ways to a proposal and to other aspects of what one
might cause. What is involved in a proposal is considered good;
one identifies with it. Other aspects of what one causes might
be matters of complete indifference or even factors in spite of
which one acts. In any case, one does not identify oneself with
all that one causes but only with what one considers good, either
as intrinsically worthwhile or as useful for attaining what is
worthwhile in itself.

This difference in practical reasoning and in attitude does
have some moral significance. As we explained in chapter eleven,
section F, morality is primarily in the relationship between a
person's choices and basic human goods. A choice is upright if
it is in harmony with the entire set of basic human goods; it is

182

immoral if it responds to some of these goods at the expense of another or others. Moreover, one in choosing does constitute oneself, maintaining openness to more abundant flourishing or stunting oneself.

Thus the proposals which moral agents adopt and undertake to carry out do determine in a primary and very special way the moral quality of their activity. The agent is committed to the proposal and must accept its content not only as somehow good but as self-defining and—if the proposal is an immoral one—as self-limiting in an unnecessary way.

As we argued in chapter eleven, section C, the consequentialist is mistaken in thinking that the morality of acts can be determined by weighing off the benefits and harms they will bring about. For the consequentialist the distinction we are making between acts and consequences would be irrelevant. But since consequentialism is unworkable, we also saw that a sound teleological ethical theory gives sense to the dictum that evil may not be done that good might follow from it—the end does not justify the means. We are now supplying a clarification of action which allows the necessary distinction between the end and the means.

One who lives hygienically (means) for the sake of health (end) might avoid contact with a patient under his or her care (bad means) for the same end. One who gives opiates (means) to relieve pain (end) might instead kill the patient (which we will argue shortly to be a bad means) to relieve pain. One who takes good care of patients (means) to earn a living (end) might perform unnecessary surgery (bad means) for the same end. In cases in which a bad means is chosen, one who chooses it is committed to it and identified with it, not insofar as it is bad, but insofar as it is a useful good. To make such a commitment the violation of a human good must be rationalized and the person who is willing to violate it stunted in responsiveness to what in itself is humanly appealing.

States of affairs which are not included in one's proposal but are merely foreseen to follow from one's causality are not willed in the same way that means are willed. One does not directly define one's moral character by reference to those effects which one causes apart from one's proposals. One's will is not set upon the realization of such effects. Since one accepts such states of affairs, one does have a moral responsibility in respect to them, but this responsibility is quite different from that which one has for what one wishes to accomplish.

This difference in the origin of moral responsibility makes possible some differences in moral evaluation. When one undertakes to execute one's adopted proposal, precisely what one is

183

doing is an act which either respects all the basic human goods or does not respect them. If it does not, then nothing can make the act good, although many things can make it more or less evil. When one merely foresees certain effects of one's effort to execute one's adopted proposal—effects which themselves are no part of this proposal—one does not in the same way determine oneself in relation to all the basic human goods.

One accepts the effects which one foresees, and so one must consider how these effects might bear upon various basic human goods. In some cases one might have a most grave moral responsibility not to accept certain effects, and a person who truly loves all the basic human goods would not accept them. But in no case can one who is accepting effects do evil that good might follow from it. Accepting effects of one's action simply is not the same thing as trying to reach an end by executing a proposed course of action as a means to that end.

Thus, for example, if Jane Doe is a surgeon who does unnecessary surgery to earn large fees, she adopts a proposal which involves mutilating another person. This appears to her to be a useful good; she rationalizes what she is doing by the good purpose to which she will put her earnings. By contrast, if John Roe is an experimenter who foresees that his experiment might have side effects which would seriously harm persons subjected to it, he need not adopt a proposal involving this harm. No matter what additional considerations are introduced, Doe's acts cannot be justified; precisely what she does is incompatible with the basic human good of life and health. Roe's act cannot be so directly appraised; its moral quality depends upon what the basic human goods require by way of other modes of responsibility.

On the one hand, if there is no compelling need for the risk, if the subjects do not give informed consent, or if other conditions are not met, then perhaps Roe's accepting of the risk of harm expresses an attitude just as careless about human goods as do Doe's activities. Here Roe's action might be seen wrong by the fact that it violates the golden rule; he would not want others to treat him as he treats his experimental subjects. Or the experiment might violate reasonable regulations of experimental procedures and thus contravene the experimenter's communally defined duties.

On the other hand, if there is an urgent need to carry out the experiments, if the subjects give their informed consent, if Roe proceeds as he would if the subjects were persons for whom he cared very deeply, if he is careful to abide by all reasonable regulations which define an experimenter's duties, then perhaps his accepting of the risk of harm to the experimental subjects is morally blameless and even commendable. Harm to the subjects is no part of Roe's proposal, only an accepted effect which he causes. Hence, in the strict sense the harm, even if foreseen, is not included in his action, in what he does. The morality of accepting this harm, therefore, depends upon the conformity of this accepting with other modes of responsibility which mediate Roe's stance toward basic human goods and this accepting. It simply is not possible that his proposal to learn by experiment can be directly against the good of life and health, for possible harm to these goods is no part of this proposal.

In sum, one is primarily responsible for one's choices. What one does, most properly, is what precisely executes the proposals one adopts in choosing. What one does constitutes oneself and shapes one's character directly. One is secondarily responsible for the effects one causes in carrying out one's actions. These effects are consequences of one's acts, not part of them. If these effects are foreseen, they are voluntary in the sense that they are accepted. But voluntarily accepted effects of one's behavior must be distinguished from chosen means to one's ends. Means are considered useful goods; they are included in one's proposals; one identifies with them. A means which is incompatible with any of the basic human goods cannot be adopted clearheadedly without immorality. Effects which are only accepted are in themselves neither compatible nor incompatible with the basic goods.

Yet in many cases effects have a bearing of great importance upon these goods. Although in some cases one might without immorality accept effects which significantly inhibit or damage some human good, this possibility is limited by various forms of responsibility. If one really is as concerned with all of these goods as one ought to be, one will not be partial to some people in accepting harmful effects. Nor will one permit effects it is one's duty to prevent. Hence, although one is not responsible for the effects one accepts in exactly the same way one is responsible for one's actions, responsibility for the former can be just as grave as responsibility for the latter.

In some cases the termination of pregnancy is brought about by the removal of a nonviable unborn child without the adoption of a proposal which is or includes the bringing about of the death of the child, but rather in the carrying out of a proposal which does include the removal of the child from the mother. In such cases an act of abortion in the strict sense is done, but such an act of abortion is not an act of killing in the strict sense. The causing of death is not part of the abortional act but is a consequence of it.

Cases which have been considered indirect abortion by those applying a traditional double-effect analysis are instances in which the death of the unborn is caused as a consequence of an act without being included in the proposal carried out in the act. For example, if a cancerous pregnant uterus is removed to stop the disease, the death of the unborn is foreseen and accepted as an effect of the operation but is not chosen as a means or part of a means to any desired end. A sign of this is the fact that in case the same operation were indicated for a nonpregnant woman, it might be done with the same purpose and carried out in the same way.

Traditional double-effect analysis, however, tended to identify direct abortion with a subclass of killing in the strict sense. Thus, a tubal pregnancy, it was argued, might be removed because of the pathology of the tube itself; an embryotomy could not be justified because the operation physically directly attacked the baby.

Our analysis would classify the removal of a tubal pregnancy from its inappropriate site of development in the tube as an act of removal, which could be chosen for the sake of preventing otherwise inevitable damage to the mother by the continuing development of the fetus with almost no hope of its survival. The death of the growing child who is removed in such a case would be foreseen and accepted but would not need to be included in the proposal adopted, and thus killing in the strict sense need not be done. We think that embryotomy can be analyzed similarly.

In criticizing a previous statement of our approach Paul Ramsey argued that it would not justify certain instances of removing a fetus which seem, intuitively, to be little different from the cases which it can be used to justify. The cases Ramsey mentions are ones in which surgery is needed to remove displaced, diseased appendix or a damaged aorta in a pregnant woman, and the only feasible approach to the site of the problem is through the pregnant uterus, with the inevitable death of the unborn child prior to the subsequent act of surgical repair of the primary problem.

In reply we point out first that whether the removal of the fetus is justified in such cases is one question; whether its removal is killing in the strict sense is another. On our analysis the proposal to remove the unborn baby from its natural site, the site required for its survival, need not include the proposal to kill the baby or to bring about its death, even though its death is foreseen as an inevitable consequence of its removal. Removal here has a different purpose: access to the site for needed surgery. The fact that the removal of the fetus is a distinct act from the subsequent surgery does not mean that this distinct act, precisly as an act which is a means to an end, is an act of killing. In the cases Ramsey suggests, the death of the child can be voluntary in the limited sense only that it is accepted as a foreseen effect.

We also point out in reply to Ramsey that our analysis does not include a thesis which he mistakenly thought to be part of the earlier analysis: abortional acts which are not acts of killing in the strict sense are automatically ethically justified. The earlier analysis included this discussion of abortion in cases in which a woman conceives as a result of rape:

> But what about the rare case in which a woman is raped and conceives a child of her attacker? She has not had a choice; the child has come to be through no act of hers. Moreover, it is not clear that her precise concern is to kill the child. She simply does not wish to bear it. If the artificial uterus were available, she might be happy to have the baby removed and placed in such a device, later to be born and cared for as any infant that becomes a social charge. Now, clearly, one could not object if that were done. May the death of· the child that is in fact brought about by aborting it actually be unintended (that is, outside the proposal) in this case? I believe that the answer must be yes.

> But this answer does not mean that abortion in such a case would be ethically right. I fail to see what basic human good is achieved if the developing baby is aborted. The victim of rape has been violated and has a good reason to resent it. Yet the unborn infant is not the attacker. It is hers as much as his. She does not wish to bear it—an understandable emotional reaction. But really at stake is only such trouble, risk and inconvenience as is attendant on any pregnancy. To kill the baby for the sake of such goods reveals an attitude toward human life that is not in keeping with its inherently immeasurable dignity. One of the simpler modes of obligation is violated—that which requires us to do good to another when we can and there is no serious reason not to do it.

We do not deny that in an argument before an imaginary moral tribunal a great many abortions might be rationalized as removal of the unborn and denied to be killing in the strict sense. But ethics is not a matter of judgments before moral tribunals, real or imaginary. It is a question of shaping one's own life, and in responding to this question rationalization gets one nowhere but deep into the quicksand of false conscience. In actual fact, as we have pointed out, many abortions are carried out precisely by way of executing proposals to get rid of unwanted children.

Even those having and doing such abortions must admit that the proposal they execute to get rid of a child amounts to a proposal to kill it. These are in fact killings in the strict sense for all those concerned who by choice adopt a proposal to kill the unwanted as a solution to the problems their survival would entail.

The second paragraph of the passage quoted above should have warned Ramsey that even in cases in which abortion is not killing in the strict sense the justification of abortion is a further and distinct question. The mode of obligation cited is what we would regard, not as a matter of charity, but as a form of responsibility even more elemental than the duties which belong to persons because of their roles in established relationships, defined by the accepted institutions of society. From the latter derive the system of rights and duties which articulate the requirements of justice, but there is much more to morality than justice, and many moral responsibilities which do not pertain to justice are more fundamental and stricter than those which do.

Still, in some cases in which abortion might be considered as a proposal which would not include or amount to the bringing about of death of the unborn child, duties would preclude the moral justifiability of adopting the proposal. A woman who willingly engages in sexual intercourse, knowing that she might become pregnant, certainly implicitly accepts the role of mother, and a primary duty of this role is to care for and protect one's children. It is true that like other duties arising from a role, this duty only binds under the condition that one is not prevented by some other obligation from fulfilling it. A woman, especially if she is already a mother, has an obligation to preserve her own life, and this obligation might reasonably seem to her to require that she consent to the removal of a cancerous uterus or surgery to repair a damaged aorta, even though such procedures would make it impossible to fulfill her motherly duty to her unborn child. But in the absence of some compelling obstacle to fulfilling a parental duty an unborn child has a moral right to the care, support, and defense of both parents who have willingly taken part in initiating its life.

Similarly, even if the proposal of abortion is not a proposal to kill the unborn, the golden rule or principle of universalizability would preclude in most instances moral justification for abortion. No one would wish others to prefer their comfort and convenience to one's own life, but most who propose abortion consider the interests of the unborn with just such a partial and biased perspective. Likewise, in any sincere moral reflection considerations of the health of the mother, when life is not truly threatened, could not be accepted as a warrant for a

188

removal of the fetus which is foreseen to cause its inevitable death.

The narrowness of the class of cases in which the proposal to abort (justifiable or not) is not equivalent to a proposal to kill the unborn can be made clearest perhaps by imagining the situation which would obtain if an artificial uterus, capable of sustaining an infant's life at any time after conception, were widely and cheaply available. The uterus would be used in cases of removal of the unborn when the intent was not to kill the child. It would not be used when the point of the abortion was to exterminate the unwanted as a solution to the problem they present.

Of the approximately one million abortions carried out in the United States each year, how many would be placed in the artificial uterus? Very few, for the unwanted baby would not be cared for in this manner. Such care would frustrate the whole point of aborting unwanted babies: to get rid of them so that they shall not live to make their claim upon their parents and upon society at large.

(pp. 385-390; 404-407)

"Toward a Consistent Natural-Law Ethics of Killing"

Apart from war and capital punishment, Aquinas discusses only one other situation in which he regards killing as justifiable. The question is: "Whether one may kill another in self-defense?" Aquinas answers:

Nothing keeps one act from having two effects, one of which is in the scope of the agent's intention while the other falls outside that scope. Now, moral actions are characterized by what is intended, not by what falls outside the scope of intention, for that is only incidental, as I explained previously.

Thus from the act of defending himself there can be two effects: self-preservation and the killing of the attacker. Therefore, this kind of act does not have the aspect of "wrong" on the basis that one intends to save his own life, because it is only natural to everything to preserve itself in existence as best it can. Still an action beginning from a good intention can become wrong if it is not proportionate to the end intended.

Consequently, if someone uses greater force than necessary to defend his own life, that will be wrong. But if he repels the attack with measured force, the defense will not be wrong. The law permits force to be repelled

189

with measured force by one who is attacked without offering provocation. It is not necessary to salvation that a man forego this act of measured defense in order to avoid the killing of another, since each person is more strongly bound to safeguard his own life than that of another.

But since it is wrong to take human life except for the common good by public authority, as I already explained, it is wrong for a man to intend to kill another man in order to defend himself. The only exception is when a person having public authority intends in the line of duty to kill another in self-defense, as when a soldier fights the enemy or a lawman fights robbers. However, even these would sin if they acted out of a private lust to kill.

Several observations may be made about this complex text.

First, although Aquinas limits justifiable self-defense to situations in which the attack is unprovoked, he does not say the attack must be unjust. Someone attacked by an insane person might kill the attacker who could be incapable of moral responsibility for his action.

Second, the intention of the one defending himself is central to the argument. Aquinas had discussed capital punishment without mentioning intention; he required a right intention to justify war. In self-defense, the intention must be to preserve one's own life rather than to harm the attacker. This restriction of upright intention leads to the important concept of measured force or proportionate response to an attack. Behavior will be selected and limited to what is necessary to protect oneself, if the intention is really self-defense.

A third point to notice is that Aquinas does not rule out the use of self-defensive force such that one foresees, with practical certainty, that the attacker will be killed. The fact that a reasonable person would expect the death of the attacker does not mean that death is intended by one using measured force in self-defense. Intentions guide and shape performances; foreseen effects of behavior that do not guide and shape it fall outside the scope of intentions.

A fourth point is that Aquinas treats as an exception to his general position killing in self-defense by soldiers and lawmen. The soldier and the lawman, however, may intend to kill, but only in their official capacities, when the intended killing is referred to the common good.

A fifth point to notice is that Aquinas rests the justifi-

cation of killing in self-defense on the natural inclination
toward self-preservation. Aquinas believes that individuals have
a paramount obligation to take care of themselves:
"each person is more strongly bound to safeguard his own life than
that of another." The argument is not that an intention to kill
is justified, but that a performance of self-defensive behavior
which also kills can be intended as self-defensive and not as
homicidal, because the intention of self-defense is possible (in
virtue of natural inclination) and justifiable (in virtue of each
person's responsibility for his own well being). If human beings
did not naturally incline to preserve their lives, an intention to
do so would only occur as a consequence of some more basic impulse;
if there were no moral responsibility for oneself, an intention
to preserve one's life by using force deadly to another could
never be justified.

For those imbued with a utilitarian outlook, Aquinas'
effort to justify killing in self-defense only if the intention
is self-defensive—not if it is homicidal—will seem at least
confused, if not dishonest. A utilitarian would urge that all
the good and bad effects of one's performance must be weighed,
and that the action is morally justified only if the net good
of acting outweighs the net good of any alternative, such as
allowing oneself to be attacked without offering resistance. For
a utilitarian, in cases in which the very same behavior would be
suited to the intention of measured self-defense and to the intention of homicide, which intention was effective subjectively would
be irrelevant. Or, better, perhaps, a utilitarian would deny the
possibility that one choosing a performance he foresees to have a
deadly effect cannot help but intend what he foresees.

I am assuming in this paper, however, that utilitarianism
is wrong in supposing that morality of action is calculated by a
weighing of good and bad consequences. The foreseeable consequences that could in any manner be considered and weighed are only
part - and not the most important part - of the reality in which
man must orient himself as he takes moral responsibility for his
self-determined action. Beyond foreseeable consequences lie the
unknown, and thus incalculable, possibilities of human goodness,
possibilities which are still to be realized in oneself and in
other persons, possibilities that will become specific only
through creative faithfulness to the "something more" of human
life.

Man calculating his action by consequences and principles
of value already known and accepted necessarily limits himself
to being no more than he already is - unless by accident. Moral
goodness, however, lies in being true to as is whom we are to
be, but are not yet nor ever have been. Only if we are first
faithful to as is whom we are to be, can this "something more,"

191

this better self, begin to gain a comprehensible outline, an outline which we must nevertheless continuously revise and adapt as we seek to realize it.

In this nonutilitarian moral outlook, whether or not another person's death is admitted within the scope of our intention is extremely important. A difference of intention can relate identical behavior in quite different ways to our moral attitude, and to the self being created through our moral attitude. If one intends to kill another, he accepts the identity of killer as an aspect of his moral self. If he is to be a killer through his own self-determination, he must regard himself in any situation as the lord of life and of death. The good of life must be rated as a measurable value, not as an immeasurable dignity. Others' natural attitudes toward their own lives must be regarded as an irrational fact, not as a starting point for reasonable community. However, if one intends not the death of another but only the safety of his own life, then one need not identify himself as a killer. One's attitude toward human life itself and toward everything related to it can remain that of a person unwilling to take human life.

Still, it may be argued that the scope of intention cannnot in reality exclude killing if one purposely performs a deadly deed, knowing it to be so, even though one's objective is his own safety rather than the other's harm. If one intends a certain objective, does he not also intend the means that are necessary for it?

I think the proper answer is "yes" if one refers to the means in a strict sense - that is, to that which is conducive to one's objective in a positive way, considered precisely insofar as it is conducive. A hired assassin whose objective is the pay he will earn only if the victim dies intends to kill the victim, even though that death considered by itself would be indifferent, or even repugnant,to him.

However, a rule to the effect that he who intends the end intends the means does not imply that one who kills in self-defense intends the assailant's death. For the other's death does not as such contribute anything directly to the objective of self-defense. The means considered strictly - a degree of counterforce sufficient to halt the attack or render it harmless - may happen to be deadly to the attacker. But if so, that is only a contingent fact. The death of the attacker is not the means of self-defense; rather, the means of self-defense happens to involve the attacker's death. The distinction is not vacuous, as is illustrated by a case in which the attacker happens to be put out of commission without his expected death occurring. If the intention is self-defense, the attacker's life is spared; if the intention is the death of the attacker, he is finished off.

Some authors seem to suppose that all foreseen effects of one's behavior are intended so long as they are accepted, however reluctantly, as the concomitants of the execution of one's objective. But this position conflicts with our ordinary-language use of the word "intentional." There may be reasons for the law to regard as intentional what ordinary moral discourse does not conceive to be such. But I think even law would not go so far as to regard all the foreseen effects of an intended act themselves intended.

I foresee that the paragraph I am now writing will be misunderstood by some readers, but I do not intend their misunderstanding. I foresee that as a result of writing this paragraph, my pen will run out of ink sooner than if I did not write this paragraph, but I do not intend my pen's running out of ink.

When I go to the dentist, I foresee that I shall suffer pain, but I do not intend the pain. I intend to keep my teeth in working order and I intend to have them repaired, but the pain contributes nothing to my objective or to the process of its realization. Pain is merely an unavoidable concomitant. True, I bring the pain upon myself by going to the dentist. But I "bring it upon" myself, I do not seek it or use it.

A human being as a moral agent is not placed within a framework of already determinate situations, as a puppet is placed upon a stage created beforehand for it. The various environments in which we live are filled with facts somehow or other related to us and to our action, but our actual life-worlds are shaped by our interests and by the ways we select to satisfy our interests. Many effects of our behavior fall outside the scope of our intentions; some effects of our behavior have no significant reference to any human concern that we know of. Consequently, we certainly do not intend all the foreseen effects of our purposeful behavior.

Yet it might be argued that we do intend foreseen effects of our purposeful behavior if these effects are relevant to human interests, particularly when such effects are necessary concomitants of the objectives we seek or the means we choose. By this criterion the death of the attacker would be intentional, even if the purpose were self-defense and the force used were strictly proportionate to the purpose. If a householder, believing an intruder is about to shoot, shoots first in self-defense, it would seem odd to say the intruder was killed unintentionally by a bullet that found its target in the intruder's brain.

This example indicates that "intentional" may be used in contrast with "accidental." The killing of the intruder is no accident, and in that sense the householder kills intentionally. Legally such killing would perhaps be classed as excusable homicide, not as an accident. For legal purposes, also, it is perhaps useful to regard as intentional any reasonably foreseeable effect of action if the action is illegal and the effect harmful, or if the harmful effect is avoidable, or if the intentional bringing about of the effect would be illegal.

Ethically, however, even if an attacker killed by defensive action is not killed unintentionally--i.e., accidentally--one defending himself with a proportionate response that will in fact be deadly need not turn against life, need not regard death (even the attacker's) as if it were any sort of good. In this sense one who kills in self-defense need not in-tend (tend toward) the attacker's death. By contrast, one who seeks anyone's death either as an objective or as a means--the hired gunman--does regard death as a good for death as such will be at least useful if not itself a source of satisfaction.

Catholic theologians, especially around the beginning of the seventeenth century, used Aquinas' justification of killing in self-defense, along with other elements of his teaching, to develop a general principle of casuistry: the principle of two-fold effect. The history of the development has been traced by others. The product of the development may be summarized as follows.

A person may guiltlessly do an act having two effects, one good and the other bad, if four requirements are fulfilled simultaneously:

1) If one prescinds from the bad effect, the act must not be evil on another ground. (There is no point in discussing the justifiability of permitting the bad effects of an act which is admitted from the outset to be murder, quite apart from those effects.)
2) The person acting must have a right intention. (Here Aquinas' analysis, which we have examined, had its influence.)
3) The evil effect may not be the means to the good effect. (One may not kill someone to inherit his wealth with a view to putting it to good use.)
4) There must be a proportionately grave reason for doing the act. (One may not use a possibly deadly drug if a safer one is available and will do.)

The first two requirements introduce no new problems. The third raises problems which we will have to consider carefully. The fourth requirement can be understood in two ways, and this ambiguity is worth a brief remark.

If we understand the fourth requirement as a demand that the good and bad effects be weighed against one another, then a limited field is being opened for a utilitarian conception of moral judgment. Since I do not believe utilitarian calculation to be feasible, I do not think any direction to engage in it can be an element in a sound ethical principle. However, the fourth requirement may be taken as a mere reminder that even if the evil effect is not our direct responsibility, we still may have an obligation to avoid it under the general principle that we should avoid and prevent evil wherever we can, unless we have some reason not to do so. One would incur a guilt similar to that of an omission if he neglected to avoid an evil effect without a good reason.

Heavy criticism has focused on the third requirement. Taken in onw sense, of course, that requirement agrees with Aquinas' analysis of justified killing in self-defense, as I have explained it. A chosen means is as much intended as is one's objective. But in another sense, the third requirement would exclude killing in self-defense, because the force used as a means of self-defense is effective to that end only in virtue of the fact that it first harms the attacker. If the required form and level of defensive force will be in fact deadly, then the one defending himself is safe only when the attacker has suffered a death-dealing counterattack. Reasoning thus, many who hold the principle of double effect do not apply it to the case of killing in self-defense. Instead they say that in such cases the intentional killing of an unjust assailant is justified.

One notable effort to criticize and broaden the third requirement was made in an article by Peter Knauer, S.J., published in the 1967 Natural Law Forum. According to Knauer, the evil effect may licitly be intended psychologically as a means to a good end, provided there is a commensurate reason for the act. Even though the good effect is in fact achieved only through the evil, Knauer claims that from the moral (as against the psychological) point of view, the evil in such a case will be "indirectly" intended. In other words, no means for the use of which there is a commensurate reason can be intrinsically evil.

Knauer suggests that the notion of commensurate reason is derived from the requirement Aquinas laid down, in his discussion of killing in self-defense, that force be measured, since an action beginning from a good end can become evil if it is "not proportionate to the end 'intended." If action achieves the good at which it aims as efficiently as possible, then that good is a commensurate reason, according to Knauer. If one settles for a partial, or short-run, or otherwise more limited realization of some value, whereas he might have sought a fuller realization of it if he had organized his action more intelligently, then his action is evil. Knauer considers evil action to involve a sort of inner contradiction: one wants the good he intends as his objective, but one fails to pursue it as efficiently as he might.

Reading Knauer's explanation, we naturally wonder how he distinguishes between ethics and any art or technique. The distinction is based on levels of generality. Art and techniques criticize or guide action so that it will be commensurate to specific objectives. Ethics includes the whole of life. For Knauer, moral theory finds behavior immoral by considering its lack of proportion to the value to which it is directed as an ultimate end.

Undoubtedly, Knauer is expressing some aspect of what is required of action in order that it be morally good. The question is whether the presence of a commensurate reason, as Knauer understands it, is a sufficient criterion of morality. We might criticize Knauer's theory both as an interpretation of Aquinas and on its own account.

As an interpretation of Aquinas, I do not think Knauer's theory is at all plausible. If Aquinas' whole discussion of the justifiability of killing in self-defense amounted to nothing more than the statement that such killing is justified if it is the only efficient way to preserve one's life, then the whole idea of intention could just as well have been omitted. In fact, Aqionas uses the notion of intention as the pivot of his discussion. Moreover, "intention" in Aquinas' discussion has not a special meaning completely cut off from the meanings it has in ordinary language.

A sign of Knauer's confusion on this matter is his use of the post-Thomistic expression, "indirectly intended," as equivalent to Aquinas' "what falls outside the scope of intention, for that is only incidental" to the action. The upshot is that Knauer lumps together, as justified by commensurate reason, two classes of situations involving killing which, as we have seen, Aquinas viewed quite differently--intentional official killings justified by the common good and killing in private self-defense justified by exclusion (which is objectively grounded) of the attacker's death from the intention that guides and shapes behavior.

Knauer is right, I think, in urging that the "effects" of

which Aquinas speaks are not extrinsic consequences of the human act but intrinsic aspects of it. Certainly, self-defense is intrinsic to an act done in self-defense and immediately realizing that purpose. Knauer also is right in insisting that human action should not be split into a purely "mental" meaning and an "external" behavior. He also assumes a realistic theory of values, which he takes to be constitutive aspects of human perfection.

But despite the virtues of his essay, and apart from its failure as an interpretaion of Aquinas, Knauer seems to me to have made the serious error of confusing a <u>necessary</u> condition of morality—commensurate reason, in his sense—with the sufficient criterion of moral goodness. The insufficiency of Knauer's criterion can be brought out in several ways.

For one thing, the requirement of commensurate reason does not show why there is a moral obligation to commit oneself to any good in the first place. Knauer assumes that action commensurate or not to a value is already going on, but this assumption sets aside several very fundamental issues in ethics. Again, the requirement of commensurate reason does not explain why we have a prima facie obligation to fulfill the duties we have in the various communities to which we belong.

More important, perhaps, is that the requirement of commensurate reason does not show what is wrong with an exclusive and fanatical dedication to any single human value. Truth, for instance, is a human good valuable apart from its consequences. On Knauer's theory it would follow that so long as a scientist pursues truth as effectively as possible, nothing he does can be immoral. The means, for Knauer, cannot be prejudged until thay are specified by the end. Suppose our scientist pursues inquiries in human psychology which can only succeed if the subjects are kept in ignorance, and which involve a serious risk of permanent psychological damage? Suppose these investigations seek experimentally to determine the conditions under which commitments such as those involved in religious or marital fidelity are most likely maintained or broken?

The knowledge pursued in such cases could be of genuine value, and the means could be proportionate to the end. Are such experiments therefore justified? If Knauer says "yes", he opens himself to justifying every sort of fanaticism, and the violation of every value but the one to which action happens to be directed. If he says "no," then he must admit that a truly commensurate reason must be proportionate not merely to one or another human good, but simultaneously to the whole ambit of fundamental human values. But how can a reason be judged commensurate to many incommensurable values? If Knauer is not to fall into utilitarianism after all, by declaring all human values to be commensurable, he will have to bring into account differences in the agent's attitude toward the circle of values. This consideration would lead back to distinctions based on intention in the sense that Knauer has tried to supersede with his simple, and oversimplified, concept of commensurate reason.

A remarkably clear example of the inadequacy of Knauer's position is furnished by a concluding footnote to his article in which he deals with some difficult questions. May a woman commit adultery to rescue her children from a concentration camp? May she engage in prostitution to avoid starvation? Knauer answers:

> I would reply first that the difficulty is by no means special to the sexual area. We have the same problem in every kind of extortion or blackmail. For example, some-one may be threatened with death if he refuses to take part in the falsification of a document.
> The question must be answered in relation to the whole context. Does life or freedom have any value if in the end one is forced to give up all human rights and in principle be exposed to every extortion? This would be in contradiction to the very values of life and free-dom. For extortion always worked after the pattern of the salami, one slice of which is taken after the other; it is a menace not only for a part but also for the whole.
> As for the woman who believes that prostitution is the only way to keep from starving, she is in reality also the victim of extortion. By acceding to an unjust extortion one can never really save anything in the long run.

It seems to me this reply is evasive. The question does not necessarily imply that the situation involves extortion; Knauer imports that idea. The woman who is trying to free her children is not giving up all human rights ("rights," of course, begs the question) nor is she in principle subjecting herself to every extortion. The hungry prostitute is not violating the value she is acting for--namely, staying alive. If she has no other way to get food, she is acting with a commensurate reason in Knauer's sense. Perhaps she would be better off on the whole chaste and dead, but for Knauer to hold that position is arbitrary.

Of course, if one wants to make "life and freedom" or some-thing similarly vague be the value sought in every action, it will always be possible to say vacuously that any act generally agreed to be immoral beforehand lacks a commensurate reason. That is like saying that sin will never make one truly happy, where "truly" begs the question. A woman engaging in prostitution to avoid starvation is surely staying alive, and may have no less compromising alternative. If she "can never really save anything in the long run," that is only because we all die sooner or later. On that score, I suppose Knauer might hold that mere human life is no value that could ever be a commensurate reason for acting.

In one set of cases, the means is a performance that leads to a specific goal ulterior to the performance itself. For example, a child does his homework (means) so that he can get good marks (end). A boy cuts grass (means) to earn enough money to buy a bicycle (end). A farmer sows (means) in order to reap (end). One makes a tool (means) in order to use it (end). As has often been observed, ends in this sense can become means to further ends. In none of these cases does the means include the behavior alone and the end its human meaning. Rather, contrary to Van der Marck, both means and end have a behavioral aspect (Aquinas' expernal act) and an aspect of human meaning (Aquinas' interior act).

In another set of cases, the means is a meaningful performance that partially actualizes a larger purpose. This larger purpose, which is the end, is not only on the side of human meaning, but also involves human existence. For example, one lives hygienically for the sake of health—the means participates in the end. One watches a drama for the sake of esthetic experience; one studies in order to learn; one gives something valuable to another for the sake of friendship; one prays for holiness. In each of these cases the means is a performance with an immanent meaning by reference to the end, which is an aspect of human being, a participation in a value which is achieved in man as he acts to fulfill his commitment, to realize his own identity. In this structure of action, contrary to Van der Marck, both means and end involve an aspect of human meaning; the means involves a performance of some sort and the end a way of being.

Van der Marck is correct in observing that a performance that is one from the point of view of natural science can be many distinct moral acts. A performance is a human act only when its human meaning is taken into account. However, Van der Marck is mistaken in drawing the conclusion that there cannot be a morally bad means to a good end. The means is not merely the performance given meaning directly by the end. The meaning of a human act as means depends on the end, but is not identical with the end. There are other factors in determining the morality of the means.

Thus, a child doing his homework (means) in order to get good marks (end) might instead cheat in examinations (bad means) for the same end. A boy who cuts grass (means) to get money for a bicycle (end) might instead sell heroin (bad means) for the same end. A farmer who sows (means) in order to reap (end) might instead allow others to cultivate the crop and then kill them

199

(bad means) in order to reap. One who makes a tool (means) in order to use it (end) can exploit slave labor to make the tool (bad means) in order to use it.

Similarly, one who lives hygienically (means) for the sake of health (end) might avoid contact with a sick person for whose care he is responsible (bad means) for the same end. One who watches a drama (means) for the sake of esthetic experience (end) might try dangerous drugs (bad means) for the same purpose. One who studies (means) in order to learn (end) might do permanently destructive experiments on human beings (bad means) in order to learn. One who gives something valuable to another (means) for the sake of friendship (end) might give up his religious faith (bad means) for friendship (e.g., marriage) with a nonbeliever. One who prays (means) for holiness (end) may subject himself to an inhuman asceticism (bad means) for the same end.

I do not rest by case against Van der Marck's position on one or another particular example. The examples merely illustrate the abstract analysis. If anyone is not satisfied with these examples, it should not be difficult to find some he will accept. Means and end in human actions are closely related, but not related as Van der Marck says. The means is not merely a performance that gets its whole human meaning from the end. Contrary to Van der Marck's dictum, there certainly can be bad means.

Other efforts have been made to overturn or radically rein-terpret the principle of double effect. However, such efforts seem to me to fall into errors similar to those into which Knauer and Van der Marck fall. It is therefore necessary for us to reconsider the principle of double effect, to see how it might be revised without abandoning the nonutilitarian theory that makes it significant and without assuming some oversimplified analysis of human action.

I think that we must distinguish between cause and effect in the order of nature, on the one hand, and, on the other, means and end in the order of human action. The preceding argument shows that in human action a means is not so exclusively determined by the end that the means might not be bad while the end is good. The means in human action therefore must be morally evaluated in itself--that is, in view of all the factors which determine its morality. The question is: if an effect in the order of nature contributes to the fulfillment of a human purpose, must the nat-ural cause of that effect be viewed as a means in the order of human action?

The third requirement of the principle of double effect-- that the evil effect may not be the means to the good effect-- usually is interpreted in a way that assumes an affirmative

200

answer to this question. Sometimes, indeed, the requirement is stated as follows:

> It is permissible to set a cause in motion, in spite of its foreseen evil effect, provided..., secondly, that a good effect also issue from the act, at least as immediately and directly as the evil effect, _that is to say_, _provided that the evil effect does not first arise and_ _from it the good effect;_... (italics added)

This interpretation of the requirement seems to me mistaken.

My reason is as follows. A means in the order of human action must be a single, complete human act (or a complex of such acts). The means cannot be a mere part of a human act. Now a human action derives its unity from two sources. One source is the unity of one's intention. ("Intention" here refers not merely to intention of the end, but also to the meaning one understands his act to have when he chooses it as a means to an intended end.) The other source of unity in a human act is the indivisibility of the performance. Both principles of unity deserve close scrutiny.

A performance may be divisible by thought or divisible in the sense that under some other conditions it could be divided, yet remain practically indivisible for a given agent here and now. Obviously, so far as the performance affects the unity of a human act, the indivisibility that is relevant is that which is defined in terms of the actual power of the agent. If I cannot here and now divide my performance, then no sort of complexity within it can in and of itself determine my action to a multiplicity corresponding to that complexity.

Now, a performance considered as a process of causation in the order of nature includes not only the bodily movements of the agent but also the inevitable physical effects which naturally follow from those movements. For example, the performance of lighting a match includes the match igniting; the performance of eating includes eliminating hunger; the performance of speaking to someone includes being heard. Insofar as the performance determines the unity of action, allowances must be made for ignorance of effects or error about their inevitability, since the immediate principle of action is judgment, into which facts enter only insofar as they are known.

It follows that when a human agent through his causality initiates a process in nature, all effects expected inevitably to follow belong within the unity of his performance insofar as that unity is a principle of the unity of action. Of course, a unified performance can belong to two or more actions in virtue of the divisive effect of intention, which is the other necessary principle of the unity of action. The point here is simply that a human act need not cease to be unified as a single act merely because there is a foreseen, inevitable complexity in the natural process of cause and effect.

For example, the distinction between moving one's fingers and a match's igniting does not necessitate the restriction of the human act, which is a means, to the movement of one's fingers. The reason is that one cannot choose to move one's fingers in that way without also choosing the igniting of the match.

If one uses the lighted match to light a cigarette, the two actions may be characterized together as "lighting a cigarette," no mention made of the match and its ignition. Here, however, the process of behavior is divisible by the agent--he may use a lighter, or use the match to light a stove instead of a cigarette, or change his mind and blow the match out without using it, or light the match for illumination, or merely to watch it burn. Because of this complexity, the performance of striking a match to light a cigarette does introduce division into action. The division is apt to be overlooked when the action becomes habitual. However, at some point the habitual smoker chose not only to smoke, but also to use matches.

When we consider the other source of the unity of action, the agent's intention, we notice that a multiplicity of non-subordinated intentions always determines a multiplicity of acts, regardless of the unity of performance. That is the point Aquinas makes when he argues that the same act in the order of nature can belong to two distinct moral categories.

Another important point is that an agent intending one aspect of a performance that is complex and known to him to be divisible may be responsible for an omission if he fails to divide it, even though he never chose the elements of the complex separately. For this reason, one who does something that might cause preventable harm to others may be responsible if he fails to divide his performance by preventing that harm. Even though only one choice was actually made--to do what causes harm--there are two moral acts, one determined by that choice and the other determined by the negligent omission.

Similarly, although a performance may be actually indivisible, a duality of action may arise from the fact that an alternative performance could have been chosen that would have served one's purpose without a foreseen harm. For example, a physician who has a choice between two equally effective drugs, one of which may in a given case have a dangerous side effect, would do two human acts if he negligently prescribed the less safe drug: he would both prescribe medication and negligently omit due care in treating the patient.

If, in fact, the agent has only a single intention (that is, a single choice made with a unified meaning, even if several harmonious purposes are served at the same time) and if there is not a related omission, then the action will be a single unit so far as its unity is determined by intention.

An act that is one both from the point of view of intention and from the point of view of the performance is one absolutely. What specific action it is, will be determined by the scope of intention, not by parts of the performance that remains a whole indivisible by the agent. The concepts of intention and scope of intention have been discussed above in reference to Aquinas' position on killing in self-defense.

My conclusion is that a good effect which in the order of nature is preceded in the performance by an evil effect need not be regarded as a good end achieved by an evil means, provided that the act is a unity and only the good is within the scope of intention. Means and end in the order of human action do not necessarily correspond to cause and effect in the order of nature, because a means must be an integral human act. If the unity of action is preserved and the intention specifying the action is good, whether the good or evil effect is prior in the order of nature is morally irrelevant. From the ethical point of view, all of the events in the indivisible performance of a unitary human act are equally immediate to the agent; none is prior (a means) to another.

According to this understanding of the principle of double effect, a woman might interpose herself between her child and an attacking animal, since the unitary act would save the child as well as unintentionally damage the agent. She could not commit adultery to obtain the release of her child, because the good effect would be through a distinct human act, and she would have to consent to the adulterous act as a means to the good end.

Again, a starving party of explorers might divide available food among the stronger members, allowing the weaker to die, since the same act would benefit the one group and harm the others. But if the stronger killed one of the weaker to cannibalize him, the killing would be a bad means, chosen in a distinct act, since killing and eating are divisible and the act is therefore not unitary.

The biblical story of Abraham's sacrifice of Isaac provides an interesting example. According to my interpretation of the principle of double effect, Abraham would have been justified in sacrificing Isaac, since the very same act which killed Isaac would have been specified by Abraham's religious obedience as an act of worship. By the same token, however, Abraham would have been <u>ethically</u> justified in refusing to kill Isaac, since the very same omission would have protected Isaac's life and left the divine command unfulfilled. But if Sarah had hid the boy, Abraham would not have been justified in torturing her in order to force her to produce him, since the good effect would have been in another human act, and the choice of torture would have been a bad means, even if the end were good.

One may expose another's shameful act to clear an innocent party; the good and bad effects are indivisible, although the bad comes first in time. But one may not cause the same harm as an example to others, since the good effect is then in a distinct act, and the evil must be chosen as a means.

As I stated at the beginning of this article, I am assuming here the unviolable dignity of human life as a natural-law principle. My purpose is the limited one of trying to work out a consistent ethics of human life by resolving difficulties that seem to be raised by limitations or exceptions that tradition has engrafted upon the basic principle that life should be respected and preserved. Thus far I have argued against justification of intentional killing; I have rejected Aquinas' defense of capital punishment and warfare. I have also accepted Aquinas' argument in favor of the justifiability of killing in self-defense, but I have rejected radical revisions of the principle of double effect and instead proposed a clarification that will allow a limited extension of its power to justify acts hitherto regarded as evil.

It remains to consider in which cases we may be justified in doing the deadly deed. How much killing is permissible under my interpretation of double effect?

In the first place, killing in self-defense, as Aquinas explains it, fits under the principle of double effect as I interpret it.

As for capital punishment, I think Aquinas was right in holding that such killing is intentional. The good effects, if any, are in other acts. Since I do not accept the justifiability of intentional killing, I do not see how capital punishment can be justified. Only if capital punishment could be viewed in some cases as community self-defense against an immediate threat could it be justified. Such might have been the case in some situations in the past, for example, when a criminal was given a choice between banishment and death.

Warfare also, it seems to me, can be justified only to the extent that the deadly deeds done in it constitute a form of community self-defense. What this means is that each act of warfare that kills must in and of itself have a good effect which is alone intended. That good effect might be defined as impeding the unjust use of force by the enemy.

Justifiable warfare thus must be defensive. But force is used unjustly not only when an attack is launched, but also when power is maintained as an instrument of oppression. Moreover, the unjust use of force is impeded when the preparation at any stage is prevented. At the same time, justifiable defensive warfare can only be a last resort, and the other conditions of double effect must be observed.

Acts of war will be justifiable only if·they are effective against the means of force being unjustly used. To demand unconditional surrender is unjust. To seek by force to overcome evil that is not using force unjustly is itself unjust. To attack noncombatants is unjust. The use of terror, torture, and reprisals is unjustifiable; the good effects, if any, are in ulterior acts.

As in self-defense, a soldier on a battlefield can shoot straight at an enemy soldier, intending to lessen the enemy force by one gun, while not intending to kill. Similarly a military camp or a factory producing military goods can be bombed. But an enemy hospital or non-military area cannot be justly attacked. The enemy soldier may not be killed if he can be inactivated otherwise, or if he has surrendered.

If criteria such as these are applied to World War II, the conclusion must be that if the United States' role in the war could be justified, still it certainly was not conducted in an altogether justifiable manner. The demand for unconditional surrender and the use of strategic bombing were certainly indefensible. On the other hand, measured force might have been justifiable had it been used merely to impede and destroy the force unjustly employed by the Axis powers.

The Vietnam war is much more questionable from an ethical viewpoint. Are the enemy forces really acting unjustly, or have they provocation? Are allied objectives as limited as we claim, or are we not more interested in preventing future consequences (the "domino" theory) than in repelling present force? Is the war a necessary and an effective means to the immediate purpose? Are U.S. forces limiting their attack to legitimate military objectives, or are they trying to gain indirect military advantages by all sorts of acts that in themselves do not lessen enemy power--acts of terror, torture, reprisal, execution of civilian suspects, bombing of non-military targets, and so forth?

The facts are not easy to assess, but it is difficult to avoid the impression that the objective of the U.S. is not so much the destruction of enemy power as it is the goining of a better negotiating position. If means proportionate to the latter purpose necessarily include some that are not directly effective toward any strictly military objective, then the killing and other destruction involved in the war are a chosen means to an ulterior end. Here the evil has entered the scope of intention.

The nuclear deterrent strategy is probably the most important subject for ethical evaluation by the principles considered here.

As I understand the deterrent strategy, the last stage would have no military function at the time it would be done. Yet only the definite intention to act at the last (countervalue) stage can amke the threat effective. The deterrent thus involves the choice of an evil as a means to a good--the good realized in another act, the enemy's present choice not to attack. The destruction of life at the countervalue stage thus cannot lie outside the scope of intention.

Of course, the deterrent involves a <u>wish</u> that it not be used. The intention to obliterate enemy non-military objectives is conditional: we will act only if forced to, and we will act at the last stage only when we have nothing more to lose. Yet this condition does not limit the moral commitment to evil embodied in the deterrent strategy, for the fulfillment or nonfulfillment of the condition is not in our power. The condition does not restrict our willingness to do evil, although it does limit our execution of this willingness.

Perhaps the United States could design a deterrent that threatened only the military capability of potential enemies. If the intention to obliterate non-military objectives were not necessary for an effective deterrent, such a threat could be justified. The problem with the deterrent strategy as it exists is not that it inhibits the unjust use of force by our readiness to oppose it, but that we are ready to destroy non-military targets. But I doubt that a pure counterforce deterrent would be effective.

Utilitarians will respond to this evaluation of the nuclear deterrent by saying that it is unrealistic. The deterrent is necessary, they will argue; therefore, it is justified. But the cumulative risks inherent in the continuous existence of the deterrent over a long period of time are omitted from this simple defense of the strategy. No end is in sight. Eventually, the worst will probably happen, for when men are ready and willing to do something when the situation indicates, the situation usually eventually indicates. The utilitarian argument will certainly seem hollow to the survivors, if any, of a large-scale nuclear war. Meanwhile, a huge share of the world's wealth that is needed for very basic human goods is being spent on weapons systems we hope we shall never have to use.

Situation-ethics will accept a negative evaluation of the deterrent as an ideal, but will join utilitarian thinking in practice. If one really believes that God needs man's sins to get His will done in this world, then he is entitled to hold a situationist view. Personally, I do not believe it. I think the deterrent is a sign and an occasion of much current public and private moral corruption. When I say that the deterrent is morally evil, I do no mean that we ought to try to dismantle it if and when world amity is established. I mean that we ought to dismantle the deterrent immediately, regardless of consequences. The end simply does not justify the means.

Communism, despite its rejection of the title, is a utopianism. Nothing would destroy it as surely and as swiftly as its success. Communism without its antithesis would be forced to admit its own inadequacy, for it would no longer have an excuse for its incapacity to create heaven on earth. The United States provides Communism with the excuses without which it could not exist. As the people of the Third World realize, in many ways there is not much difference between the U.S.A.and the U.S.S.R.

Of course, the world's problems would not all be solved if the nuclear deterrent were renounced by us and if Communist ideology were falsified by its subsequent inevitable failure. However, those who have reached economic self-sufficiency might more readily face the challenge of poverty if our attitudes were not thoroughly corrupted by the antilife commitment inherent in the deterrent strategy. At present, our effort to deal with poverty is being directed increasingly into the suppression of human life in its beginnings. Both at home and abroad, more programs of contraception, sterilization, and abortion are replacing constructive programs of development. The policy of the United States is increasingly clear: to eliminate poverty by eliminating poor people.

This observation brings us to another issue in which the revised formula of the principle of double effect may be tested-- the problem of abortion. In treating this topic I shall assume that the unborn are persons, and that killing unborn persons must be evaluated on the same basis we use in evaluating the killing of any other human beings.

The usual formulation of the principle of double effect justifies certain operations in which the death of the unborn is an inevitable consequence. Examples are the removal of a cancerous, gravid uterus and removal of a fallopian tube damaged by the presence in it of an ectopic pregnancy.

By my reformulation of the principle of double effect, some additional operations involving the removal of a nonviable fetus could be justified. An example would be when the pregnancy itself was dangerously overloading an ill mother's heart and kidneys. In such a case, I think the fetus may be removed, because although it will certainly die, the very same act (through a humanly indivisible process) lessens the strain on the mother and contributes to the mother's safety, which alone need be intended by an upright agent.

Another example would be the crushing of a baby stuck in the birth canal. The very act of crushing and removing the baby, an act in fact destructive of its life, saves the mother from otherwise perhaps inevitable death. On the same principle, one would be equally justified in cutting away the mother to rescue the baby. Of course, if the baby is crushed more than necessary to relieve the mother or if the mother is cut more than necessary to release the baby, the excess damage would lie within the scope of intention and the act would be evil.

If abortion can be extended to some cases such as these, the next question, of course, is where the line can drawn. Is abortion to be considered justifiable for any woman who wants one, on the ground that the intent is not to kill the child but only to avoid a "compulsory pregnancy" or to contribute to solving the "population explosion"?

If we bear in mind the point assumed in this discussion—that the same rules must apply to killing the unborn as to killing any other persons—a negative answer is not difficult to sustain. If a person is killed because he is unwanted or because he considered surplus, clearly the precise intention is to kill. The motive for the killing is to get rid of the one killed; getting the victim out of the way is not an intention other than the intent to kill him, but a formulation of the end for which killing is the chosen means.

This conclusion may become more evident if one considers what would be done in such cases of abortion if there existed an artificial uterus into which the publicly or privately unwanted baby might be transferred. Such a device might be used in cases of genuinely therapeutic abortion. But the unwanted baby would hardly be cared for in this manner. To do so would frustrate the whole point of aborting him—which is, of course, to get rid of him in order that he may not live to make his claim upon his parents and society.

Interesting problems are presented by certain intermediate cases. If an abortion is not directly lifesaving but does have a true therapeutic aspect, need the child's death be intended? Can the abortion be justified? Similar is the case of abortion resulting from rape. In both cases, the fetus might well be placed in an artificial uterus, if one were available. What is desired is not that the baby be disposed of, but that the mother not continue to be pregnant.

I think this distinction is sufficient to establish the possibility that the baby's death would be outside the scope of intention. But this fact does not by itself show that abortion in such cases is justified. A person does not reasonably prefer his own health to his own life; one does not reasonably kill himself to avoid embarrassment, discomfort, and inconvenience. To kill the baby for such reasons, therefore, indicates quite clearly that what is at stake in the action is not human goods as such, but the good of some people (pregnant women) in preference to the good of others (unborn babies). Such a preference is a form of invidious discrimination, based on a prejudice against the unborn. Abortion in such cases lacks a proportionate reason.

Prospective defect seems to me a wholly unjustifiable excuse for abortion. If the benefit is to others, the abortion is chosen as a bad means to a good end. The benefit can hardly be to the unborn child itself. Where there is life, there is hope; no one is healthier dead. The argument for abortion in such cases seems to me to gain what little plausibility it has from the supposition that the unborn child is like a product coming along a production line. If the product does not meet all specifications, it is put into scrap by an inspector.

Of course, this concept assumes that we know just what is required for a good human life, that we have a simple check list to determine whether or not an individual is an adequate person. This simple-minded assumption, which also underlies utilitarianism generally, happens to be false. Human goodness is composed of many incommensurable aspects. Some of the most important are not available for inspection. Many "defective" persons have added new facets to our ideals of human goodness and greatness.

Many other examples of acts involving the destruction of human life could be analyzed. However, the preceding applications of the revised principle of double effect to warfare and to abortion ought to be sufficient to suggest the way in which I propose to work out a consistent ethics of killing on the basis of the natural-law principle that human life as such is to be respected and preserved.

Roman Catholic readers will notice that my conclusions diverge from common Catholic teaching. They should note that I do not justify intentional killing, although I somewhat broaden the range of cases in which killing would be called "indirect." At the same time, I deny that any good end can justify the direct killing of a human being.

As a philosopher, I cannot subordinate my inquiry to theological principles. As a Catholic, however, I propose my philosophic conclusions for consideration in the light of faith. I do not propose philosophy as a substitute for the magisterium of the Church. In my view anyone who genuinely believes that the Catholic Church is what it claims to be would be foolish to adopt in preference to its moral teaching any other practical norm whatsoever. Human reason cannot compare with divine wisdom. Still, human reason must not be despised--I speak still as a believer--for the exemplar is dishonored when the image is despised.

(pp. 73-83;85-96)

"Against Consequentialism"

(cf. 7: CONSEQUENTIALISM)

PUBLICATIONS

"Moral Objectivity and the Cold War," Ethics, LXX (July, 1960), pp. 291-305.

Contraception and the Natural Law (Milwaukee: The Bruce Publishing Co., 1964), pp. xiii+245.

"The First Principle of Practical Reason: A Commentary on the Summa Theologiae, 1-2, Question 94, Article 2," Natural Law Forum, 10 (1965), pp. 168-201; reprinted in Modern Studies in Philosophy: Aquinas: A Collection of Critical Essays, ed. Anthony Kenny (Garden City, New York:Doubleday & Company, Inc., 1969), pp. 340-382.

"Man, Natural End of," The New Catholic Encyclopedia, vol. IX, pp. 132-138.

Abortion: the Myths, the Realities, and the Arguments (New York and Cleveland: Corpus Books, 1970), pp. ix+559. Spanish edition: El aborto: mitos, realidades, y argumentos, trans. Luis Bittini (Salamanca: Ediciones Sigueme, 1972), pp. 717.

"Toward a Consistent Natural-Law Ethics of Killing," The American Journal of Jurisprudence, 15 (1970), pp. 64-96.

"The Value of a Life: a Sketch," Philosophy in Context, 2 (1973), pp. 7-15.

"Unqualified Values and Ethical Decisions," Philosophy in Context, supplement to 2 (1973), pp. 5-11.

"American Catholic Higher Education: the Experience Evaluated," in Why Should the Catholic University Survive? ed. George A. Kelly (New York: St. John's University Press, 1973), pp. 39-55.

Beyond the New Theism: A Philosophy of Religion (Notre Dame and London: University of Notre Dame Press, 1975), pp. xiii+ 418.

Free Choice: A Self-Referential Argument, with Joseph M. Boyle, Jr., and Olaf Tollefsen (Notre Dame and London: University of Notre Dame Press, 1976), pp. xi+207.

"Dualism and the New Morality," Atti Del Congresso Internazionale (Roma-Napoli - 17/24 Aprile 1974) Tommaso d'Aquino

nel suo Settimo Centennario, vol. 5; L'Agire Morale,
(Napoli: Edizioni Domenicane Italiane, 1977), pp. 323-330.

"Against Consequentialism," American Journal of Jurisprudence,
23 (1978), pp. 21-72.

Life and Death with Liberty and Justice: A Contribution to the
Euthanasia Debate, with Joseph M. Boyle, Jr.,
(Notre Dame and London: University of Notre Dame Press,
1979), pp. xiii+521.

"Charity and dissenting theologians," Homiletic and Pastoral,
(November, 1979) pp. 11-21.

"Fidelity," unpublished address.